The Invisible History of Museum Computing

American Alliance of Museums

The American Alliance of Museums (AAM) is the only organization representing the entire museum field, from art and history museums to science centers and zoos. Since 1906, we have been championing museums through advocacy and providing museum professionals with the resources, knowledge, inspiration, and connections they need to move the field forward.

The American Alliance of Museums' mission is to champion equitable and impactful museums by connecting people, fostering learning and community, and nurturing museum excellence.

Books published by AAM further the Alliance's mission to make standards and best practices for the broad museum community widely available.

American
Alliance of
Museums

The Invisible History of Museum Computing

The Behind-the-Scenes Magic of Museum Technology Professionals

Paul Marty and Katherine Jones

ROWMAN & LITTLEFIELD
Lanham • Boulder • New York • London

Published by Rowman & Littlefield
An imprint of The Rowman & Littlefield Publishing Group, Inc.
4501 Forbes Boulevard, Suite 200, Lanham, Maryland 20706
www.rowman.com

86-90 Paul Street, London EC2A 4NE

British Library Cataloguing in Publication Information Available

Library of Congress Cataloging-in-Publication Data Available

ISBN 978-1-5381-8383-0 (cloth : alk. paper)
ISBN 978-1-5381-8384-7 (paperback)
ISBN 978-1-5381-8385-4 (electronic)

∞™ The paper used in this publication meets the minimum requirements of American National Standard for Information Sciences—Permanence of Paper for Printed Library Materials, ANSI/NISO Z39.48-1992.

This book is dedicated to all those in the museum technology profession who struggle; may the stories shared herein light your way in dark times.

Contents

Preface

In the fall of 2020, at the height of the COVID-19 pandemic, we embarked on a project to chronicle the history of the behind the scenes, invisible work of museum computing. We reached out to a wide range of current and former museum technology professionals, asking if they would be willing to share stories from their own personal experiences working with computers in museums. We collected over forty hours of oral histories comprising nearly 400,000 words of transcribed text from more than fifty museum technology professionals working in the Americas, Europe, Asia, and Australia from the 1960s to the present day.

We asked our oral history participants to tell us stories about the behind-the-scenes work in museums that most people do not see: the invisible labor, innovative experiments, and unexpected challenges that underlie so many museum technology projects. We recorded these oral histories in 2021, and after a year spent transcribing, editing, and organizing, we made the original recordings and transcripts available online at https://ohmc.cci.fsu.edu/. To help future researchers and historians of museum computing, each of our participants agreed to share their oral histories under a Creative Commons Attribution 4.0 International license (CC-BY), which allows for their unrestricted reuse provided that appropriate credit is given to the original source.

We were inspired to tackle this project because we wanted to preserve stories that could help put a human face on the history of museum computing. When it comes to museum technology projects, too many people only see the finished product and miss the extensive work that takes place behind the scenes. We hoped that these stories would provide useful insights into the wide-ranging responsibilities and all-too-often unseen activities of museum technology workers and help everyone understand that those are not magic elves working behind the scenes, but real live people who need continued support and encouragement from their institutions.

The oral histories we recorded vividly document how the challenges and opportunities facing museum technology professionals have evolved and recurred over the decades, covering such topics as the underlying invisibility of information infrastructures, the dangers of losing institutional memory and organizational knowledge, and the increasing demands placed on museum technology professionals over time. These histories offer insights into the important work of generations of museum technology professionals in support of metadata standards, collections management, interactive exhibits, online experiences, and other digital initiatives.

When we embarked upon this project, we knew we would capture powerful moments in the history of museum computing, many of them never recorded before, and all of them in the words of the very people who made the magic happen. Our participants shared amazing stories on such topics as the chaos that ensues when an entire content management system vanishes, the unexpected challenges of working with open-source software for the first time, the difficulties of implanting RFID tags in fish, and the unintended consequences of teaching a mobile app to talk to your collections. Their memories provide an entertaining sweep from the first mainframe computer systems at the Metropolitan Museum of Art in the 1960s, to early databases at the Smithsonian Institution, to the first websites at the Berkeley Art Museum, to engaging interactives at the Cleveland Museum of Art, to online chatbots at the Field Museum today.

We knew we had a unique opportunity with this project to shine a light on the people who work behind the scenes to make the magic of museum computing happen. When we first started talking about this project at conferences, the feedback we received from people hearing these stories for the first time can be boiled down to three words: "I feel seen." Museum technology professionals who had worked behind the scenes for years—often with little recognition for how much they have accomplished, how far the field has come, and how much their hard work has paid off—found in this project powerful stories of transformation and accomplishment.

But what we did not expect from this project was the boundless enthusiasm for the field of museum computing that pervades these histories. As we stepped back and took a look from a 30,000-foot view at the oral histories we had collected, as we analyzed these histories looking for themes that transcended more than sixty years of museum computing, we found ourselves surprised and encouraged by the sense of joy, excitement, inspiration, enthusiasm, and yes, even magic that we saw shining across the decades. And so, we knew we had an obligation to the field not only to share the history we captured but to convey that sense of delight, that spirit of enthusiasm, in an effort to inspire the next generation of museum technology professionals.

This book brings together the most engaging and inspirational stories that we collected and uses them to present an illustrated history of museum computing from the 1960s to the present day. We could not have accomplished this without the contributions of our oral history participants, who kindly offered their unique, illuminating, and insightful stories about museum computing to this project. These participants are listed here, in alphabetical order, along with a short description of the memories they provided in their oral histories:

- Greg Albers. Memories from the J. Paul Getty Trust, and more, from the 2010s forward.
- Jane Alexander. Memories from the Cleveland Museum of Art, and more, from the 2010s forward.

- Howard Besser. Memories from the Berkeley Art Museum/Pacific Film Archive, Canadian Center for Architecture, and more, from the 1970s forward.
- Jonathan Bowen. Memories from the Science Museum, Museums and the Web, and more, from the 1980s forward.
- David Bridge. Memories from the Smithsonian Institution, and more, from the 1960s forward.
- Lori Byrd-McDevitt. Memories from the Children's Museum of Indianapolis, Wikipedia Foundation, and more, from the 2000s forward.
- Seb Chan. Memories from the Powerhouse Museum, Cooper Hewitt Smithsonian Design Museum, ACMI, and more, from the 1990s forward.
- Kate Collen. Memories from the National Postal Museum, Smithsonian Institution, and more, from the 2000s forward.
- Aaron Straup Cope. Memories from the SFO Museum, Cooper Hewitt Smithsonian Design Museum, and more, from the 2010s forward.
- Ruth Cuadra. Memories from Cuadra (STAR) Associates, the J. Paul Getty Trust, and more, from the 1970s forward.
- Costis Dallas. Memories from the Benaki Museum, CIDOC-CRM (ICOM), the University of Toronto, and more, from the 1980s forward.
- Max Evjen. Memories from Arizona State University, the Shedd Aquarium, the Michigan State University Museum, and more, from the 2010s forward.
- Silvia Filippini-Fantoni. Memories from the J. Paul Getty Museum, Indianapolis Museum of Art, North Carolina Museum of Art, Newark Museum of Art, and more, from the 1990s forward.
- Eleanor Fink. Memories from the Smithsonian Institution, J. Paul Getty Trust, and more, from the 1970s forward.
- Diana Folsom. Memories from the LA County Museum of Art, the University of Oklahoma Gilcrease Museum, and more, from the 1990s forward.
- Megan Forbes. Memories from the Museum of the Moving Image, LYRASIS, and more, from the 2000s forward.
- Jeff Gates. Memories from the Smithsonian American Art Museum, and more, from the 1990s forward.
- Cathryn Goodwin. Memories from the St. Louis Art Museum, Princeton University Art Museum, and more, from the 1990s forward.
- Josh Gorman. Memories from the National Museum of American History, Smithsonian Institution, and more, from the 2000s forward.
- Michael Haley Goldman. Memories from the United States Holocaust Memorial Museum, and more, from the 1990s forward.
- Douglas Hegley. Memories from the Metropolitan Museum of Art, the Minneapolis Institute of Art, and more, from the 1990s forward.
- Cathy Heller. Memories of her father (Jack Heller) from SUNY-Stony Brook's Institute for Computer Research in the Humanities, the Museum Computer Network, and more, from the 1960s forward.

- Nik Honeysett. Memories from Cogapp, the J. Paul Getty Trust, the Balboa Park Online Collaborative, and more, from the 1980s forward.
- Deborah Howes. Memories from the Art Institute, the Metropolitan Museum of Art, and more, from the 1980s forward.
- Kathy Jones. Memories from the Florida State Historic Preservation Office, the Harvard University Peabody Museum, and more, from the 1970s forward.
- Norbert Kanter. Memories from the Kunst- und Ausstellungshalle der Bundesrepublik Deutschland, and more, from the 1990s forward.
- Sarah Kenderdine. Memories from the West Australian Maritime Museum, École Polytechnique Fédérale de Lausanne, and more, from the 1990s forward.
- Rob Lancefield. Memories from the Wesleyan University Davison Art Center, the Yale Center for British Art, and more, from the 1990s forward.
- Andrea Ledesma. Memories from the National Archives, the Field Museum, and more, from the 2010s forward.
- Matthew MacArthur. Memories from the National Museum of American History, Smithsonian Institution, and more, from the 1990s forward.
- Martha Mahard. Memories from the Harvard University Fine Arts Library, the Boston Public Library, and more, from the 1990s forward.
- Shelley Mannion. Memories from the British Museum, the University of Lugano TEC-CH Program, and more, from the 2000s forward.
- Paul Marty. Memories from the University of Illinois, Florida State University, and more, from the 1990s forward.
- Darren Milligan. Memories from the Smithsonian Learning Lab, Smithsonian Institution, and more, from the 2000s forward.
- Marla Misunas. Memories from the San Francisco Museum of Modern Art, and more, from the 1990s forward.
- Dana Mitroff Silvers. Memories from the Berkeley Art Museum/Pacific Film Archive, San Francisco Museum of Modern Art, and more, from the 1990s forward.
- Chuck Patch. Memories from the Historic Collection of New Orleans, the Museum Computer Network, and more, from the 1980s forward.
- Sam Quigley. Memories from the Museum of Fine Arts Boston, Harvard University Art Museums, the Art Institute, and more, from the 1980s forward.
- Mia Ridge. Memories from the Melbourne Museum, Museum of London, Science Museum, British Library, and more, from the 1990s forward.
- Richard Rinehart. Memories from the Berkeley Art Museum/Pacific Film Archive, the Samek Art Museum, and more, from the 1990s forward.
- Peter Samis, Susie Wise, and Tim Svenonius (in a joint history). Memories from the San Francisco Museum of Modern Art, and more, from the 1980s forward.

- Scott Sayre. Memories from the Minneapolis Institute of Art, the Corning Museum of Glass, and more, from the 1990s forward.
- Tina Shah. Memories from the J. Paul Getty Museum, the Field Museum, and more, from the 2000s forward.
- Koven Smith. Memories from the Indianapolis Museum of Art, Metropolitan Museum of Art, Denver Art Museum, and more, from the 2000s forward.
- Marty Spellerberg. Memories from the Art Gallery of Ontario, the Museum of Contemporary Art in Chicago, and more, from the 2000s forward.
- Rob Weisberg. Memories from the Metropolitan Museum of Art, and more, from the 1990s forward.
- Layna White. Memories from the UCLA Grunwald Center for the Graphic Arts, San Francisco Museum of Modern Art, and more, from the 1980s forward.
- Holly Witchey. Memories from the San Diego Museum of Art, Cleveland Museum of Art, and more, from the 1980s forward.
- Bruce Wyman. Memories from the New England Aquarium, Denver Art Museum, and more, from the 1980s forward.
- Diane Zorich. Memories from the Harvard University Peabody Museum, Smithsonian Institution, and more, from the 1980s forward.

We are grateful to each of them for their participation in this project, and we offer them our most sincere thanks; this book would not exist without their help. Each of these participants shared inspiring stories about their behind-the-scenes work in museum computing, examples of which are featured as quotes in the chapters that follow. Please note that the quotes from our oral history participants provided in this book have been slightly edited for clarity.

Most people do not get to hear these stories. The museum professionals who engage in the work of museum computing do so in darkness. Yet they are real people who work extremely hard behind the scenes, performing magic that most people never see, and that few people understand. Almost never do we get the chance to look behind the curtain to glimpse this important work in action, so let's pull back that curtain together, and reveal the magic of museum computing.

ORAL HISTORIES OF MUSEUM COMPUTING

For the original recordings and transcripts of the oral histories featured in this book, please see:

Marty, Paul, and Katherine Jones, eds. 2021. *Oral Histories of Museum Computing*. https://ohmc.cci.fsu.edu/

Introduction

AN ORAL HISTORY OF MUSEUM COMPUTING

> I think technology . . . technology's lost its magic. There is no magic in mobile devices now. There should be, but there isn't. . . . But for a while, it *was* magic, and those magic shows were amazing.—Oral History of Seb Chan

Museums are magical places, and for more than six decades, museum computing has helped bring the magic of museums to life—behind the scenes, in the galleries, and online. It may come as a surprise to some readers that museum professionals have been using computers to support their work for more than sixty years. In fact, museum professionals were early adopters of computing technologies, using mainframe computers in the 1960s to build databases and organize information about their collections, personal computers in the 1970s and 1980s to develop collections management systems and run digital kiosks in their galleries, the Internet and the World Wide Web in the 1990s and 2000s to share images, collections, and exhibits online, and emerging technologies like artificial intelligence and virtual reality to offer new interactive experiences for their visitors in the 2010s and beyond.

The chronological history of computers in museums has been explored elsewhere, and it is not the intention of this book to revisit those grounds. Instead, this book provides a unique perspective on the history of museum computing—one that reveals important historical trends that drove the field of museum computing forward over the past sixty years. To accomplish this goal, this book uses select quotes from a one-of-a-kind collection of oral histories gathered by the authors from current and former museum technology professionals around the world to shine a light on the invisible, behind-the-scenes work of museum computing. Note that in this book, we use the term "museum technology professional" to refer collectively to all the different individuals who have worked to introduce computers into museums: registrars, librarians, curators, collections information managers, information technology workers, web developers, social media managers, and many more.

Beyond a simple history of chronological events, this book provides a critical analysis of key trends in museum computing that collectively drove the profession forward from the 1960s to the present day. By drawing upon the oral histories we collected from our participants, we are able to offer in this book an "annotated history" of museum computing where we share engaging quotes from the museum technology professionals who participated in this oral history project, place their memories in the appropriate historical context, and use their personal stories to tell the history of museum computing from the perspective of the very people who lived through it.

The quotes from our oral history participants that we have selected to share in this book bring to life the history of museum computing in a way that has never been done before, while our commentary about the overarching trends that influenced the field of museum computing explains their historical significance and why they continue to matter today as museums move forward into their shared digital future. Filled with a positive spirit of inspiration, innovation, and boundless enthusiasm, this unique history explores the changing roles and responsibilities of museum technology professionals over the past six decades in a way that provides clear guidance to those wrestling with their own digital initiatives today.

Working unseen and behind the scenes, museum technology professionals successfully pulled off one of the greatest magic tricks in the history of computers. They took us—museum professionals and museum visitors alike—from a world where curators were steadfastly opposed to the use of computers in the galleries, to a world where no museum exhibit is complete without interactive technologies. They took us from a world where museum directors refused to allow images of their collections on the Internet because they worried visitors might decide to stop coming to the museum, to a world where millions of high-resolution images of museum artifacts are freely available online through open-access initiatives. And they took us from a world where the official curatorial voice was the sole arbiter of the information resources provided by museums, to a world where data-driven evaluations, human-centered design, and a culture of participatory design and inclusion bring diverse voices into all aspects of the museum's collections and exhibits. How did this happen?

These evolutionary changes took place slowly but surely in museums around the world. The museum technology professionals who orchestrated these transformations were rarely in the public eye, and few people know just how hard they had to work to change deeply rooted individual and institutional perspectives and philosophies about the purpose and role of technology in museums. This book offers a once-in-a-lifetime opportunity to look behind the scenes and learn about the accomplishments of the people who made the magic happen. Vividly illustrated with entertaining stories from the museum technology professionals who led the way in this history, this book shines a light on the magic of museum computing in a way that underscores the significance of this history for museums past, present, and future.

Understanding this history is critically important because when it comes to the design and implementation of museum technology projects, too many people only see the finished product and miss the extensive work that took place behind the scenes. They see the product, but not the process. They see the noun, but not the verb. They see the end of the trick, but not the magic itself. By pulling back the curtain on the magic of museum computing, this book helps museum professionals respond to several important needs as they wrestle with digital initiatives in their institutions today:

1) This book meets the need to make visible the invisible work of museum technology professionals in ways that support their efforts and recognize their contributions to the field. The fact that the accomplishments of those who work in the museum technology sector tend to be invisible to museum visitors, administrators, board members, and the general public can pose significant challenges for digital leaders in museums. By bringing these rarely heard, behind-the-scenes stories of museum computing to a broader audience, this book helps to shed light on this important history. The more those who are not museum technology professionals understand the valuable but invisible work of museum computing, the more the behind-the-scenes work of museum technology professionals can be protected and supported moving forward.
2) This book meets the need to document the history of museum computing in a way that can help modern museum professionals move forward with a deeper understanding of the changing nature and purpose of technology in museums. There is a clear need to preserve this history before it is lost to time, especially given the invisible nature of the work of museum computing, and the difficulties the profession has faced in documenting its own history over time. Without an understanding of the past, it can be difficult to explain why museum computing is important and how it affects museums today. By documenting the historical work of museum technology professionals, this book helps museum professionals at all levels improve their overall understanding of the value of museum technology at a pivotal time in the history of museum computing.
3) This book meets the need to articulate the case for funding and continued support for current and future museum computing projects. The more the behind-the-scenes work of museum technology professionals remains unseen, the more that work tends to be undervalued internally by museum leaders and ignored externally by the broader community. As a result, it can be difficult for museum professionals to acquire the resources necessary to develop and sustain technology projects over time. By bringing to light these untold stories of the museum technology profession, this book

helps museum administrators better understand the personnel and financial resources necessary to support museum technology projects, helps museum professionals better understand the nature and importance of museum computing, and helps museum technology workers better advocate for their own value within the museum environment.

4) This book meets the need to keep the knowledge of the field's past accomplishments alive so that museums can build on the past instead of constantly reinventing the wheel. Without that knowledge, museum technology professionals find themselves stuck in unfortunate "cycles of forgetfulness" where they keep repeating previous work or previous ideas because they do not remember what others have done in the past. Even if one does not work directly with museum computing, a collective understanding of what has been accomplished in the past can be extremely valuable for solving the problems facing the museum technology community today. By ensuring that the history of museum computing is not forgotten, this book encourages museum technology professionals to learn about the historical trailblazers who led the way and use that knowledge to move their institutions forward in a positive manner with museum technology.
5) This book meets the need to inspire the next generation of museum technology professionals to take up the mantle and continue the work of museum computing. The museum technology profession can be a difficult one to pursue, often with limited resources and a lack of long-term sustainability. When one considers the challenges the profession has had to overcome, it is amazing how far the field of museum computing has come in just a few short decades. Understanding the historical trends that helped to move the field forward, and seeing the enthusiasm and passion that enabled this community to develop and grow, is both encouraging and inspirational. By emphasizing the groundbreaking work that took place in museum computing over the past six decades, this book conveys a positive message of growth and enthusiasm that will help inspire the next generation of museum technology professionals.

Meeting these needs provides clear takeaway lessons for museum technology professionals today as they move their own institutions toward a future of digital maturity and advocate for the future of digital leadership in museums. By shining a light on the innovative spirit of positive growth and the boundless enthusiasm that carried the field of museum computing forward over the past sixty years, this book inspires current museum technology professionals to overcome challenges and shape the future of technology in their own institutions. By drawing upon the lessons of the past to help shape the future, this book provides guidance for current museum professionals as they work to understand the important role that digital initiatives have played, currently do play, and will undoubtedly play in the future as museums move forward.

To accomplish these goals, we asked our oral history participants to share stories about the work they have done behind the scenes at museums with computing technologies. We told them we were looking for stories that may never have been shared before, stories that preserve memories that few people know or might guess happened, and stories that document how often the hard work of the museum technology profession goes unseen both inside and outside the museum. We asked our participants to help us bring the story of their profession to life by sharing memories that put a human face on the history of museum computing. By capturing, preserving, and sharing these stories—the secret histories of museum computing—we hoped to take the extensive work of museum computing that happens behind the scenes, and bring that history, and the accomplishments of museum technology professionals, into the light.

In collecting these stories, we intentionally kept our focus on the action of our oral history participants themselves—what they did as *they* made this history. We did not want stories about computers in museums as much as we wanted stories about the people who made museum computing happen. Throughout this project, we use the word "computing" as a deliberate choice to draw a direct historical connection to the pioneers of the field. Among museum technology professionals, "computing" is the verb used to describe the activities of the people who worked to introduce computers into museums, while "technology" is the noun that describes the tools they used as part of those activities. By emphasizing the verb over the noun, we are able to keep the focus on what our participants accomplished throughout this history.

To analyze these stories, we took three passes through the transcribed oral histories, using a process of coding and memoing that allowed important historical themes to emerge naturally from more than forty hours of recordings and nearly 400,000 words of transcribed text. The goal of our analysis was to identify key historical trends that transcended the past sixty years and could represent important factors that drove the history of museum computing forward over time. We approached this work with no preconceived notions, and we intentionally let the stories drive our analysis of the oral histories we collected. Thus, instead of grouping together stories that were from the same time period (such as the 1970s or the 1990s), or stories that covered the same specific technology (such as collections databases or interactive exhibits), our approach allowed us to identify important themes and concepts that featured in multiple oral histories, and that cut across different time periods and technologies (such as overcoming resistance to change, or building institutional capacity).

Combining a carefully curated selection of the stories we collected with our commentary on those stories allows us to present a compelling and exciting behind-the-scenes history of museum computing. The oral histories drive the chapters, while our annotations and explanations show how the challenges and opportunities facing museum technology professionals (such as the process of integrating emerging technologies in the galleries or behind the scenes) manifested time and again throughout this history. With each memory shared, we explore its significance to the history of museum computing, discuss important takeaways and lessons learned, and comment on how each story relates to the chapter's theme. The resulting analysis brings multiple voices and perspectives from more than fifty individuals into one integrated whole where each chapter weaves seamlessly in and out of the topics, time periods, and technologies that connect these histories and the lessons they represent for the museum profession.

Our analysis of these oral histories identified important themes and concepts that highlight and connect the fascinating work that has taken place below the waterline in museums. Over the past six decades, the purpose of technology in museums evolved from connecting systems and networks to providing access to information resources and collections content, to offering meaningful and engaging experiences to diverse audiences, to helping people around the world embrace our shared humanity through the power of museums. The oral histories we collected vividly document how the technological challenges museums faced and overcame in the past continue to have significant implications for museum leaders and professionals today.

Recognizing that the history of museum computing is not about technology but about people, this book presents a critical analysis of this important history as seen through twelve different conceptual lenses. Each lens is presented in its own chapter and offers a different perspective on the history of museum computing in a way that demonstrates how the overarching concepts that drove this field forward remained the same even as the technologies used in museums changed. The twelve chapters that comprise this history are as follows, each exploring a different theme that transcends the past sixty years of museum computing:

1) *Invisible Work* explores the challenges posed by the underlying invisibility of information infrastructures in museums and the double-edged sword that museum technology professionals face as they perform their important work unseen and behind the scenes. This chapter stresses the need for museum leaders to support museum technology professionals as they work on museum computing projects, and to strive to make their invisible contributions visible to all stakeholders across the institution.
2) *Evolving Roles* explores how the roles and responsibilities of museum technology professionals evolved along with changing technologies in museums, with a particular focus on the evolution of collections management systems. This chapter stresses the transition that took place as the nature of museum computing evolved over the decades from smaller, more internally focused, individual technology projects to larger, more externally focused, multi-institutional digital initiatives.

3) *Institutional Knowledge* explores the dangers of losing institutional memory and organizational knowledge as needs and priorities change with respect to technology projects in museums. This chapter stresses the importance of building internal capacity, recognizing professional expertise, and emphasizing the process over the product if museums are to break out of the cycles of forgetfulness and preserve the institutional knowledge needed to sustain museum computing.
4) *Increasing Demands* explores the difficulties involved in keeping current with constantly changing technologies—whether one is working behind the scenes, in the galleries, or online—with a particular focus on the use of digital images in exhibits. This chapter stresses the increasing demands that were placed on museum technology professionals over time to learn new skills, adopt new technologies, take on new tasks, and implement new tools to support computers in museums.
5) *Creative Innovation* explores the factors that fostered a creative spirit among museum technology professionals and helped the field of museum computing move forward through the development of inspirational projects in an environment of constant change and technological growth. This chapter stresses the need to overcome barriers to innovation and keep alive the positive spirit of creativity that helped museums to adopt innovative approaches to using computer technologies to engage their audiences.
6) *Experimental Freedom* explores how museum technology professionals enthusiastically embraced the freedom to experiment with emerging technologies to explore new ideas through cutting-edge projects that pushed the envelope of museum computing. This chapter stresses the importance of taking risks in traditionally risk-averse institutions like museums and the boundless enthusiasm that stemmed from the excitement of learning something new, and the fun of figuring things out along the way.
7) *Disruptive Technologies* explores the underlying tensions, fears, and frustrations that emerged as new computer technologies caused disruptions for museum professionals and museum visitors in the galleries and behind the scenes. This chapter stresses how the museum technology professionals' ability to overcome fears and resolve confusions prompted a seismic shift in attitudes about museum computing that helped everyone better understand the benefits of integrating new technologies into museums.
8) *Radical Change* explores how new ideas about providing access to digital images and collections data changed the nature of the museum experience and the responsibilities of museum technology professionals. This chapter stresses the importance of the evolving social obligations that encouraged museums to adopt open data and open-access policies for their collections information and images and embrace the idea of making their digital information resources broadly available as a public good.

9) *Digital Leadership* explores the attitudes and characteristics of the individuals and institutions who led the way in helping museums embrace new technologies and support technological innovation. This chapter stresses the evolution of museum technology professionals from invisible, behind-the-scenes workers to institutional leaders and innovation champions who worked together to bring about organizational change in their own institutions and professionalize the field of museum computing worldwide.
10) *Professional Networks* explores how belonging to a professional community provides access to a network of peers that can help museum technology professionals reach their goals, share lessons learned, and solve problems together through the power of collaborations, consortia, and other communities of practice. This chapter stresses the value of professional communities for helping museum technology professionals overcome challenges, share knowledge, and shape the future of museum computing.
11) *Changing Mindsets* explores how new ideas about the role of the museum in the life of the visitor encouraged museum technology professionals to shift the focus of their efforts from the museum and its needs to the museum's visitors and their expectations. This chapter stresses the importance of museums developing a culture that emphasizes data-driven evaluations, iterative design, and user testing as an integral part of shaping the way museums engage with their audiences through computer technologies.
12) *Inclusive Philosophies* explores the evolving philosophies that guide museum technology professionals as they work to make their collections more inclusive, challenge implicit biases and assumptions, and bring more diverse voices into their information systems. This chapter stresses the difference museums can make in the lives of their visitors, no matter who they are or where they live in the world, and the opportunity museums have to encourage diversity, promote social justice, and help make the world a better place.

Museums today find themselves at a challenging crossroads where digital initiatives are more important than ever, but advocating for those initiatives continues to be extremely difficult. The more the valuable work of museum technology professionals remains unseen and unsupported, the more likely it is that the invisible nature of this work will pose a danger to museums in times of change, and the less likely it is that museum leadership will prioritize digital initiatives in the future. By shining a light on the behind-the-scenes magic of museum technology professionals, this book pulls back the curtain on the history of museum computing in a way that will help lead the profession into a more positive, more magical future, together.

SUGGESTIONS FOR FURTHER READING

Ellin, Everett. 1969. "Museums and the Computer: An Appraisal of New Potentials." *Computers and the Humanities* 4 (1): 25-30.

Jones-Garmil, Katherine. 1997. *The Wired Museum: Emerging Technology and Changing Paradigms*. Washington, DC: American Association of Museums.

Marty, Paul F. 2007. "Museum Professionals and the Relevance of LIS Expertise." *Library & Information Science Research* 29 (2): 252-276.

Marty, Paul F., and Katherine B. Jones. 2008. *Museum Informatics: People, Information, and Technology in Museums*. New York: Routledge.

Marty, Paul F., and Katherine B. Jones. 2022. "Making it Visible: An Oral History Project Shines a Light on the Invisible History of Museum Computing." *Museum* (Nov/Dec): 22-27.

Parry, Ross. 2010. *Museums in a Digital Age*. London: Routledge.

1

Invisible Work

> So long as those systems aren't visibly breaking or causing trouble in some way, they can be pretty invisible. I mean, in a good sense and a bad sense, they're a little bit like plumbing. If they're working, it's great; if they're not, you really know it. But you often don't think about whatever sorts of ongoing maintenance and proactive engagement they require that takes very specific kinds of knowledge.—Oral History of Rob Lancefield

One of the challenges facing museum technology professionals is that their work tends to be invisible, both inside and outside their institutions. This form of invisibility typically manifests in two ways: first, their work tends to be invisible to other people—in the sense that if you can see what I am doing, then I am probably not doing my job; second, the underlying infrastructure that supports their work also tends to be invisible, even to people who use that infrastructure every day—in the sense that if you can see that infrastructure, then something has likely gone terribly wrong.

The invisible work of technology professionals is naturally not unique to museums. The problems of invisible labor pervade a multitude of institutions and disciplines. Digital initiatives and technology projects often require extensive behind-the-scenes work that few people see, and even fewer people understand. This kind of invisibility offers a certain degree of autonomy but also the potential for misunderstanding the technology professional's actual job.

Many of our oral history participants commented on how the inherent nature of invisible work can be a double-edged sword for museum technology professionals. On the one hand, when no one is watching what you are doing all that closely, you have a kind of freedom that can be helpful. But on the other hand, when no one sees what you are doing or understands why it matters, it can be difficult to get the resources you need to support your work. Shelley

Mannion, for example, in her oral history, reflects on her experiences developing digital learning programs at the British Museum:

> There's the invisibility of the work that happens in museum technology departments, in maybe the invisibility to people from outside—meaning visitors, or the public, or the people who consume the things that we produce—but there's another really interesting layer of complexity to this, which is the invisibility *within* the museum of our work. . . . I feel like that invisibility works in two ways. It works in our favor, and it also works against us. It works in our favor in the respect that it allows us to experiment and do things that the institution maybe wouldn't formally sanction. . . . An example that I'd use is my work at Samsung Digital Discovery Centre at the British Museum . . . which was designed to create digital learning programs for families and for schools. . . . Where I feel like I benefited from invisibility is that nobody was really that interested in what was happening . . . there wasn't a lot of scrutiny about what I did. I had a lot of autonomy, and not only was that satisfying from the point of view of building my skills, and taking ownership of something, and having the freedom really to make my mark on it, but equally, it meant that there were a lot of things that I got to do that I genuinely don't think, with more interest, oversight, and more scrutiny, I would have been able to do. . . . Of course, the downside of that is that you have incredibly few resources. . . . Being a museum technology person means that it's all on you. . . . I can remember this slightly harrowing moment when I realized that I'd advertised and got bookings for a family workshop around Augmented Reality, and I literally didn't know what I was going to do. . . . I had maybe two weeks, and I remember sitting, kind of slightly panicked, in my bedroom in my tiny apartment in London, being like, "Okay, I really have to get it together now. I have to research AR and figure out how, in two weeks' time, I'm going to design some sort of digital learning experience for these families that are going to come in and have the expectation of doing AR at the British Museum."

Flying under the radar can be a powerful thing. Many of our participants mentioned how having the autonomy to work on projects without anyone looking over your shoulder means you have the freedom to explore ideas and develop projects the way you want without any interference from the institution. Richard Rinehart, for example, describes building one of the world's first museum websites in this environment at the Berkeley Art Museum and Pacific Film Archive:

> It was one of those things where the institution was only peripherally involved—in fact, largely unaware of what we were doing. When we launched the website. . . . I think it was probably among the first ten museum websites developed in the world. . . . It was interesting to me how we started this under the radar, like we were the Morlocks, and we were building our own machines, and nobody knew, up above, what we were doing until they came out, and it turned out to be quite a useful tool.

Deborah Howes echoes these comments as she describes the relative freedom and lack of expectations one had when designing websites at the Metropolitan Museum of Art at a time when no one was watching what you were doing, and few people even knew what the web was:

> I stayed at the Met for thirteen years, and at that time . . . nobody was really watching us that closely about what we were doing. It was such an unknown. . . . There were no expectations. There were five people at the Met when I started who had email addresses—and they were not "metmuseum.org"—and so when I would talk to curators about, "Let's do this on the web. . . ." They were like, "What is that? I don't know what that is."

Unfortunately, while no one watching over your shoulder has its advantages, the difficulties that accrue when no one understands what you are doing—when your own work is invisible—can be dangerous. There are no magic elves working behind the scenes in museums keeping technology projects running. Rob Lancefield reminds us that technology only keeps working because there are real people doing this work and that this kind of invisible labor poses risks:

> Whatever sorts of platforms and systems and tools and software are in play, it's ultimately people who make these things work, who keep them working for other people, who answer a technical support email to help people, who help them figure it out when they can't figure out what the issue is. . . . And all of that can be invisible in ways that can pose continuing risks that can be difficult to communicate.

It is perhaps understandable that audiences from outside the museum might not recognize or understand the behind-the-scenes work of the museum technology professional. When visitors interact with museums online, for example, they may not think about the people who work behind the scenes to make that interaction possible. Sometimes the people performing that work can be so invisible that outside audiences might not even realize there is an actual person, and not a machine, working in real time behind the scenes. Andrea Ledesma, for example, describes answering questions as an invisible worker on Twitter for the National Archives:

> I ended up getting an internship with the National Archives in D.C., and I was placed with their social media and education team. And, looking back on it, it was a really wild project because I knew I wanted to work with visitors. I wanted to work with the Internet and technology . . . and at the time, the National Archives had a traveling Civil War exhibition . . . and at the end of that exhibition there was a podium where you could tweet at the exhibition something that you wanted to know more about or something that you learned, and then that would respond. And lo and behold, that Twitter account responding

> was me, the intern, watching the Twitter feed, and sort of sitting there, like a Mechanical Turk, like, "Oh, this fun fact about this particular battle? Yes, I have a spreadsheet of responses, and I will go in and respond for you."

When we visit museums in person and interact with immersive visualizations and other digital exhibits, we may not think about how much work was required to create those interactive displays before they are installed on the gallery floor. Even experienced, professional designers can easily underestimate how much time these digital projects can take, or how challenging the work can be. Sarah Kenderdine describes the extensive time and effort involved in creating high-quality image visualizations in museum galleries:

> Everything is slow in visualization. It's not fast; it's slow. I've got a young software engineer working for me and we're working on a small project together. It's two 82-inch LCD screens on a rotating platform . . . for browsing Buddhist objects for my Atlas of Maritime Buddhism. And he said to me, "When you gave me this job, I thought it would take three weeks, and we're still working on it six months later." And it's the difference between making things that are good enough, and then the next bit is so hard and so painful you don't want to do it. And the effort that it takes—people don't have a clue.

When we look at the collections of digital images freely available for us to access online, we rarely consider the challenges museum professionals had to overcome in order to make those images available for outside audiences to download and use. The ease with which one can search for and retrieve high-quality digital images of museum artifacts belies the complexity involved in putting those images online in the first place. Ruth Cuadra describes the invisible work that had to take place in the background in order to make open-access images available worldwide:

> We've done a lot. The Frick just announced a huge upload of free images. The British Museum has done it. But all of that has a lot of things going on in the background, having to do with: What are the decisions about the size of what someone can download? What are the copyright—copyright is a big part of that that people don't realize. "Oh, they have all these images! They're letting us use them." All of those images were vetted as being available under their particular copyright restrictions. Nobody has any idea that all that is going on in the background.

While this kind of background work may be naturally invisible to outside audiences, it is quite a different matter when internal audiences, such as museum administrators, do not recognize or understand the work that needs to happen behind the scenes for museum technology projects to succeed. This can be particularly challenging when it comes to museums making decisions about long-term investments in digital resources. Eleanor Fink, for example, describes the difficulties museum administrators faced in understanding the invisible work necessary to support the underlying digital infrastructure at the Smithsonian American Art Museum:

> There was very little understanding of the needs for documentation standards as they evolved in the museum community, especially by museum administration. There was, and in many respects there still is, a lack of understanding about the effort and work that goes into cataloging and maintaining good documentation. There is particularly a lack of understanding of the importance of sharing data and adhering to international standards. When we brought the first computer into SAAM to begin adding the information from our collection management system . . . there was a lot of work that had to be invested in maintaining the data that just was not, I would say, known by the administration. And today, to some degree, I think it's the same. Although we've come a long way, I think that museum administration and trustees are seduced by the shiny technological things and are hesitant to understand and invest in a long-term digital infrastructure in order to maintain and upgrade systems, keep staff trained, and adhere to international standards so that data can be shared. Progress has been made, but the lack of understanding of what's involved in documenting, and the commitment that has to be made in order to maintain and provide good data, is still an issue.

This kind of invisibility can be particularly dangerous for museum technology professionals. When people do not understand what you are doing, it can be difficult for them to determine where you belong in the organization, or even if you belong at all. Dana Mitroff Silvers describes how it was unclear which department was responsible for the museum's website or where the web belonged in the organization when she started working as a web developer for SFMOMA:

> When I applied for the job at SFMOMA, it was called "Web Manager," but I don't even know what the title was. This was 2000 or 2001. It was still pretty old school in that it was considered a graphic design job. The question was always, "Is this marketing? Is this graphic design? Who owns this thing? Where does it go? Who owns the content?"

When people do not understand what you are doing, they may not understand the importance of investing in digital skills or hiring people with those skills. As Jane Alexander reminds us, with the prevalence of personal computers and modern-day digital devices, museum administrators may think that technology work is the sort of thing that anyone can do, and as a result, may not recognize the need to invest in people with specific technology skills:

> Museums need to invest . . . museums need people with technical backgrounds. . . . I mean, sometimes we're like, "Well, we all use digital." It reminds me of the 1980s, when we all got Macs, and we had Paintbox on our Macs, and it was like "Oh, we don't need a graphic designer. We all can make our own signs."

When people do not understand what you are doing, they may not take your work seriously. Mia Ridge describes the challenges she faced developing software at the Museum of London and the difficulty of being taken seriously in terms of the experience required to do the job well:

> I ended up doing a Master's in Human Computer Interaction, because I was building software and sometimes it wouldn't be used, and I was like, "I need to know why it's not being used because we're investing time." We didn't have anything like requirements engineering, or understanding user needs—it wasn't on the radar. And I was sick of people saying things like, "My 12-year-old could make a website. Why is this taking so long?" Or thinking that their opinion was as valid as mine. At that point, I probably had 10 years' experience working on the web, and was like, maybe I didn't have a piece of paper. I didn't have a Ph.D. or anything to say I've been doing this for a long time.

When people do not understand what you are doing, they may not realize your work is real work that requires real expertise. You might have to keep explaining what your work is, why it matters, and why it is core to the museum's mission. As Matthew MacArthur explains, reflecting on his role at the National Museum of American History, the job of the museum technology professional is so new, especially in comparison to other, more established museum roles, that people may not realize that this work is highly skilled with its own discipline and required knowledge base:

> When it comes to the care of physical artifacts and putting them on display, there are very well-defined roles from conservation to exhibit designers to fabricators. . . . Nobody's marching down to conservation and telling them, "Here's a bottle, you should be really using this stuff," or going in to the fabricator, and grabbing their tools. But with digital tools, a lot of people know a little, and they know just enough. Like maybe, back in the day it was, "I made a Geo page," or "I made my little site," or "I have social media accounts, and therefore I can be somewhat of an authority on this." And I'm not saying that's totally untrue, but as anyone who's run institutional social media knows, it is very different from running one's personal accounts. And then, if you get into the aspect that we're actually trying to be educational about it, and teach history, there's just a lot of skills that come into play. It is a highly skilled job, and yet, sometimes it is hard to explain even to people who know us very well, to colleagues, or to our managers. We find ourselves sometimes in the position of feeling like we're constantly explaining what it is that we actually do . . .

> because there is not really as much of a shared knowledge and understanding as there is in some other kinds of disciplines in the museum.

When people do not understand what you are doing, they may take your work for granted and think of you as free labor. When the cost of the technology worker's time is invisible, museums can end up making strategic decisions that may not be in their best interests and can result in the underfunding of museum technology projects. Rob Lancefield explains how the invisible costs of staff time hid the true cost of the project when selecting a Collections Management System for the Davison Art Center at Wesleyan University:

> The cost of licensing a system? That was very visible. The costs of staff time to develop in-house because there happened to be somebody working there who was really interested in doing it, and had thought some about data modeling in other contexts before museum work, and was getting paid to be there anyway? That was effectively invisible. . . . It looked like, "Wow, cool. All those people at the Davison Art Center have to do is pay 159 bucks for a FileMaker Pro license. . . ." It looked cheap, and in a cash sense, it was . . . although of course it was zero-sum with other work that could have been done. . . . The invisibility of the very significant amount of time it took for an already on-staff person to design, build, and manage an in-house system drove an institutional decision unavoidably towards going with an in-house system, even though . . . adding up all of the various indirect but definable costs of that approach, surely that exceeded what would have been paid to, in that case, Gallery Systems, had we moved to EmbARK back in like 1998 or whenever.

It is in this environment of invisible labor, therefore, that museum technology professionals design and develop the underlying infrastructures that keep the museum's digital projects running, and shape the work of the museum behind the scenes. Building and supporting those infrastructures is extensive and time-consuming work that is not only critically important to the museum but also essentially invisible to most users of the museum's digital resources. As a result, museum technology professionals spend a great deal of their time building invisible infrastructures behind the scenes that few people will see but many people will use. Kate Collen, for example, describes the extensive, behind-the-scenes work required to establish digitization procedures, scan postal proofs, and make the resulting digital images available online at the National Postal Museum:

> We had about 35,000 very rare objects. They were called certified plate proofs, which were the final print of the postage stamp that was signed and certified prior to it going and being printed by the Bureau of Engraving and Printing. We have these original sheets of stamps. And they're very rare. . . . But they had never been digitized because of their rarity, because of

> their value, their fragility. . . . So I ended up writing a grant to a Smithsonian committee in order to be able to digitize these . . . and we ended up, for a number of reasons, outsourcing the digitization to National Geographic. . . . We'd courier them from the Postal Museum . . . down the street to the main National Geographic headquarters. And there they would be digitized using a high-resolution scanning back camera. Metadata would be embedded into them. We'd take the images on two terabyte drives, and then we'd courier the objects back. But the back end of that project was numbering them, making sure that they were cataloged in TMS, hiring a registrar to do that, hiring volunteers, culling the collection, getting curator buy-in. The curators wanted to see the digitization facility. The head of preservation wanted to visit it to make sure it was a safe environment. We had to negotiate with National Geographic to be able to store our objects in their vaults when we left them for a week of digitization and then came back, got those objects and brought new objects. It was a highly choreographed project, but in the end, I believe, about 2,500 high resolution objects ended up online. Over 20,000 of them were fully cataloged in the CMS at the end of the project. It made a previously unavailable collection available to the public through our online research portal and collections website.

Just getting the museum spaces and storerooms ready for that digitization work to take place requires extensive and challenging behind-the-scenes work that is invisible to most end users. Setting up a physical workflow, resolving infrastructural problems, and strategic planning are all necessary first steps before the first picture can be taken. As Diane Zorich reminds us, when it comes to the invisible work of mass digitization and digital imaging at the Smithsonian Institution, clicking the shutter is the easy part:

> Moving these collections from storage to a digitization station and back safely, in our facilities, that is a real challenge. We have very old buildings. We have offsite facilities. We have over 1,000 storage spaces total, from every broom closet that has something in it to huge spaces in our Museum Support Center in Maryland. . . . Most of the storage areas were chosen in some of the buildings because there's no internet drop. Nothing can be done there, except storage. But we need to sometimes bring internet drops in to be able to use barcoding and scanning. . . . Some areas don't have electrical outlets. We have to put in electricity, drop electrical wire, so we have to bring our facilities people in. It's a huge checklist of things that we go through before we even click the first shutter. It could be months of planning before you actually do anything. And you need the entire staff of the museum to know that.

Similarly, getting the galleries ready for visitors to bring their own devices into the museum requires a lot of behind-the-scenes hard work that most visitors do not see. Infrastructural requirements become more complex as more visitors bring their own smart devices into museums and attempt to access information about the museum using those devices. Scott Sayre describes the invisible work that goes into building an infrastructure that seamlessly supports visitors using their own devices to access content at the Corning Museum of Glass:

> We're talking about people either having iOS or an Android device in their pocket and really aiming our content for that, at the same time knowing that particularly people who are traveling have concerns about their batteries, and using their phone, their minutes, and things like that. So the first thing we did was really build an infrastructure to support Bring Your Own Device (BYOD), and we were able to do that from the ground up in that we had a robust open Wi-Fi network that when you logged onto it, it pushed our content right to your device, so basically the minute you logged onto our Wi-Fi, our mobile experience was right there on your phone. We put in charging stations throughout the entire museum, and developed a signage system and little sitting areas that were dedicated juice-up stations to make sure that we were addressing everything that people really needed. The other thing that we did was make sure the museum shop was carrying support accessories—headphones, batteries, and things like that—so there were lots of different ways to support people using their own devices throughout the museum.

Yet as important as these underlying invisible infrastructures are for museum professionals and museum visitors alike, they are also dangerous. Information infrastructures tend to be invisible only up to the point when they fail. It can be challenging when your users only become aware of your infrastructure when they can no longer use it. Richard Rinehart reflects on this difficulty in his oral history as he explains that he was late to his interview because of a failure of invisible infrastructure in the form of a bridge coming down:

> I was late because of a bridge coming down. And while I was frustrated and embarrassed to be late, as I was waiting there, it did occur to me that I was frustrated by the failure of some invisible technology. . . . We don't notice this kind of invisible infrastructure until it fails us, and that was not lost on me. . . . And as I was passing the highway workers who were working on getting this bridge up and running, I sort of felt a kinship in a way. I know what it's like to be one of the Morlocks, down in the subterranean chambers, laboring away at machines, whose purpose and impact I perhaps don't fully grasp, but laboring nonetheless in darkness, while the masters above reap the benefits until we smash the machines.

In particular, the inherent nature of invisible infrastructures can cause problems because they can look like they are working fine, right up to the moment that they fail. Invisible work is risky work. Invisibility can mask underlying problems with information infrastructures and make it hard to explain the need to support those infrastructures over the long term, especially when people cannot see what is happening behind the scenes. One could easily be convinced that if an infrastructure is currently working, then it must be fine with the level of support it currently has. Unfortunately, as Rob Lancefield explains, that is not necessarily true:

> The super-tricky part is communicating the importance of keeping invisible work happening and able to continue happening. . . . It can look like "working properly" is just the natural state of those systems when in fact, it's a condition that comes about, in large part, only because of the expertise that staff are applying to those systems every day to keep them running in ways that people don't notice, because they are working. . . . The only way any of this stuff works is when people know how to keep it working and make it work better. And the more invisible that is, the tougher it can be to help people understand why it should not be left in a fragile state. . . . When things are working, it can mask the fact that there can still be a dangerous degree of fragility.

It can be hard to help people understand just how fragile these invisible infrastructures can be, and why they cannot be left alone to fend for themselves. Getting additional support for invisible work is tricky, and this lack of understanding about the underlying fragility of these invisible infrastructures can make it hard to get resources you need to sustain those infrastructures. Matthew MacArthur explains how the evolution of websites at the National Museum of American History shines a light on the challenge of supporting invisible infrastructures over the long term, and all the things that can go wrong as digital resources disappear and websites fail:

> In the early years . . . a lot of resources went into very beautiful exhibition websites designed by some great designers and companies that we worked with. What happened is that these websites started accumulating over time. They were all one-offs, because we would work with different companies, and as time changed, the technologies would change. And we found ourselves accumulating a collection of these unique snowflakes of websites. And looking back from the perspective now, we were just setting ourselves up for an infrastructure and maintenance nightmare because each site was unique to maintain. When a site broke, it broke uniquely. The Smithsonian would update its servers, and things would break. So, we really started changing our mindset about that in the early 2000s, where you know, we started saying, "Hold on, let's stop thinking so much about these one-off projects, and start thinking about making investments in technology platforms that were reusable, that would unify our approach somewhat, and that we could update over time." And so we've been grappling really for the first time in a very serious way as an institution with lifecycle issues. . . . Our more successful content has a way of getting embedded in the school curricula, so it's not a super simple calculation. Sometimes we take things down, or they break, and teachers start writing to us and say, "Hey! My class was doing this today. What the heck?" . . .

> So it's a little messy, but we have leadership who gets this, and is helping us transition our mindset to build more sustainability into the process.

Of course, getting that investment of resources from leadership is not easy. It is difficult to get support for your work when people do not see what you are doing, and not all museum administrators will be able to sustain invisible infrastructures, especially during times of change; unfortunately, that is precisely when invisible infrastructures are at their most vulnerable and most easily forgotten. The fate of the Getty Information Institute, established in the early 1980s to help museum professionals organize and share information about their collections, provides a cautionary tale. As Eleanor Fink explains, the lack of understanding about the behind-the-scenes work of the Getty Information Institute and its significance to the field, combined with all the stress and moving parts leading up to the opening of the Getty Center, led to the Information Institute's closure in 1997:

> I would say, in many respects, it was a lack of understanding among the trustees of what the true value of the Getty Information Institute was. . . . The very fact that the Getty Information Institute was shuttered, so to speak, is typical, I think of the lack of understanding. Of course, we had briefings with the trustees. We were all directors of the different institutes. . . . Each of us had separate budgets and leadership activities. We met with the trustees every month to inform them about our activities. But there was so much going on before the opening of the Getty Center, and so many cost overruns, that . . . although I briefed the trustees on several occasions on the Getty Information Institute's leadership role, they tended to forget. The trustees' main interest was always the museum and its collecting. They didn't seem to appreciate how many organizations and institutions around the world counted on what we produced. The Getty Information Institute's circle of supporters didn't come to the Getty Center.

For many museum technology professionals, not only are their work and their infrastructure invisible, but so are the people who depend on that work and rely on that infrastructure. To keep their work going, and to make sure the infrastructures they build are not shut down, it is essential that museum technology professionals have support from museum administrators. Once again, however, this can be a double-edged sword. Gaining that support or receiving recognition for your work has its own consequences. It calls attention to your activities and raises questions of control. As Shelley Mannion describes, when people finally do see what you are doing, when your invisible work becomes visible and you become part of the fabric of the institution, you risk losing the very autonomy that made you successful in the first place:

> When the Eye of Sauron is turned on you, it means all the stakeholders are looking. Suddenly, the business recognizes that you're doing something interesting, and it's like . . . suddenly people are interested, and everybody has an opinion about it. . . . It suddenly feels like this wonderful autonomy that you've had, where you've been able to be self-directed. . . . Suddenly, then, you have to begin to justify everything. . . . I mean, it's great, right, because you want the attention. You want visibility for your work. You want resources for your work. You want it to become part of the fabric of the institution. In order to genuinely transform the institution, you need to be close to the centers of power of the institution, where decisions are made, where the influencers are, and so on. But equally, you then surrender a great degree of your autonomy and freedom because now you're working within a set of constraints and . . . it just becomes so much more political.

Peter Samis describes a similar transition from skunkworks to scrutiny for his digital team, and the corresponding loss of creative freedom, as he reflects on the changing nature of digital work at SFMOMA over time:

> Digital is part of everything that the museum does now . . . and it's also scrutinized from the top level in a way it wasn't before. We started out as a skunkworks . . . and now we're at a place where that digital creative impulse has been in a sense, subordinated or subjugated by the top-level strategies of the museum, and so people no longer have the creative freedom to do the kinds of things we were free to do.

Tim Svenonius echoes these comments about losing autonomy at SFMOMA as the institution recognized the work they were doing, and their work became more visible:

> One of the things that characterized those days, in my mind, was that even though the museum had a graphic design department, they had no dealings in multimedia . . . so essentially, we had oversight on matters of image production, color correction, batch processing, interface design, visual design . . . so many things that later, once our activities were more visible and recognized by the rest of the institution, we started losing that autonomy. These little pieces of self-sufficiency were taken away from us. Where ultimately the graphic design department had to approve everything, and . . . a lot of things gradually became much more institutionalized.

Nevertheless, despite the risks, when your work is invisible, you have to make an effort to show people what you did, and how it got done. As Seb Chan reminds us, reflecting on his time at the Australian Centre for the Moving Image (ACMI) in Melbourne, you have to explain your work if you want other people to understand what you have accomplished:

> With the I.T. teams here, everything is below the waterline. Everything that you see as a visitor—almost all the work that happens to make that seem seamless is invisible. . . . You have to tell people about the work you're doing. You can't just show what got done. You have to show how it got done, and what it achieved, because otherwise, people don't realize how much work it actually was to get to where we've got to.

If no one sees your invisible work, then it can be difficult to get the support you need to continue your work in the future. It is essential therefore to give credit where credit is due. Susie Wise, for example, describes her efforts to shine a spotlight on an army of unseen, invisible workers at the launch of a digital exhibit at SFMOMA:

> I remember having a party to celebrate the exhibition launch . . . and deciding to print, as part of the remarks to kick off the party, a list of everybody who'd worked on all the different things. . . . I had it as a scroll, and at the party I just threw it, so that this paper—it was probably from some dot matrix printer—rolled out with the names. . . . It was like a whole software development team. . . . It was just an army of people, totally invisible to almost everybody at the museum, and I look back on it now, and it's kind of an act of leadership to just be like: "This is how many people it actually takes to do this work!"

When all that people see is the end product of technology work, it's easy to miss the effort involved in the process of creating that product. It is essential that we find ways to protect the invisible technology workers who labor behind the scenes building invisible infrastructures and recognize their valuable contributions to the work of museums today. It is worth taking almost any risk if it prompts future investments that can support the invisible work of museum technology professionals and sustain the invisible infrastructures of museum technology projects. By investing in the digital literacy skills of their employees and the technology needs of their institutions, museum administrators can help support museum technology professionals and shine a light on their important yet invisible work in museums.

SUGGESTIONS FOR FURTHER READING

Marty, Paul F. 2012. "Unintended Consequences: Unlimited Access, Invisible Work, and the Future of the Information Profession in Cultural Heritage Organizations." *Bulletin of the American Society for Information Science and Technology* 38 (3): 27–31.

Marty, Paul F. 2016. "The Cobbler's Children: Invisible Work and Information Professionals in Museums." In *Annual Review of Cultural Heritage Informatics*, edited by Jennifer Weil Arns, 19–22. Lanham, MD: Rowman and Littlefield.

Nardi, Bonnie, and Yrjö Engeström. 1999. "A Web on the Wind: The Structure of Invisible Work." *Computer Supported Cooperative Work* 8 (1): 1–2.

Sayre, Scott. 2015. "Bring It On: Ensuring the Success of BYOD Programming in the Museum Environment." In *Museums and the Web 2015*, edited by Nancy Proctor and Rich Cherry. Silver Spring, MD: Museums and the Web. https://mw2015.museumsandtheweb.com/paper/bring-it-on-ensuring-the-success-of-byod-programming-in-the-museum-environment/index.html

Star, Susan Leigh, and Karen Ruhleder. 1996. "Steps Toward an Ecology of Infrastructure: Design and Access for Large Information Spaces." *Information Systems Research* 7 (1): 113–138.

Star, Susan Leigh, and Anselm Strauss. 1999. "Layers of Silence, Arenas of Voice: The Ecology of Visible and Invisible Work." *Computer Supported Cooperative Work* 8 (1): 9–30.

Zorich, Diane M. 1999. *Introduction to Managing Digital Assets: Options for Cultural and Educational Organizations*. Los Angeles, CA: Getty Trust Publications.

2

Evolving Roles

> The museum administration wanted the Registrar's Office, where I was at the time, to come up with a recommendation for a system that would track the museum's finances, membership, donors' contributions, the art collection, and, oh yeah, attendance, too. So we spent some time looking for that magical unicorn system . . . and guess what? We never found it.—Oral History of Marla Misunas

The roles and responsibilities of museum technology professionals have changed dramatically since computers were first introduced to museums in the 1960s. As the purpose of museum computing evolved from installing systems and connecting computers to providing access to information resources and collections content, first internally and then externally, to supporting new forms of engaging experiences for museum audiences, starting in person and then moving online, museums recognized the potential of information technologies, and the job of the museum technology professional changed in response to new systems and technologies.

These changes were challenging for two key reasons: first, what you were doing on the job—the tasks you were asked to complete—kept changing as new technologies entered the museum; and second, why you were doing the job—the reasons you were asked to complete those tasks—kept changing as new ideas evolved about how those technologies could be used in the museum. For museum technology professionals, these changes were part of a process of co-evolution, where the tasks they completed and the technologies that drove those tasks changed constantly alongside each other in response to ever-changing internal demands and external expectations for museum computing.

One of the best ways to observe this co-evolutionary process in action is to examine how museum technology professionals used computers to organize and manage information about their collections, and how that task evolved over time with the available technologies. In some cases, early efforts to digitize information about museum collections were driven by a single individual, usually because they had information they wanted to save electronically, and they recognized that digitizing this information would be useful in the future. Often no one asked them to do this, no one understood why they were doing it, and no one else was even interested in the idea. Howard Besser, for example, in his oral history, describes his early experiments with building one of the first computer databases at the Berkeley Art Museum in the 1970s:

> I started working as a volunteer for the Pacific Film Archive, part of the University Art Museum in Berkeley in 1972. . . . We got a grant from the National Endowment for the Arts specifically for cataloging our Japanese collection, and so I was essentially doing computerized typesetting that would also feed into an eventual database, but at that point we had no capabilities of databases. We started that project in about 1977 or so, where we were typesetting the records of different films. . . . The administration of the museum decided, "Hey, let's take our regular printed calendar, and let's make a souped-up version using computers to typeset the calendar." So they hired a very expensive designer and I worked with the designer . . . who was only interested in what the calendar looked like . . . but I was interested in saving the records that we were doing. At that point in time, Pacific Film Archive was showing about 15 films per week, and the calendar included all of the information about the filmmaker, the stars, the date, the distribution company, as well as a synopsis of the film. And I was interested in saving all of that, and making sure that we had that in such a way that it could enter a database. So I developed a very simple user interface, where the computer would ask you director, film title, filmed date, running time, etc. And then it would nicely typeset all that but also save all the information in machine-readable form. The museum was really only interested in the immediate issue of typesetting . . . but I was struggling and making the process a whole lot more complicated in order to save those records.

In other cases, museums started using computers to organize, manage, and share information about their collections because of institutional efforts specifically intended to digitize museum resources. A growing number of museums recognized that creating digital versions of their collections records would enable them to cooperate and share information in a more standardized way using computers. This would only work, however, if there were some common system or computer platform that they could all use to coordinate information about their collections in digital format. In the late 1960s, institutional efforts to organize digital collections information started to ramp up as museum professionals began to explore institutional approaches to solving this problem. Cathy Heller describes how her father, Jack Heller, led the development of a new database system shared across a consortium of museums that would eventually become the Museum Computer Network:

> In 1965, New York University established the Institute for Computer Research in the Humanities. . . . In 1966, my dad and the Institute came to the attention of the staff at the Metropolitan Museum of Art and began exploring a project to create an electronic index of the Met's collections. . . . The Museum Computer Network was born out of a cooperative computing project in the New York City area in 1967, under the direction of my father. The organization began as an informal grouping of museums with the goal of automating registration records. . . . The vision was for a shared national and international museum data bank that would not only improve museum management practices but would provide unprecedented access for researchers. . . . Fifteen New York area museums joined forces to explore ways that an electronic index—a data dictionary—of the Metropolitan Museum's collections could be used beyond the Met and other museums. . . . My dad developed a system called GRIPHOS—General Retrieval and Information Processor for Humanities Oriented Studies—which was based on a data dictionary that could be used by diverse institutions participating in the project. It consisted of a tagged record format that allowed for the description of individual objects with separate linked records for the artists' biographical information and for reference citations. . . . The GRIPHOS system provided information storage, search, and retrieval infrastructures for the museum records.

Whether the impetus to digitize collections information came from individual or institutional efforts, it is important to remember that almost all of this work was conducted on mainframe computers in the 1960s and 1970s, where museum professionals would need to connect to the mainframe through a laborious process using punched cards to upload digital records. The nature of this technology directly shaped the task of the museum technology professional and changed the job almost overnight as museums learned how they could use these new systems to support their activities. Kathy Jones describes using GRIPHOS in the Division of Archives, History, and Records Management in Tallahassee, Florida, and how the passage of the Historic Preservation Act in 1966 drove the adoption of database technology for recording information about artifacts:

> After I graduated, I went to work for the Department of State. . . . The Historic Preservation Act was passed in 1966 and that created a State Historic Preservation Office (SHPO). Before that time, all of the records of archaeological sites and properties had been kept by the universities in the departments of anthropology. Suddenly we have the SHPO and the files start moving there . . . and with all of those site files moving to one central office, it meant that there was a need for a database. On or before 1974, the SHPO had licensed GRIPHOS from the Museum Computer Network. . . . We had to run it on a large mainframe at another state office. We kept all of the punched cards, which allowed us to put data into the system, in file cabinets in a large office in the Old Leon County Jail, because that was our home. My first office actually

> was in a holding cell, and that was kind of convenient because you could lock it up at night and not have to worry about your stuff. . . . Our division became the repository for artifacts that had been recovered from archaeological sites under that 1966 Act, so we had to start processing them and taking care of them as if we were a museum. I don't know if all of my colleagues were prepared to do that, but we learned quickly on the job, and it became apparent that we could use GRIPHOS to record artifacts too.

In some ways, the fact that much of this work was being done on common mainframe computers made it easier to share systems and standardize cataloging methods across multiple museums. On the other hand, this depended on everyone having access to the same technology hardware and software, and the question of which systems could run on which computers became very important as competing database systems were developed to record information about museum collections at different institutions. At that time, one's choice of database system was inextricably linked to the available underlying technology (for example, GRIPHOS was written in PL1, and as a result could only run on IBM mainframe computers). David Bridge explains how this interconnection between software and hardware affected the development and adoption of the SELGEM database system at the Smithsonian, perhaps one of the first examples of open-source software, in the early 1970s:

> One of its strengths was that it was generalized, it wasn't just designed for insects or mollusks. . . . SELGEM was a very flexible system, and so I could sit down with you today, and you say, "I've got these 50 interviews and I want to get some keywords and people, dates, and times," and we could have a database for you tomorrow. . . . SELGEM was developed in COBOL, and in absolute pure anti-standard COBOL, which means that you could move it to any other computer that was available in the '70s. GRIPHOS . . . and other systems were built on IBM mainframes, which is perfectly logical, since they had the largest base of installed machines. They also had assembly language code some place in the middle of the program, which meant that it wasn't as transportable. So all the little museums, universities, and whatever that had CDCs, or Sperry Rand, or whatever kind of computer, they couldn't run that software. And it certainly was not the intent of the Smithsonian to have a killer app like that, I built it myself just for Natural History, but it was done in a general enough way that all the other Smithsonian museums, and at least 100 others that we gave it to, implemented it. . . . It just made perfect sense.

This co-evolution of technologies and tasks continued as the field moved from mainframe computers to superminicomputers to personal computers. As the computing technologies available to museums evolved, so did the job of the museum technology professional. Computers became smaller and more broadly available and started offering new features that changed not only what museums could do with the technology but also what museums wanted to do with the technology. For example, museum technology professionals quickly discovered that computers in museums could be used not just to record information about museum artifacts, but also to communicate with others. David Bridge explains how a VAX superminicomputer purchased to support the move of museum collections at the Smithsonian ended up being used for email communication in the early 1980s:

> We were running a DEC VAX 750. The Smithsonian acquired that system to support the move of Smithsonian collections from many different places in Washington, D.C., to the new Museum Support Center in Suitland, Maryland. . . . The Marine Mammal Collection, for example, was in the Alexandria Torpedo Factory, the old military building, and we just took VT100s and printers over there, and plugged them in with modems, and documented the collection that was being moved, and then we took it all out and put it someplace else. . . . We got the VAX computer to support the move, but then I found out that it had email on it, and wonderful communications capability. The Museum Support Center is about eight miles outside of downtown, off the Mall, which was a big problem for a lot of people because it's the first time you couldn't just walk to the other end of the building, or walk to another building to meet with somebody. So I started email to talk to our HR people and financial people and stuff like that. . . . The whole VAX computer was set up to be a networked kind of device . . . which meant that it was widely accessible from all over the place.

This co-evolutionary process continued with the introduction of personal computers into museums in the 1980s and 1990s, dramatically changing the potential of museum technology and the responsibilities of the museum technology professional. As computers became both more prevalent and easier to use, many more museums could purchase a computer and create their own databases to keep track of their collections. The personal computer revolution led to an explosion of digital information systems in museums, as some institutions decided to build their database systems in-house, while others purchased systems from an ever-growing number of off-the-shelf options. This was a brave new world, as Costis Dallas describes:

> When I joined the Benaki Museum—the Benaki is the largest private museum in Greece, it's got collections from Cycladic figurines and classical Greek art to folklore objects and ethnographic collections, and 19th century painting, and jewelry, they've got a lot, really—I started working with the Department of Drawings and Paintings . . . and I started creating this kind of database using CDS/ISIS to start documenting that collection. It was interesting because I had a curator who was very interested in that. She was supporting the project because she felt this was going to be a useful thing for her. For her, the whole process of computerization was nothing different to just transferring the records about these paintings and drawings and prints onto something

> like a manual card catalog—I mean, this was the analog that she had in mind, right? So, in many ways, this is how we started doing the work. . . . It was like a brave new world.

The rise of personal computers in museums quickly changed the landscape of the museum technology profession, prompting many new individuals to get involved in the field for the first time. Cathryn Goodwin describes how the chance to work with computer databases in museums launched her own career at the St. Louis Art Museum:

> I had very purposefully volunteered at the St. Louis Art Museum because I read in their annual report that they were going to be "automating" their collection, as it was called in 1990, and I had gone back to school, and was getting a dual degree in museum studies and information management. And this was exactly what I wanted to do in the museum that was in the town where I was living, so I started volunteering, and I literally as a volunteer, photocopied every object record in the museum to be sent off to what was then Willoughby, and the Quixis database, which was our first collection system. We scanned, we photocopied every session record, and we had to stamp them because, of course, the photocopies were all black and white, and any color coding that was in these documents was lost, and so we had to recreate the color coding, and rapid data entry was done by the vendor. The whole collection was put into this very, very, very basic database at the time, which, of course, had no images. It was all text-based, black screen, blue letters, you know, that whole look. At that time, my computer at the museum when I was volunteering, had two floppy disk drives. One to start the operating system, and the other to save your data.

As the available tools and information systems kept changing, an increasing number of curators and other museum professionals started to realize just how important computers were going to be for museums, and how many new opportunities would arise with collections databases. Sam Quigley, for example, describes the process of recognizing the benefits that database systems could bring to museums like the Museum of Fine Arts, Boston:

> In the '80s, I happened to be one of the curators who had drunk the Kool-Aid of technology and realized that computers were very useful for what we do. We do list-keeping, and ideally, we broadcast from those lists, or some facsimile of them. I was an early advocate and an amateur, but fairly successful amateur programmer. My initial chosen tool was that old faithful, dBase III, but a friend of mine was into DataEase, a so-called fourth generation language, which was really cool, and I developed a little database which got bigger over the course of time for the musical instruments collection and, ultimately, that was seen as something valuable, also for the European Decorative Arts department, of which the musical instruments collection was a part. And so, I did another

> DataEase program for them, and that was particularly useful in their planning a large move that they were doing. . . . We tried actually sharing databases online, using a little tiny network. Well, that soon became kind of cumbersome, but it opened up some eyes. And I think that it was around that time that I started advocating for the idea that the MFA might "really benefit" from getting serious about this stuff.

With this recognition came new opportunities and new challenges for museum technology professionals. New ideas about how database systems worked, why they were necessary, what they could be used for, and who could benefit from their use led to the realization that museum databases might actually be useful to more than a handful of curators and registrars. This was a significant change for many museums. Suddenly, museum databases were no longer viewed as a novelty of limited interest to a small number of people, but a valuable set of data that could be useful to a wide range of potential users. Koven Smith describes coming to the realization that people other than museum registrars were going to want to use the data he was collecting at the Indianapolis Museum of Art:

> My work at the IMA was as the collections database administrator, and I was the first person hired in that position that had any real kind of technical chops at all. . . . I was really the first content-focused technology role that the IMA had, because I wasn't in there just installing desktops. I was working directly with the museum's most important content. And like a lot of museums in those days, they'd been through two or three other collections management systems before Argus, which they were using at that time. There was all kinds of data all over the place, really not normalized, not aligned with any kind of controlled vocabularies or anything like that. And there was a whole users' group of poor Argus users, all of us long suffering, who were trying to figure out how to get things out of the data, because we were starting to get demands and requests to use this data in other ways. That was when for the first time we thought, "Oh, this isn't just like a fancy card catalog; this data may have usability beyond just this system. And others, other than just registrars, may want to use it."

New ideas about the purpose of computer systems in museums also went hand in hand with the growing realization that the museum's records would need to be made available to audiences outside the museum. This was also a new idea for many museum professionals. In the early days of museum computing, most database records were developed for internal use only, with little consideration given to how those records might look to outside observers. As Josh Gorman explains, new ideas about providing open access to previously closed museum data posed challenges for early adopters of computer databases like the Smithsonian:

> We have collections data that goes back to some of our first systems, which were created in 1968. None of that data about our collections was created with the notion that anyone outside the museum would ever use it . . . that the information would be deployed and leveraged by users in any fashion outside of a very narrow group of collections managers, registrars, and curators. There was just no notion that anyone would ever want to see this, that anyone ever would, which severely complicated the ways in which it was entered, and what we had to do to prepare that data to go out, especially with respect to some specific risks around privacy and different security questions, and then the whole notion of reputational risk. You know, the idea that the collections data may be sloppy. It may be incorrect. It may just be embarrassing in some places. . . . So it resulted in us having to spend a long time pulling apart the threads of these other really complicated issues in order to make that happen.

And with these new ideas, the role of the museum technology professional changed. Suddenly museums needed more than simple databases to keep track of their records internally; they needed integrated collections management systems that could help coordinate all of their collections-related activities for global audiences. Once again, new ideas about the purpose of museum computing led to new roles and responsibilities for museum technology professionals. Everyone from museum registrars to slide librarians found their jobs changing as they were asked to explore new ideas for organizing and sharing data with people inside and outside the museum. Kathy Jones describes working as a registrar at the vanguard of museum computing:

> I became a member of the Registrar's Committee of AAM, which was instrumental in how we were processing becoming technologists really early on in the museum world when we thought we were dealing with paper records. But no more. We were dealing with computers, and we needed to know how to standardize our data so that we could eventually talk across platforms, or understand how to migrate data from one platform to another. So that was really important for me very early in my career. . . . That, to me, was important foundational work for the field. Thinking about how registrars became the people who were the early providers of computer information. . . . Being a registrar helped me tremendously in understanding the whole life cycle of an object and what museums needed to do to keep information about it . . . and really helped me prepare for the rest of my career working with databases.

New ideas about sharing information more broadly also meant that museum technology professionals had to find new ways to share collections data through common metadata standards and controlled vocabularies. While establishing shared metadata standards for digital records had long been a concern for museum professionals (dating back to the early days of GRIPHOS), this struggle faced new difficulties with the proliferation of databases following the personal computer revolution. With different museums organizing their collections in different formats following different standards, museums needed to find better ways of organizing and sharing information among institutions and individuals. Unfortunately, this was not a simple task. Eleanor Fink describes her early work organizing information in slide libraries before the introduction of computers, where not only do different institutions organize their slides differently, but different users of those slide libraries search for information in different ways as well:

> Even before I started working at the Smithsonian American Art Museum, I was very interested in how you organize knowledge. The reason for that is that while I was in graduate school, the department of art history asked me if I'd like to help out in the slide library and organize the visual materials. I thought it would be a great way to study for tests, so I said yes. Soon I discovered that each professor organized visual materials differently. There was no consistency or overall logic to the organization of the slide library which made it difficult to find slides. . . . Each followed a different schema for overall organization of their visual materials. One method was by period: ancient, medieval, modern, etc. Another was by type: monument, paintings, sculpture, etc. I learned that there were different ways you could organize knowledge, but at that time—before computers—that meant you were limited to choosing only one schema for physically filing the slides. The one method was based on what worked best for patrons. If your patrons had different needs or multiple interests, you might include cross reference cards. In essence, access to knowledge at this stage was more or less one-dimensional. . . . When the museum's fellows came to my office to look for visual materials, I soon learned that they weren't necessarily interested in searching by period, type, or even by a certain artist. Most often, they were interested in finding images that depicted certain things or specific subjects. For example, they might ask me for images depicting women with white parasols, children playing games, and other genre scenes from different decades. Their interest in finding certain subjects depicted in images kept deepening my whole framework for how to organize visual materials and provide access for research purposes. I realized more and more that the one-dimensional approach was going to be too limited. You needed something that was multidimensional.

Without a common frame of reference or shared standards for organizing information, providing this kind of multidimensional access to collections data is extremely difficult, whether one has access to computers or not. Eleanor Fink describes working on early computer projects at the Smithsonian American Art Museum, and the difficulties they encountered due to the lack of national standards for controlled vocabularies:

> By the 1980s, the Smithsonian American Art Museum had five large computer-based research projects numbering over 500,000 records on the subject of American Art. . . . It occurred to me that it would help if we produced an

"index by artist" drawn from the five databases that could serve as a finding aid. So I asked the Office of Computer Services to produce a comprehensive artists listing. The result indicated huge spelling discrepancies and inconsistencies with the way names were formatted. Good access to information stored on computers depends on consistency. I began to seek sources for art data standards and artist authorities. I discovered there were no standards for managing art information aside from cottage industry examples. I ended up creating my own subject thesaurus to help the scholars who were primarily interested in things depicted in works of art. It was quite elaborate. I would have preferred to use a standard vetted by the museum community, but museums were inventing their own local standards at this stage. There were no national standards. I visited the Library of Congress, to find out more about NACO, a national authority for names of authors. I pointed out that artists were represented in the collections of hundreds of museums, and that museums would benefit from having access to an artist authority like NACO's authority for authors. I asked if NACO would consider expanding its services to include names of artists. They looked at me and said, "Well, who would be the authority to validate which form of an artist's name would be used?" Fast forward a few years, and I would end up taking a leave of absence from SAAM to spend a few years at the Getty to head and establish the Getty Vocabulary Program.

In this environment, it was museum technology professionals who stepped forward to create standards for museums where there were none before. Eleanor Fink explains how her work evolved as she developed metadata standards and controlled vocabularies at the Getty:

> My transition to the Getty happened because of my research on standards and exploration of where to find art documentation standards and name authorities. One day, John Walsh, who was the Director of the Getty Museum, and Henry Millen, who was an advisor to the Getty and head of the Center for Advanced Study in the Visual Arts in the National Gallery of Art, came to see me. They looked at my comprehensive artist listing and said it was excellent. They mentioned that the Getty has several research databases, and staff discovered similar problems with name inconsistencies and lack of a name authority. At the time, the Getty was developing the Provenance Index, the Witt Computer Index in the U.K., the Census of Antique Art and Architecture Known to the Renaissance, and the Bibliography of the History of Art. They were all created on different platforms by different scholars. They said they were very interested in my own efforts to identify standards and name authorities. And so, in essence, their visit led to an invitation from the Getty to create and set up the Getty Vocabulary Program. When I got to the Getty, I hired staff and together we focused on the Union List of Artists Names, and the Thesaurus of Geographic Names, and then later metadata standards like the Categories for the Description of Works of Art and Object ID, both metadata standards I initiated.

The metadata standards developed at the Getty as a result of these efforts proved extremely useful for museums around the world. Ruth Cuadra describes how projects such as the Getty Provenance Index helped coordinate museum records, and provided a source of authority:

> One of the goals of the Getty Provenance Index, from way back at the beginning, was to eventually connect those provenance records: This is the sale of a painting by Rembrandt to an image of that painting. It's the obvious thing. People come to the Provenance Index, and they think they're going to see the pictures of the art that's being described. But that turns out to be nearly impossible, except for a small handful of Old Masters, because we have a lot of records that say, "landscape with a cow." And we know the artist, but which landscape? Which cow? Which version? Who owns it? There are ten copies of that image of that painting. Which one does the Provenance Index think is the one to be shown? You can't really do all of that, and that's where linked data will be very valuable when we get to it. Because out there, there are ten museums that have an image of the landscape with the cow, and we can link to them. We don't have to say, "We think this one is the authority, or this is the right one to go with this provenance record, but here's some possibilities," and we can link to them by the artist's name, by the title, by the owning organization, and so it's a way of expanding the root of what's in the Provenance Index to a much larger universe and potential for research.

As part of their efforts to develop standards for sharing collections data, museum technology professionals had to learn how to work across a wide variety of institutions—not just museums, but libraries and archives as well. Richard Rinehart explains the importance of integrating information from libraries, archives, and museums through interoperable metadata:

> There were a lot of metadata schemas and standards being formulated. . . . A lot of the projects that we were doing, like Museums and the Online Archive of California, purposefully involved museums, archives, and libraries. We were trying to hit really the eternal triad of cultural heritage to get everybody involved, and get everything to be interoperable. . . . I wanted people to be able to discover cultural heritage data and share it behind the scenes. . . . That's still the dream, and it's definitely happening.

This focus on sharing information across institutions also drove efforts to develop collections management systems that could meet information needs across different collections. Chuck Patch, for example, describes his efforts to find a collections management system that would work across the library, archives, and museum divisions at the Historic New Orleans Collection:

> I interviewed for this job at the Historic Collection, and I was there for the next 21 years. . . . I became the Director of Systems there . . . and here's where we

started actually dealing with museum automation, because really early on, in the late '80s, I got obsessed with the idea of integrating museum, library, and archival information because we had three divisions in this very tiny museum. There was a total staff of maybe 60 people, and the library wanted to get software, the archives division wanted to get software, and I was damned if I was going to buy three different systems for this place when we were all basically in successive rooms or buildings. You know, how ridiculous was it that we would have three completely separate divisions dealing with the same types of information . . . the same subject, the history of the city, and the Gulf South in general, and yet we were requiring researchers to trek from one place to another to get any information when we had it all there.

Integrating collections data across libraries, archives, and museums was not the only challenge; so was sharing information resources across different kinds of museums. Art museums, science museums, history museums, and more all have different ways of describing their collections, and identifying a common standard that can work across those types of collections is not easy. Kate Collen describes the process of making it possible to search across collections databases from many different museums at the Smithsonian Institution:

Now the Smithsonian has one overarching collections website. It's collections .si.edu. That was another project I worked on where we had to map data from our TMS system. And there were, I think, ten museums, using different instances of TMS at the Smithsonian when I was there. Each had different types of collections. Each had different ways they were using the system. So this large data mapping project took place . . . so now, the public can go in and they can search the Smithsonian's website. But previously you had to navigate to 19 different museum's collections websites. . . . If you just wanted to search for a bicycle in the Smithsonian's collections, you'd have to go to 19 different websites. That's no longer the case, fortunately.

All of these efforts took time. Not only do different institutions have different collections, but the people who work at those institutions often run in different circles, and may not even know each other or realize that they have the opportunity to work together. Kathy Jones describes starting work on a shared repository for the visual collections at Harvard University in the 1990s:

I went to the College Art Association Conference that was held in Boston and gave a talk about digitizing collections. There were two people from Harvard who were in the audience—one was from the Fine Arts Library, Martha Mahard, and the other was from the Graduate School of Design Library, Ann Whiteside, and we got together after that. We worked about two Harvard blocks away from each other, but we had never met. . . . Through that effort, Harvard Libraries . . . supported a project to begin to tie all of the repositories that had visual collections together. And that came together under the name

> of Visual Information Access, or VIA . . . so that all could be represented. . . . I thought that was kind of a miraculous thing, where anyone could look through all of the Harvard collections and see images of everybody who had an elephant, or something like that.

Collaborating across collections in this way presented difficulties that became more apparent as more institutions worked to share their collections data. Martha Mahard explains how a lack of standards for describing images at Harvard posed challenges for the Visual Information Access project from the very beginning:

> We wanted to make a catalog for visual resources. Harvard was incredibly rich in visual resources, and had made no attempt to describe them in a consistent way, or make them available across the university . . . and that led to a really intense collaboration that was fantastic. Kathy and I managed to convince the library administration to take on this project and to support it, which would bring in the museums as well as library collections and try to create an online catalog of image collections. Now right at the beginning, we hit the problem of no standard descriptions! Everybody called what they had something different! And you can't do that in a catalog . . . but it showed the difficulties of crossing disciplines, and combining an art-related collection of images with a scientific collection. It was just so hard.

As a result, museum technology professionals needed to find new ways to make it easier to connect and share information across different institutions. Ruth Cuadra describes the goal of linked open data projects to connect collections of all types:

> The goal for linked data is to encourage access in terms of making this data linkable . . . to other kinds of cultural, historical information that may be out there. The linked data world is big and small at the same time. It's a huge undertaking. . . . We are developing a data model in conjunction with a consortium that worked on something called linked.art, which is a data model for museums that's been developed. . . . Everybody who uses linked.art will have systems that can talk to each other. If I say, "I want to know what this museum has that was done by Rembrandt, and what they said about Rembrandt, and how does it compare to what we say about Rembrandt," then we can pull data together from multiple systems and massage it locally and do all kinds of visualizations. . . . The ability to link between resources that may occur in collections in different locations is really the key to the future of research using cultural heritage materials.

Efforts to develop information systems that can link collections data and represent knowledge relationships using the semantic web in museums require extensive work at an international scale. Costis Dallas describes the early days of developing the Conceptual Reference Model for the International Council of Museums' International Committee for Documentation:

> One of the things that I was involved with after the CIDOC 1990 meeting was the Data Modeling Working Group at CIDOC, in which a lot of the work was really going in the direction of building a system and a generic model for museum documentation. . . . We were in the triennial meeting of ICOM in 1995. We were to work on the model, and suddenly there was this meeting room in which people opened and stitched together pages with printed parts of the model. It was like the whole floor was full of representations of boxes, connected with arrows. . . . The first conversations, of course, were met by disbelief. I mean, our colleagues thought, "Who are these guys from Greece who are saying these crazy things about semantic information systems and semantic models?" But then this got traction, and Martin Doerr joined the Data Modeling Group . . . and this model went on to become the CIDOC-CRM, the Conceptual Reference Model, which applied these abstractions to allow specialization, to allow event centricity, so that we are able to show the life of objects, cultural objects, cultural heritage objects, material culture objects as a biography in which events are in the center . . . that sees the object as a living terrain for events, for the lives of communities whose meanings are invested through this history of events.

As museums embrace new ideas for sharing collections data, the work of museum technology professionals to connect museum collections continues to evolve. As Costis Dallas explains, linked open data has the potential to usher in a future where different museums can integrate their resources and contribute collections data in ways that transcend institutions:

> We started at that time understanding and seeing the need to be able to undertake initiatives that run beyond institutions . . . the need to see cultural heritage and collections not as isolated little animals, but as vibrant participants in this ecosystem in which we are connected with one another . . . to focus on information integration, to focus on existing collections, and how these collections need to be connected with one another. . . . How can we do that in ways where we can get access to the knowledge, and add better knowledge representation? How can we do that in ways that preserve and perhaps enrich that information? . . . What I think is really the next frontier is not so much the museum as institution, and the museum collection as an institutional resource, but this institutional resource becoming a public resource, becoming a social resource, becoming a cultural resource in which communities will be able to go back and use that object and add to it. I'd like to see more fluid information systems in museums.

As the computing technologies available changed over time, the roles and responsibilities of museum technology professionals shifted, evolving from individual efforts focused on smaller, more localized, internal projects to larger, externally focused, multi-institutional initiatives. The choice of technology in use at the museum directly affected the job of the museum technology professional as the overarching task of museum computing transformed from keeping track of collections data for the museum's own internal purposes to making collections data available for discovery by institutions and individuals worldwide. Throughout all of these changes, as the museum technology profession moved from meeting internal needs to fulfilling external demands, they kept their eye on the common goal of providing access to information.

SUGGESTIONS FOR FURTHER READING

Baca, Murtha, ed. 1998. *Introduction to Metadata: Pathways to Digital Information.* Los Angeles: Getty Information Institute.

Chenhall, Robert G. 1973. "Sharing the Wealth." *Museum News* 51 (8): 21-23.

Coburn, Erin, Eliza Lanzi, Elizabeth O'Keefe, Regine Stine, and Ann Whiteside. 2010. "The Cataloging Cultural Objects Experience: Codifying Practice for the Cultural Heritage Community." *International Federation of Library Associations and Institutions* 36 (1): 16-29.

Doerr, Martin. 2003. "The CIDOC CRM: An Ontological Approach to Semantic Interoperability of Metadata." *AI Magazine* 24 (3): 75-92.

Marty, Paul F. 2007. "The Changing Nature of Information Work in Museums." *Journal of the American Society for Information Science and Technology* 58 (1): 97-107.

Marty, Paul F. 2014. "Digital Convergence and the Information Profession in Cultural Heritage Organizations: Reconciling Internal and External Demands." *Library Trends* 62 (3): 613-627.

Misunas, Marla. 2010. "Collection Management in Museums." In *Encyclopedia of Library and Information Science*, edited by Marcia J. Bates and Mary Niles Maack, 1124-1134. New York: Taylor & Francis.

Vance, David, and Robert G. Chenhall. 1988. *Museum Collections and Today's Computers.* Westport, CN: Greenwood Press.

3

Institutional Knowledge

> What are realistic expectations for handing projects off? What are realistic expectations for making these things sustainable? We don't have a history of handing complicated projects off. . . . Something gets built, and it runs, and it works, but the people behind it leave . . . and so, all of the history around the project is lost.—Oral History of Aaron Straup Cope

As the roles and responsibilities of museum technology professionals changed over time, it became increasingly important for museums not only to develop the technology skills of their employees but also to preserve knowledge about how technology works in museums. Our oral history participants spoke often about the importance of preserving knowledge, as well as building internal capacity and internal expertise. As museum technology professionals worked on increasingly complicated projects, it became critically important to keep lessons learned in-house and to preserve institutional knowledge about the inner workings of museum computing.

Unfortunately, building institutional memory and organizational knowledge can be difficult, especially when one considers the inherent invisibility of museum technology work. When one does not understand the work involved in a technology project, one might be tempted to outsource that work. Yet the more technology work is outsourced—the more museums focus on the product instead of the process—the more likely institutions are to lose key expertise with museum computing. As museum technology professionals come and go, the internal knowledge needed to support the museum's digital projects and technical infrastructure can get lost, and as a result, museums have to keep reinventing the wheel. To break out of that cycle, museums need to build internal capacity and invest in the skills of their technology workers.

Building institutional capacity and preserving institutional knowledge is especially important given the increasing demands placed on museum technology professionals over time. Many of our participants spoke about the value of long-term experience and internal knowledge when working on museum computing projects. Many problems that museums face require long-term expertise in the field, and museum technology professionals often rely on their lived experiences to recognize issues and provide structural solutions to systemic problems. Rob Weisberg explains in his oral history, for example, how his long-term experiences and perspectives influenced the creation of a new digital infrastructure for managing publications at the Metropolitan Museum of Art:

> When people ask me "What do you think your enduring legacy will be in the department?" I just say immediately, "It's the spreadsheet." Where the story comes from is one of the things I started noticing when I'd worked on all of the books for a few years, because I was the only person who had a role in all of the books. What I found was that I seemed to be the person who knew that we were going to be sending three books out to the printer on the same day. . . . Back then, there wasn't a lot of organizational scheduling software, so I made a whiteboard in my office with construction paper and tape and colored markers to make my own Gantt chart. And that was fine for me, because it would help me flag when there were potential conflicts, but it obviously wasn't shareable, and so I started suggesting to people that we make our schedules shareable, at least within the department. And since I had some sort of influence over the workflow, I went through a process of just trying to bring people together, and Excel was the only program that everyone had in common and felt comfortable using, even if it was just as a grid, and not for any of its formulas. I started trying to convince people, "We need to have a regular status meeting, and we need to have kind of a document that's core for this, and that document should list all of our schedules and information for all of the books in one place, and we should just sort of go through it now. . . ." There was a bit of a fear of sharing the information too widely. . . . It wasn't easy. . . . But over time . . . the spreadsheet became more and more a core document of the department. . . . People come in now and have no idea that there was a time where we didn't have something like this, and we didn't share this kind of information, we didn't put it on the server, we didn't make it easy for multiple people to access. . . . I think it's the ultimate story because it's not about the technology. . . . The spreadsheet itself always ended up being the non-threatening core of our shared workflows. And to me, it's the ultimate expression of people over technology, and people over process, and the simpler, the better . . . the more invisible, the better . . .

Museum computing projects often require specialized expertise and involve different individuals working on solving difficult problems over long periods of time. Working with complicated data sets, for example, can be fraught with challenges. Certain database problems can be so complicated that solving them requires multiple individuals, each with their own unique skills, working across multiple software platforms to take data in an unusable format and convert it into a more useful form. Michael Haley Goldman shares a story in his oral history about the extensive and long-term behind-the-scenes work at the U.S. Holocaust Memorial Museum that was required to make data about Holocaust survivors available online:

> When I first started at the museum, I was in a group that was called the Registry of Holocaust Survivors. . . . My colleague, Vadim Altskan, who was part of our team that did a lot of archival acquisitions, got involved with the National Archives of Uzbekistan. . . . As Nazi Germany invaded the Soviet Union, you have a huge number of people who were evacuated East . . . and there was a collection of these individual documents from Uzbekistan that we were going to photograph, and in the process of photographing them, they actually created a database of all the information. They were these little cards that you had as an evacuees-status person, basically asking for care and work and things like that. . . . We're doing a ton of microfilming work on these kinds of collections, and there was a database with it, and Vadim acquired the database, kind of as an afterthought . . . and what we discovered was this set of CDs, with what turned out to be a standalone application that you could load onto a machine, and it would allow you to search through this finding aid of the documents. And, of course, we couldn't really do anything with it. . . . Enter yet another colleague. . . . Michael Levy. . . . He had the CDs and started kind of digging through them, and after a fairly prolonged process . . . he was able to get in and rip the data out from this standalone application, but then of course it was using some kind of proprietary character system, so then he had to figure out a way to convert it into Unicode so that you could actually have it as a Cyrillic data set, and this took a fairly long period of time. . . . I remember sitting down with Vadim, who was the only one of us who actually knew the Cyrillic alphabet and . . . we were able to kind of pull out a Latin alphabet version of this database. A little bit more time passed, and we brought in Randy Davis, who was working on moving things online . . . and he was the one to figure out a way to transfer this data . . . into a tool that allows you to search names across all of these different types of digital historical data sets. . . . So there's something about the sheer number of us that had to touch this really complicated, strange thing to make it something that could be publicly available. . . . We have millions and millions of records about individuals from databases like this—created by us, created by partnerships, created by other organizations—that is part of an online tool that tries to bring together this information . . . and that's one of the tools that we make available.

Naturally, all of this can be expensive, time-consuming, and complicated work. Just assembling the necessary personnel with the required skills and technical knowledge can be difficult. As a result, many institutions are tempted to outsource technology work where they can. Unfortunately, many museum computing projects cannot be handed off to someone else to complete, especially those that require groups of people with specialized expertise working over a long period of time. Many of our participants spoke about the risks of outsourcing technology work, explaining that asking someone else to solve your technology problems for you often just brings new problems. Marla Misunas shares a story about the problems that arose when SFMOMA tried to outsource a massive data entry project in the 1990s:

> SFMOMA's system was just the kernel of this interim database with object locations and bare bones object information, put together out of a number of different departments' FileMaker databases—you can imagine what that was like. Every department had their own set of records, meaning they could alter their own records without bothering anybody else's records, which is bad for data integrity. . . . More than one object record for the same thing had slightly different titles, slightly different credit lines, and it was obvious we really needed a centralized database. We had roughly 15,000 things in the collection, and all their corresponding paper records, which translated to 15,000 object files in hundreds of binders. We didn't have the staff to input everything into our new system, and the new system wasn't ready. The museum administration decided the way to get this done was to have a third-party service microfilm all of the binders. They boxed up the microfilm in crates, and sent it to a company in Australia that had won the project, being the lowest bidder. . . . To make a long story short, the company went bankrupt in the middle of our project, and we had crates and crates of microfilm in Australia, where probably most of the records had been entered on a first pass into something like FileMaker. . . . We were desperate to get this material back in whatever condition we could, and we knew it was going to take a long time to clean up. It took us a full year to clean up everything. The records got into the database, but it took a long time, and it took another long time to get the different departments—Curatorial and Registration and Conservation and Exhibitions—to not only trust the data but actually use the database. It was at least a five-year rollout, and not everybody used it even at the end of that period.

Unexpected problems when outsourcing museum technology projects can result in additional work for the institution, and when errors occur, they can erode trust in both the system and the process. Marty Spellerberg describes what happened when the Art Gallery of Ontario outsourced the development of the content management system for their new website:

> The Art Gallery of Ontario was doing this expansion, with a new Frank Gehry remodel of the building, and they hired the web team a year out from the reopening. I was on the internal team—it was me, and my colleague, and a boss—and we worked on that for the year. We were working with an outside agency that had been chosen, and we were facilitating with them, and this crazy thing happened where the outside agency, they heard what we wanted, and they said, "Okay, well, we think that there's this developer, who we want to bring on to work with you guys." And so we were working with this developer, and he was building out the CMS implementation, and he had it on his local machine—all his work—and he disappeared! Like, he just disappeared

> one day. We didn't hear from him. He didn't show up for a meeting. We called the agency. We were like, "Hey, do you know where this guy is?" They said no. The agency called around. They called his family. No one ever found him. And no one ever found the code either! It completely threw off our timelines. . . . We ended up taking the design that we'd been working on and applying it to all our old stuff. We just applied the design. Everybody was like, "Yay! A new website!" It wasn't really a new website, but it looked like a new website. And when the agency finally got around to delivering the new back end, we just sort of quietly put that in, and then that was that. But that experience really influenced how I approach my work, and my work when I was building out projects.

Unfortunately, the dangers of outsourcing go beyond missing consultants and collections data. On a deeper level, outsourcing poses an almost existential threat to museum technology professionals. When museums outsource technology work, they are neither building internal expertise nor acquiring internal knowledge. Even if your museum is lucky enough to get the product you paid for, and even if that product works as intended for many years, what you did not get was the in-house knowledge of the process behind the development of that product. Other people got those skills, not your museum. And that in-house knowledge often lasts a lot longer than the product itself. Sarah Kenderdine talks about the importance of investing in developing internal expertise in-house, instead of outsourcing projects:

> The way that museums work, quite honestly, when you're talking about museums trying to procure new media, they don't invest in-house. They go out-house and they don't learn much in that process. They tend to go to tender. The guys come in. They build it. They leave. That's it. It's gone. It's over. And so, for ages, I was really advocating for museums to build really robust engineering facilities.

Many of our participants spoke about the importance of museums investing in the technical expertise of their own staff, and not outsourcing technology projects to others. Naturally, some museums may not have the necessary technology literacies in-house and will have no choice but to outsource their technology projects. But in those situations, as Seb Chan explains, one still has to be strategic about those choices and ensure that the museum is investing their time in developing skills that will help the institution in the long term:

> The complexity of technical literacies that are required are broad, and institutions need to spread that literacy across them. . . . Some will outsource all of that, but if you outsource it, you need somebody really technically knowledgeable, so you don't get ripped off, and you make good choices. If you outsource it, it brings a whole other set of difficulties. . . . I talk about institutional muscles needing to be built around particular things, strategically choosing what you

> want to build those muscles in, but you got to build muscles in things you're going to exercise with. There's no point going to work out at a gym if you're not going to keep working out at the gym.

Similarly, there can be circumstances where outsourcing is simply not an option at all. Some information needs can be so institution-specific that it would not be feasible to outsource the museum's work to others. Megan Forbes, for example, explains why the Museum of the Moving Image was unable to outsource the development of its collections management system, but instead had to develop their own system in-house:

> Moving Image had tried to find a proprietary system to manage their collection. . . . They had hired a consultant to help them with this search, and basically, the consultant came back and said, "I have to be honest. None of the proprietary systems really work for your collection." A lot of them presume that you have an art collection, or that you have an anthropology collection, or that you have your botanical garden, or whatever it is, but Moving Image was kind of this kooky collection where everything in the collection they had because of its relationship with something that wasn't in the collection. Like you have the "Luke Skywalker" action figure because it's related to "Star Wars" the movie, which is a thing they didn't actually have, so then, how do you catalog "Luke"? Who's the artist for this action figure? And how do we capture all of those other relationships around things like licensing and distribution and manufacturing? . . . They released it when the first movie came out, and then they changed the name of the first movie when the second movie came out, and so you have to look at the package, because even though Luke looks the same, it's not the same one. . . . I need to know that this is the "Luke" from "A New Hope" because the licensing was different then. Warner Brothers owned the licensing, and then Lucas took over the second film, and then that's when they started calling it "Episode IV" . . . so Luke is always the example that I use for, "Why couldn't you just use Past Perfect, or why couldn't you just use TMS?" and, I'm like, "Let me tell you why."

For most museums, the question of outsourcing museum computing projects comes down to balancing the relationship between what activities can be done in-house and what activities need to be outsourced to others. In those situations, it is important that the museum have someone who can serve as a bridge between those two sides of the relationship. As we learned from our oral history participants, this is a role that the museum technology professional often plays. Jeff Gates, for instance, describes his work to coordinate between in-house staff and outsourced teams at the Smithsonian American Art Museum:

> From the very beginning, we needed people within our organization who could be the intermediary between the outsource companies and the project

> managers and the stakeholders of these projects. The content and its contextualization would always be the museum's responsibility. Knowing enough about the technologies we'd be using and the content we wanted to present allowed us to be good go-betweens between our outside contractors and the museum. . . . In 2011, I worked on a project co-sponsored by the Smithsonian American Art Museum and the National Museum of African American History and Culture. It would be a website for teachers using our combined African American artworks. It was called "Oh, Freedom." I was the tech representative on the project, and I ended up designing the site. When I spoke to the project manager about her priorities, one of the most important was the ability for teachers to upload lesson plans they could share with other teachers. This was not something that we could create from scratch in-house, so I went looking for a CMS that would fit most of the project's priorities. The one that most closely delivered was a content management system called Omeka. George Mason University had designed it expressly for cultural institutions. I had never worked with a content management system at the development level before. . . . Every night I came home thinking I was going to fail big time. I had never felt so inadequate. Luckily, I was able to reach out to people within the larger Smithsonian community and to the developers of Omeka to help me, and together, we made it work. The more I got to know Omeka, the better I could see how to fit my stakeholders' priorities into the CMS's structure. . . . Knowing the stakeholders as I did, and having experience with last-minute changes that always occurred, I became the "technology project manager." My job was to make sure the content came to me in its final iteration at a much earlier stage than usual. . . . I had to be attentive to the stakeholders' needs while knowing the application landscape well enough to justify my choices. This is a typical story of how technology interfaces with content, and how technologists and content producers must communicate with each other. My job was to see into the future of our interactions to spot potential problems before they became actual problems.

Museum technology professionals with the in-house knowledge and technical expertise to solve complex computing problems for the museum can be invaluable. As a result, as Jeff Gates explains, it can be challenging for museums when the people with that knowledge leave:

> When people leave, their experience often goes with them. And with time, that history—and the lessons we learned—disappears. When I retired at the end of 2018, I was the person who had been in our department the longest. Sometimes I could say how we solved a similar issue in the past. . . . It can be helpful knowing how we handled a similar issue twenty years ago. Before I left, I spent months outlining procedures for projects I worked on. I do not know if they ever needed to use them. But they were there if they did.

The dangers of losing institutional knowledge when people move away are well known, and it is important for museums to find a way to preserve knowledge when people leave the institution and pass that knowledge on to the next person. Sam Quigley reflects on the loss of knowledge in the field, as people leave and take their knowledge with them:

> The problem is not having a database. We've got lots of databases walking around, in fact. They're on two legs, and when they retire, they walk right out the door. We had huge troves of knowledge about our collection that were suddenly inaccessible to us.

This is especially dangerous for museums when there is only one person in the institution who understands the museum's technical initiatives—a situation that is all too common for museums that can afford only one museum technology professional. When they leave, much is lost. Layna White reflects on her work contributing data from the UCLA's Grunwald Center for the Graphic Arts to the Online Archive of California (OAC) using a tool developed by Berkeley, and the dangers of losing her knowledge, given that she was the only person there doing that work:

> The Grunwald was a super, super small place, and I was left alone in a good way, I suppose. I was the person that worked on the content to get three finding aids for the Grunwald contributed to the OAC via that tool. And when I say, I think it was a good thing, one might also say, "Was that really a good thing?" It allowed progress to be made . . . the project got done, while everyone else was doing many other things . . . but when I left, I took that knowledge with me about how to operate the tool that was developed by Berkeley, and also perhaps I took some of the energy about participating in the OAC with me. . . . So it's interesting to think about that. . . . It enabled the project to get done, because I could focus on it, and I was trusted to do it. That was great. It happened. And then I took it with me. I took the knowledge with me about that project and the use of that tool in this case.

Museum technology professionals are often overworked, undervalued, and underpaid, and institutions that cannot compete in terms of compensation will naturally find it challenging to retain skilled workers. When employee turnover is high and institutional memory short, it can be difficult to keep museum computing projects going and carry knowledge forward over time. Once a critical mass of people leave, it is all too easy to lose important institutional knowledge. Paul Marty shares a story from the World Heritage Museum at the University of Illinois that underscores the difficulty museums can have preserving knowledge about their collections over long periods of time:

> This museum had a fantastic collection of Roman lamps, and one day we got a phone call from a detective in San Francisco. He said that somebody had recently passed away in San Francisco, and in his will, had confessed to

stealing some Roman lamps from the World Heritage Museum, back when he was a student at the University of Illinois in the 1950s. One of his dying wishes was that these lamps be returned to the museum. So, this detective was calling to arrange the transfer of these lamps back to the museum. And of course, we were very happy to get these lamps back, but we didn't tell the detective that we had no idea these lamps had ever been stolen.

When it comes to collections management over time, this loss of internal knowledge can include everything from basic inventory records to more complicated research reports. As Paul Marty continues, not only did the museum not know that some of their lamps had been stolen, they had also lost access to research reports about the collection's historical significance:

> We had the opportunity to put some of the Roman lamps out on display. It was an exhibit about daily life in ancient Rome. We only had room for a handful of lamps, maybe two or three, and there were literally hundreds to choose from. And all we had in the database system was this sort of tombstone data, and in that, all these lamps looked exactly the same. They're all made of terracotta. They're all about the same age. They're all about the same dimensions. How do we know which of these lamps are significant? How do we know which of these lamps are worthy of being put on display? Is there any way to find that out? And at this point, I can remember the chair of the Classics department said that back in the 1960s, there was a student in Classics at the University of Illinois who did her master's thesis on this collection of lamps. And if we could find a copy of that thesis, it might tell us which of these lamps were worth putting on display, and which weren't. But of course, he didn't know the name of the student, he didn't know the title of the thesis. We had no idea how we could ever find that thesis. Certainly, it wasn't digitized anywhere, probably it wasn't even in the library system. For all we knew, the museum had a copy, but we'd never be able to find it, so we gave it up. It's a great example of how there's so much behind-the-scenes knowledge in museums that is basically hidden. And if we don't find that information, and try to get it in some sort of format where at least it's findable, then so much is just lost.

In our oral histories, we repeatedly heard our participants emphasize the value of preserving documentation if museums are to avoid losing institutional knowledge when people move on. Having this kind of documentation is important not only to individual museums but to the global community of museum technology professionals as well. Seb Chan talks about the importance of documenting projects, sharing knowledge, and building a community where people can learn from what others have done:

> I think it's about documenting as you go, and publicly doing it . . . that sort of communication of the process as you go is really important. I think that's been key to the practice. . . . There were a bunch of us who were writing furiously

> about what we were doing, and the act of writing, the warts and all . . . we were seeing it as being part of a community of people, a global community of peers.

This approach to documentation can help build a professional technology community that is willing and eager to learn from each other—a community that transcends time, preserves knowledge, and shares it from the past to the future. Holly Witchey explains how museum technology professionals could benefit from making it a practice in the field to pass lessons learned about museum computing forward, and to learn from the people who came before us:

> I would say that a great problem that was caused by the professionalism of technology in museums was this desire, when you got into a new museum, to throw away what had been done before, and start over again. . . . I think in my life I have not been as grateful to the people who came before me as I should have been. And I'd like to make up for that now, and encourage the people in these positions to practice gratitude. If the person who had the job before you is still living, call them up and say, "Hey, I'd like to know what you've done." What if we made it a practice that one of the things you do is you call your predecessor and keep a record for a predecessor? What if we just instituted that as a best practice? Before you start to do anything new, find out what came before.

One of the reasons this approach to knowledge sharing is so important is that, when it comes to museum technology projects, the lessons that one learns from working on a project are often much more important than the outcome of the work itself. After all, the end product of any given technology project may very well be obsolete in just a few short years, but the lessons learned from that project have the potential to last much longer. As Bruce Wyman explains, if we are to move the field of museum computing forward as a professional community, then we need to put a greater emphasis on documenting the lessons learned from our work:

> I think it ends up being critically important not to document individual products, but the things that have been learned and the techniques that have been learned because those create longevity about how we do this field. Because this isn't a field of technology, rather, it's a venue of communication, and how we do that sort of stuff and how we apply that stuff . . . and when you start to see those patterns, it really changes how you begin to think about stuff and how you begin to articulate and architect things.

When it comes to preserving institutional knowledge, recognizing that the process is more important than the product is a critical first step for museum technology professionals. As Aaron Straup Cope explains, focusing on the tangible project outcomes over the intangible lessons learned can doom museums to a vicious cycle where museums can neither develop nor sustain the internal expertise they need to support technology projects on their own:

> There's never enough time, there's never enough money, and there aren't enough people because there's never enough time and there's never enough money. And when there is money, it gets put into questionable resources for which there isn't enough time or money or people to sustain them properly. So you end up in this vicious circle: in order to address short term needs, you hire outside vendors, who produce something that's very expensive that isn't designed to be sustained, and you don't have the staff to sustain. So nothing happens, until the next round of funding, when you hire another expensive vendor to do the same thing. . . . This is the challenge, and what people don't want to think about is, what do we need to change in order to deal with that dynamic?

Solving this problem requires a change in perspective that can be a difficult concept for many museums. Technology professionals who work in museums are typically funded to complete specific projects, and as a result, we tend to think about technology work in terms of project outcomes, but that is not where real change or learning happens in museums. Instead of focusing solely on the end product, we should strive to create an environment where we build the institutional knowledge needed to find systemic solutions to structural problems. Seb Chan talks about the importance of changing the core by folding technical skills and knowledge into key institutional processes and general operations for the museum:

> A lot of work has been really influential and important, but it never got folded into general operations, where it would have gotten supported, all because general operations hated the idea of having to change the legacy stuff. There's this big friction around, how do you do experimental projects that then change the core? . . . The key to the experimental stuff is to always find ways to build them into what the core business and core operations are, and if you can't do that, make it the new core business. . . . By the time I left the Powerhouse, there were 50 different projects that had their own microsites and webpages, and it was just symptomatic of the way things got funded. It was good, because lots of stuff got done, but it was also difficult. A lot of people who worked on those teams went off to other things and ran other groups, and we have realized that this is a challenge of "How do you institutionalize the good stuff and change the core operations?" And I think that's very difficult, when it's incremental and project-based, and so work like the Cooper Hewitt and all this work here in Melbourne at ACMI—this last decade, for me—is about the institutionalizing the previous decade of work. Rather than taking a project approach, can you rebuild the entire museum around the notion of "building-in" technology and innovation and constant iteration of insight and learning?

This is a challenging task for most museum technology professionals. It is all too easy to spend time focused on one-off projects, and it is common for many small projects and microsites to be left behind in museums as technology projects and technology workers come and go. But our focus should not be on those one-off projects. Bruce Wyman explains his strategy for building infrastructure and institutional capacity for future initiatives at the Denver Art Museum:

> That was the secret thing in Denver: Every time we did something, it was never a one-off project. I always did it as if we were building the infrastructure that we would use in later products . . . it was always this long-term, incremental art . . . so that at some point, you have a pretty strong compendium of tools in the toolbox that you can use to do almost anything.

When one looks at institutions that have implemented this strategy successfully, one sees the importance of thinking carefully about how technology work can become a long-term, integral, and organic part of the museum's core activities. Sometimes the only way to keep technology projects going is to make them part of the fabric of the institution. Jane Alexander, for example, describes how the process of developing the Collection Wall at the Cleveland Museum of Art was integrated into the core processes of the museum:

> Our digital asset management system spoke to the collection online, and pulled all the metadata from our current collection management system, and that was really our first sort of, "Okay, here's how content will work," and it also made me really understand what kind of content is collected when we talk about art. And so, our Collection Wall really became another project that was a proof of concept in that there were ways people wanted to do things and make it look cool, and we would curate things all the time, but as everybody knows in museum world, once something's done, nobody has time to keep it updated and going. It has to be organic, part of how the museum works.

By integrating our growing technical knowledge into the core fabric of the institution, we can build internal capacity, preserve institutional knowledge, and avoid reinventing the wheel every time someone leaves or a new person is hired in the museum. Through a renewed focus on understanding internal knowledge processes, documenting technical activities, and sharing that knowledge with a broader community, we can break out of the cycles of forgetfulness that have trapped so many museum technology professionals over the decades. The more we emphasize the process over the product, the more we will recognize the value of in-house technical expertise, the dangers of outsourcing technical activities, and the need to break down the silos of knowledge that separate so many museum departments. Working together in this way, museum technology professionals can ensure that the knowledge needed to support and sustain museum computing is not forgotten, and help encourage the next generation of museum technology professionals to take museum computing to the next level.

SUGGESTIONS FOR FURTHER READING

Ball, David, and Carleton Earl. 2002. "Outsourcing and Externalisation: Current Practice in UK Libraries, Museums and Archives." *Journal of Librarianship and Information Science* 34 (4): 197–206.

Cameron, Fiona, and Sarah Kenderdine, eds. 2007. *Theorizing Digital Cultural Heritage: A Critical Discourse*. Cambridge, MA: MIT Press.

Dodge, Ryan. 2016. "Technology: Are Museums Keeping Pace?" *MUSE: The Voice of Canada's Museum Community* 35 (1): 40–45.

Harrison, Jeff. 2000. "Outsourcing in Museums." *International Journal of Arts Management* 2 (2): 14–25.

McLeod, Alyssa. 2015. "Mapping the Way to a More Digitally Inclusive Museum." In *Museums and the Web 2015*, edited by Nancy Proctor and Rich Cherry. Silver Spring, MD: Museums and the Web. https://mw2015.museumsandtheweb.com/paper/mapping-the-way-to-a-more-digitally-inclusive-museum/

Parry, Ross, Doris Ruth Eikhof, Sally-Anne Barnes, and Erika Kispeter. 2018. "Development, Supply, Deployment, Demand: Balancing the Museum Digital Skills Ecosystem: First Findings of the One by One National Digital Literacy Project." In *Museums and the Web 2018*, edited by Nancy Proctor and Rich Cherry. Silver Spring, MD: Museums and the Web. https://mw18.mwconf.org/paper/development-supply-deployment-demand-balancing-the-museum-digital-skills-ecosystem-first-findings-of-the-one-by-one-national-digital-literacy-project/

Paterson, Lucie. 2017. "Transforming a Museum through Product Management." In *Museums and the Web 2017*, edited by Nancy Proctor and Rich Cherry. Silver Spring, MD: Museums and the Web. https://mw17.mwconf.org/paper/transforming-a-museum-through-product-management/

4

Increasing Demands

> I was a maritime archaeologist, working at the West Australian Maritime Museum . . . and I had an extremely clever boss . . . very clever man, and he said to me, I think it was 1993, and he said, "Sarah, there is something called the World Wide Web, and I want one."—Oral History of Sarah Kenderdine

Over the past six decades, museum technology professionals were constantly being asked to learn new skills, adopt new technologies, take on new tasks, and implement new tools. The nature of museum computing changed rapidly as new technologies offered new opportunities, new opportunities led to new responsibilities, and new responsibilities brought new challenges. The rapid pace of change for information technologies in museums is well documented in the oral histories we collected, which make it clear that if one did not keep up with the increasing demands of new technologies in museums, one would quickly be left behind.

Keeping current with constantly changing technologies—whether those are behind the scenes, in the galleries, or online—poses unique challenges for museum technology professionals. While different individuals and institutions naturally adopt technologies at different rates, when one looks holistically at the history of museum computing, the overall trend one sees is a steady march of technological progress. The adoption of each new computing technology leads inevitably to the next as museums learn how these tools can help them accomplish their goals and reach their audiences. Keeping current with technologies as they change over time is extremely important and places significant new demands on museum technology professionals.

An excellent example of the increasing demands that stem from this technological snowballing can be found in the museum's use of digital images, from the early days of digital imaging behind the scenes to the integration of digital images into exhibits, to the evolution of interactive digital experiences, in the galleries and online. While digital images had been used in museums since the 1960s, digital imaging technology became much more mainstream in the 1980s and was adopted by museums with great fanfare. Howard Besser, in his oral history, describes the reaction to an early demonstration of his work with high-resolution digital images:

> In 1985, we developed a prototype system where you could do a query across a network, using simple text fields, and get an image that would show up on your screen. . . . In the spring of 1986, both the American Library Association (ALA) and the American Association of Museums (AAM) had their annual meetings in San Francisco. . . . We had done all our development work on Sun Microsystems . . . and they rented booths for us at both the AAM and ALA conferences, and it was a huge hit. Most people, at that point in time, had never seen a high-resolution image on a computer before, and certainly not on these Sun workstations that were about 1500 pixels across. At that point, most computer images were like Pac Man style, or like the early Mario Brothers—very blocky, you couldn't see any detail. We were showing images that were really pristine and looked like a photograph. And it just became this huge hit. . . . At some point in late '88 or early '89, the New York Times came out, interviewed me, and did the cover story for the Sunday Art section on what we were doing. It ended up being this really incredible, although very difficult project that was really way, way, way ahead of its time. You know, this is the 1980s. This is before the web. The first web browser was in 1993, and we were doing this in '86, as kind of the big debut of our system.

This reaction to the introduction of digital images was natural for museum professionals and museum visitors alike. Everyone likes seeing pictures of museum artifacts, and digital images can improve access to visual information resources for a wide variety of users. Marla Misunas describes how revolutionary it was for museums when digital images first started to appear in collections management systems:

> We worked with the company that became Gallery Systems. We were one of twenty museum partners working with them to create the best museum system, including images—hugely innovative at the time—in the early '90s. Nobody had images in their databases back then! Here we are a visual field and we just had descriptions. . . . People began to depend on images—it's so much easier to find something if you know what it looks like. Eventually, having images in the database became the direction that everybody was going in. . . . We were scanning transparencies and people started seeing images in our internal database, which was pretty exciting.

The introduction of digital images in museums allowed for all kinds of new opportunities, not only behind the scenes with collections management systems but also in the galleries and beyond. While some institutions had been experimenting with putting computer kiosks in the galleries for their visitors, the introduction of high-quality digital images took these interactive experiences to new levels, and museums started exploring new ways of bringing digital images of their collections to their audiences. In the early 1980s, most museums did not have computers capable of displaying digital images, so they often turned to other technologies—videodiscs, for example. In her oral history, Deborah Howes describes how the Art Institute worked with Voyager, one of the first companies to focus on producing videodisc content for museums, to create and distribute digital images of their collections for school children:

> Bob Stein at Voyager said, "We're doing pretty well making these videodiscs out of museum collections . . . would you be interested in making a videodisc just for children?" This is like 1988, and the . . . Mac computer didn't have the capacity to show images on its screen yet . . . they would have an RS232 connector to a videodisc player and monitor, so it was a two-screen solution, and Voyager is saying: "Let's choose 250 objects that you think would really be interesting to children, and we'll make an interface using HyperCard . . ." and I said, "I want to do that because we have a lot of teachers here who use this technology. . . ." We rented these high-end studios where we would project transparencies onto a wall that would be like the size of a movie screen, and in the same room, there would be a digital moviemaker camera that would capture the projection, and that became the digital file. . . . There was no other way to make these images, other than this high-end Hollywood technology, that was clearly beyond any museum's ability. It took us about a year to get everything right, including the interface, but when we finally published it in 1991, the whole world had shifted to CD-ROMs . . . but in '93, the CD-ROM came out . . . exactly the same content, just in a much neater package, because now the images are coming up on the computer screen, and that was bundled with the Apple education distribution. When a school would buy an Apple package, they got the "With Open Eyes" CD-ROM from the Art Institute of Chicago, and it became the number one art CD-ROM of that moment. That was the one that everybody had. If they were using art in the classroom, they all had it. And those 250 or 350 images became the core set for almost everything else that was done at the Art Institute of Chicago.

One of the challenges facing museum technology professionals is that the technologies used to create and disseminate digital images changed very quickly, going from projectors and standalone videodisc players to scanners and personal computers with integrated CD-ROM drives in just a few short years. At the same time, expectations about the technologies that one could reasonably assume would be available to museums, in schools, or at home changed as well. So many changes in such a short amount of time meant that keeping current with these new technologies was difficult, but these changes also opened up new opportunities for museum technology professionals who were interested in reaching new audiences in new ways. Peter Samis, for example, describes the power of multimedia technology to bring museum content to audiences in new ways.

> I was never into technology for its own sake, but as a communication-creative-synthetic production tool. . . . I was into writing, I was into film, I was into photography. To bring them all together and be able to tap into archives and bring that material together . . . multiple voices in multiple approaches to understanding something, instead of boiling it all down to one paragraph of jargon in a label, I thought, "Wow! We can unpack this stuff!" That was really interesting to me. . . . Voyager had just come out with the first CD-ROMs like Beethoven . . . and my mind was blown. I saw the potential of how we could communicate in completely new ways that had never been invented before using these tools. . . . I had been a docent already at SFMOMA for years, so I understood how clueless some people are when they arrive in the galleries, and they look at a pile of rocks on the floor or they look at a monochrome canvas on the wall. And here I was now, with my Master's in Art History, working as a curatorial assistant, and I felt, "Okay, now we have a tool to restore some of the context the white cube of the gallery strips away."

Very quickly, museums started realizing the potential of interactive multimedia tools to add content, context, and new dimensions to the way they tell their stories. The introduction of this technology into museums pushed museum technology professionals to create new experiences. Howard Besser describes an interactive kiosk that he designed for the Canadian Centre for Architecture in the early 1990s:

> 1992 was the 350th anniversary of the founding of the city of Montreal, and the 150th anniversary of the establishment of the country of Canada. . . . The Canadian Centre for Architecture had been working for many years on an exhibit that would open that summer called "Opening the Gates of 18th Century Montreal." They were planning a really big deal with fireworks, the Mayor present, the Vice Premier of Canada, lots of TV coverage, and the centerpiece of this exhibit was a set of videos of 3D models of the city of Montreal across the 18th Century, and a kiosk with a user interface that allowed people to wander around different areas in a 3D model of the city. . . . The exhibit included three-minute videos of 3D flyovers showing buildings colored in different colors for the French versus the British, and how that changed over time. . . . Perhaps the most challenging part of this exhibit was this interactive touch-screen kiosk that had . . . a 3D mode where you could touch the arrows on the screen, and kind of like a video game, you could move forward, backwards, turn, move left, move right, and you could see how far apart the buildings were and what the spatial relationships looked like.

Developing these kinds of digital exhibit kiosks at that time involved cutting-edge technology, and required high-end computing equipment that was very expensive. All of these tools were still very new, and museum technology professionals frequently encountered unexpected and unprecedented problems. Solving these problems was not easy. Howard Besser, continuing his story, describes the extreme pressures they faced when they discovered an unanticipated hardware problem just four days before the grand opening of the exhibit:

> We had really expensive hardware . . . Silicon Graphics Crimson . . . just the one computer, the size of a piece of luggage, cost us a million dollars to buy . . . and we had contracted out the building of a computer enclosure with a fan so it could sit in the gallery, and not get bumped. . . . We had specced out everything around this enclosure. . . . On Friday, four days before the exhibit opened, we put the computer and the touch screen into the enclosure. Everything fit fine. It was the end of the day. I had to pick up someone at the airport at 5pm . . . and I took a darkroom thermometer, and I put it in the enclosure, and went to the airport. Luckily, rather than hanging out with the person who I picked up at the airport, I came back, and I checked the thermometer, and it was over 100 degrees. I then checked the documentation, and it said, "The computer should never operate above 80 degrees. . . ." And I panicked. . . . The only viable solution was to remove the computer from the enclosure, and just have the touch screen in the enclosure, but we couldn't put a million-dollar computer in an open gallery. . . . So I called both the computer company and the touchscreen company, and I asked how long the wires could be between the computer and the touchscreen, and of course they couldn't give me a definitive answer because no one had ever asked that before, but they said it was probably something like 10 to 20 feet. So, I found some extra cables . . . and we got floor plans for the building, and discovered that the only possible place to put the computer was in someone's office directly below the gallery. . . . Yes, we had to drill through concrete. We had to get lots of people involved: the Director, the Assistant Directors, maintenance people, exhibition people, conservators and even the person in whose office we planned to put the computer. . . . We finally did it, but we had another problem. . . . You had to click on things in order to get the computer and the application to start, but the screen was in the gallery, and the computer and the mouse were one floor below. So we had to get the security people to borrow their walkie-talkies, and we were like, "Okay, move the mouse one inch to the right, half an inch up. Okay, now click. No, you missed it. Down a little bit. Click. . . ." We had to boot it that way about once a week with the walkie-talkies. . . . It's amazing, but by far, this was the most high-pressure kind of thing that I'd found myself in because this was 15 to 20 years of research. This had the attention of the entire country. . . . There was just way too much pressure to try to make it work, but we did make it work, and that was pretty amazing.

Despite the costs and the occasional rough learning curve, the potential for interactive multimedia to serve as a powerful tool for reaching visitors was so strong that museums started investing in hiring in-house personnel who had the skills to design and develop interactive multimedia. Given the costs involved, this sometimes required contributions from wealthy benefactors and other important financial contributors. Scott Sayre explains the source of the funding that took him from producing documentaries at the University of Minnesota to developing interactive multimedia at the Minneapolis Institute of Arts:

> We were expected to produce one or two mini-documentaries on what we saw as emerging trends in technology . . . and one of the things that we went to cover was an early Interactive Videodisc program that was developed at the Minneapolis Institute of Arts . . . the interactive directory to what you could do at the museum. I was there with the crew shooting this, and the woman from guest services said, "Do you know much about this kind of stuff?" And I said, "Oh yeah, I've written my dissertation on this, and this is an area that I've been working on." And she said, "You know, we've been looking to hire a Director of Interactive. . . . You should really talk to the Director of the Museum. I think there might be an opportunity for you here. . . ." I ended up landing this job, and it was probably the first one in the country, or maybe the world, to be forming an internal interactive media group in a museum, and this was early 1991. The backstory on this was that the Director, Evan Mauer at the time, had been on a plane and happened to be sitting next to Bill Gates. And Bill Gates asked him what he was doing with technology in the museum, and Evan had said, "Nothing, but what should we be doing?" And Bill had told him that he should really be looking at interactive technologies, that they were the up-and-coming learning technologies for museums, and then Evan went and met with General Mills, and got $1.5 million dollars that was basically sitting at the museum when I was hired to start this project, so I mean, what an incredible opportunity to be given!

Throughout the 1990s, those opportunities kept coming for museum technology professionals, with technologies often changing faster than one could keep up. Scott Sayre describes the rapid pace of technological change at the Minneapolis Institute of Arts and the challenges of keeping current with digital imaging as they moved from exhibit kiosks to the World Wide Web:

> We played with a lot of early technology. . . . I remember having my first experience with JPEG, and this sounds totally nerdy but what you could do with a JPEG image and how quickly you could load it was just magical, and so I remember buying these JPEG decompression cards for the Macs that we were putting in the galleries. And they would work magic because images could actually appear within seconds . . . and we're doing all sorts of work with DeBabelizer, which was a tool to force images down into a very small palette of colors, and that all that was fun, and we got really good at it, but so much of that work just got thrown away because better things came very quickly, and all of a sudden we were working with thousands and eventually millions of colors . . . and then QuickTime came out and blew our minds and all this is like

> crazy exciting, we're having a really hard time keeping up with it, and then. . . . I went to a meeting and was introduced to Mosaic right when it came out, and immediately went back to my team, and was like, "We're dropping everything. We're gonna. . . . This is good. This is going to be amazing."

The release of NCSA Mosaic, the world's first graphical web browser, in 1993 represented a sea change for museums. Of course, museums had been working with the underlying infrastructure of the Internet, and figuring out how to get their institutions online, long before the introduction of the web. David Bridge, for example, describes the process of collecting the funds needed to get the Smithsonian connected to the Internet and set up the Smithsonian's first Internet server:

> I was walking through the cafeteria in Natural History, and Richard Thorrington and Barbara Smith said, "Come over here and sit down. We've been hearing about the Internet. Can we get connected to the Internet?" and I said, "I have no idea, but I will find out. . . ." We managed to cobble something together, and get it put into the budget request, which was rejected in January of 1991. . . . And we had two or three people who were really adamant that we needed to get connected to the Internet, and so I went around to them and said, "We can try again next year, and we may have the same results, and that will still be 18 months before we can get connected, or maybe we can pass the hat and we can fund this, at least at a minimal level." And so, I collected $72,000 from about a dozen different offices and organizations within the Smithsonian. The Library contributed $23,000 or something, but a lot of people put up $5,000, saying "I want my organization to be on." And I remember the Head of Research at Natural History in a meeting said, "We have to decide whether we're going to be a first-rate research institution in the world, or a second-rate one." And they put in $10,000.

But once the web emerged as a force, and museums started setting up websites, it quickly became clear that there was a great deal of interest in museum websites, not just from museum professionals, but from museum visitors as well. Jonathan Bowen describes building the world's first directory for museum websites, the Virtual Library Museum Pages, and seeing firsthand just how much interest there was in museums on the web:

> I started looking at Mosaic in about 1993 . . . and because my wife is in museums, I thought, "Well, I'll look for some museum things. . . ." I noticed a few museums, so I thought, "Well, I'll just do a little list of museums that have anything on there. . . ." I made a collection of those, and then I noticed also that Tim Berners-Lee with some colleagues had set up this Virtual Library, because this was pre- any real search engines, so if you wanted to find anything, you needed some sort of index page to help you find things. Well, I just emailed off to them and said, "Look, I'll volunteer to do the museum section," and they

said, "Fine," so I just set it up on our web server, and fairly quickly. . . . I realized that the number of people accessing the museums pages far outstripped any interest in any of the research going on. . . . It was several times more for the museums than everything else on the server.

The more people were interested in museums, and the more museums started getting online, the more the technology started to snowball. Jonathan Bowen, continuing his story, explains how he came to the realization that the number of museum websites was growing exponentially:

> One of the curators decided to have an exhibition called the "Information Superhighway," which dates it, and they had a little workshop meeting of about one day, where they invited people along . . . and everyone else was giving these talks about how wonderful the web was going to be in the future, whereas my talk was, "This is what I've been doing for the last year or so. Here are all the statistics of access. This is what's going on." So, I guess that made a bit of a contrast—what most people were looking at was the future, whereas I was saying, "Well, it's already happening. Yes, it's going to be very exciting." I mean, one little statistic . . . the accesses were going up. They were doubling every three months at that time. So, I did my little calculation, "You know, it's going to be millions and millions. . . ." Of course, it leveled out a few years later, so we didn't keep going up exponentially, but at that time it really was exponential.

All of a sudden, there was a veritable explosion of museum websites. It seemed as if everyone was talking about museum websites, showing off museum websites, and trying to figure out how to build museum websites. Museum conferences, especially those with a technology focus, featured sessions devoted to the topic. Rob Lancefield, for example, describes learning about websites for the first time at the Museum Computer Network conference:

> At MCN 1995, a good number of the presentations were showing off and talking about museum websites—this fairly new thing—and how they were made and all of this. So that seemed pretty interesting. And I got back from MCN, got a big fat book on HTML 2.0, and played around with my favorite text-editing software, and a pretty early version of Photoshop. I learned a little bit about Apache and launched our museum website early in '96. Pretty minimal, but it was fun to do. And suddenly we didn't have to put ink on paper to let people know when the gallery would be open.

Despite the enthusiasm of museum technology professionals who were ready to jump on the World Wide Web for the first time, many of them faced an uphill battle, especially in the early days, when few people had seen a website or understood what websites were. Richard Rinehart, for example, describes the reaction he received when he proposed making a website for Berkeley Art Museum/Pacific Film Archive:

> We made the website, which launched in 1994, when I got there. And I remember, when I first got to the museum, it was the year that I got there, and I had just come from the library, and I was some whippersnapper, and didn't know anything or anybody. And I said, I think at a staff meeting or something, I said, "I'd like to create a website for this museum. I think that'd be a great way to reach the public." And of course everybody's like, "Web? What? What's a Web?"

Despite this reaction, museum technology professionals pushed ahead with building early websites, even when others did not see the potential or understand what they were doing. Dana Mitroff Silvers describes working on the Berkeley Art Museum/Pacific Film Archive website with Richard (Rick) Rinehart at a time when the majority of the museum staff had no idea what they were doing or why anyone would want to do that:

> I was working at the Berkeley Art Museum / Pacific Film Archive in the '90s. And they had one of the very first museum websites to go online. I think it was among the first 500 domains. And Rick—because that's the kind of person he is—said, "I'm going to do this. I'm going to put up a website!" And he just did it! At the time he was the IT guy. These [website manager] roles didn't even exist. Rick was the guy who managed all the Mac workstations. And he just put up the first website . . . to which people were like, "Wait, what the hell is he doing?" I was working in the education department as a program assistant creating paper-based guides for schools and families to come into the museum and go around with a paper tour. And I said to Rick, "Hey, why don't we put this online?" And Rick said, "Yes, go for it. Here's a little booklet on HTML 1.0. There's a computer in the hallway that has Photoshop on it. I'll teach you some basic HTML, and you can go for it! Oh, and here's a scanner." Now this wasn't part of my job. Nobody knew what I was doing. I told my supervisor, and she said, "Why would you do that? Why would you want to put this stuff online? That's weird. That makes no sense." And I just did it. I would stay late, and taught myself some HTML. . . . Rick explained everything to me. I didn't even know what metadata meant. I didn't know what a digital image was. I didn't know any of this. And Rick just taught me, and I apprenticed myself to him. And I started putting our Family Guides online on the website. And then I started getting really interested in it, and realized, we could put this online and that online. And we can have a clickable JPEG file that could be a visual image of the museum. Because we were thinking so literally at that time, like, "Oh, we'll have a map, and you click here because that's where that object is—it's on this floor in this corner. So you'll click on it and it'll load a new page and that'll have the information. . . ." At the time, my supervisor still used a typewriter. And she was actually one of the holdouts who used a typewriter for many, many years. She literally sat in her office on her typewriter, and here

> I was putting all this material online. And that opened up this whole world for me. Because I had been doing all this in-person, traditional, education stuff, and I was like, "Wow, why wouldn't you put this online?" It seemed amazing, and to me like a no-brainer.

Naturally, it took time for museum technology professionals to figure out what information they wanted to put online and how they might organize web pages for their institutions. They had to create web structures and information architectures on their own with little prior experience, testing out ideas about user experience, interaction design, and graphical elements as they went along. Kathy Jones describes the kinds of decisions they had to make while creating the first website at the Peabody Museum at Harvard University:

> I was at the Peabody in the time of the magical 1990s when all of us were able to do things like digital imaging or create multimedia products. And the early website that my team and I created for the Peabody and other Harvard museums was during that period. We based it on a little book called "*The Treasures of Arts and Science at Harvard University*." And I thought that it would be okay to use the material for each museum because it had been funded by the Provost's Office and vetted by the Office of General Counsel. So I felt that there would be no copyright issues. And we didn't run into any. . . . We reserved the domain names for the Harvard museums. Many of them still have those in place, like https://peabody.harvard.edu/. We also formed an internal committee to look at the different departments that should be represented on the website, and to begin thinking about how you would create consistency or cohesion in the pages that you were presenting, a main page then maybe departmental pages and other subpages. So we were thinking about that. . . . We did a lot of work.

Diana Folsom shares a similar story about her early work developing the website for the Los Angeles County Museum of Art, and how they based their initial design ideas on the museum's print brochures and the colors of the I.T. guys' cars:

> We created our own website in about 1997. We were in the I.T. department, just sitting in the back room, and just re-typing what we saw in either a brochure or the collections catalog, and plugging that information online. And that was about it. At one point, I think the colors chosen were colors to match one of the I.T. guys' cars. There wasn't a whole lot of thought about user experience then. It was just trying to figure out how to make a few pages, recreate a few brochure-like pages, and stick it online. As many things begin, it was kind of quiet and just having fun together. Just trying things out. Experimenting a bit. We were the little elves behind them, making the magic happen.

Slowly but surely, people started to realize that all museums were going to need a website and that this medium was too important for the design of those websites to be left to chance. Simply posting some random text and images online was no longer going to be sufficient. Museums were going to need to make an effort to formalize the design and development of their websites, a realization that placed even more demands on the museum technology professional. Deborah Howes describes how she was recruited to the Metropolitan Museum of Art in order to formalize their early web presence:

> In '95, the web was discovered by the Metropolitan Museum of Art, and someone I used to work with at the Art Institute, Kent Lydecker, was at the Met, and Kent is saying to the Director, Philippe de Montebello, "This is going to be big. This web thing. We really need to focus on what the educational message of this is going to be." And Philippe's like, "Well, you could be right." In '95, not many museums had websites, but the Met did. Someone had run out again with their 8-bit flip phone and taken a picture of the facade of the museum with a prominent yellow taxi in front, almost obscuring the building, and that was the homepage for the Metropolitan Museum of Art's website. And when you clicked "Enter," you had to fill in your email address, because they didn't want just anybody coming into the website, you had to be registered as a visitor. And then the next screen was "Which floor would you like to see? First, second, or third?" No pictures. I mean, it could not have been more inside baseball in any way. . . . And so Kent's calling me like, "Have you seen the Met's website?" I'm like, "Uh-huh." And he's like, "Do you think you could come to the Met, and help us?" And I'm like, "You betcha!"

Slowly but surely, people started to realize that museums were increasingly going to rely on the web as a primary means of communication to help them reach their audiences and spread their message more broadly. Matthew MacArthur describes the evolution of his work with websites at the National Museum of American History, and the process they went through convincing people at the museum about the opportunities afforded by the web:

> Reflecting on those early years at the museum, I think our main job really was to evangelize the possibilities of the web. This was very new. It was not in many people's workflow, or in their budgets. Of course, it fit in very nicely with the mission of the museum to serve audiences in the whole nation, and even internationally. The web, of course, greatly expanded the opportunities to reach those audiences who couldn't come to the museum. And of course, we were learning at the same time what it meant to manage and staff and run a website project. But really, at our museum then, and to a good extent today, exhibition projects were really the driver of funding and institutional effort. And so, we would schedule meetings to talk to project teams for upcoming exhibitions and really just kind of sell this idea of why they should be interested in trying to have some kind of web presence. We were starting to figure

> out for ourselves and for the museum what were the strengths and weaknesses. Some of the museum's first efforts were very literal like, "Here's a map of the gallery. Click on this room. . . . Click through the labels . . ." and it was very much getting out of that mindset, which can still be valid in some cases of the gallery as an organizing metaphor, but of course, we saw that there were so many opportunities when you went beyond that, and really started to see a website as its own project with its own opportunities and strengths.

Once people realized the importance of the web for museums—as soon as everyone figured out just what the technology could do, and why it mattered—everyone wanted a website, and they wanted those websites to be professionally designed. Just keeping up with the increasing demands for website development became a new and ongoing challenge for museum technology professionals. Matthew MacArthur describes that tipping point at the National Museum of American History:

> For some period of time, we were trying to drum up work, basically, but at some point, the tables turned. Everybody got it. Everybody wanted a website. It became sort of an expectation, even from funders and stakeholders and internally, that these projects were going to have an awesome website. So then it became, well, like too much work, you know. It was a gatekeeping problem, unfortunately, which continues today. Unlike the constraints of the physical building, where we have only so much floor space and so much capacity . . . digitally, it's sort of infinite space. And so figuring out how to define that and to manage workflow and everything like that, is kind of a perpetual challenge.

All of a sudden, convincing museums to go online was no longer the problem. Instead, museum technology professionals had to grapple with new and unprecedented ideas about what to do with the World Wide Web, figure out how to meet rapidly increasing demands for museum websites, and learn how to keep current with constantly changing Internet technologies. Designing and developing museum websites suddenly became a professional task with long-term goals and managerial responsibilities. Darren Milligan describes the changing nature of his job at the Smithsonian as new ideas about website management evolved over time:

> I went from someone who learned how to do some HTML to someone who was really not a webmaster but a software project manager, which is very different. . . . The people who were webmasters at the Smithsonian when I started, many of them are still here, and they were such generalists. I think, 15 years ago we had to be. We were taking the photographs that are on the web page, and editing the photographs. We were writing most of the content, editing the content, coding the pages, launching the pages, and sometimes taking care of the servers. You were a team of one in many ways, and what's been

> wonderful, as our digital teams have grown, and there's been more emphasis and funding and resources for outreach and for online platforms is to see the specialization. I've had the opportunity to really dive deeply into education, while there's a dive into scientific research, or other areas of deeper specialization, which was not a reality 15 years ago. We were all teams of one.... So, my role has really gone from somebody who's stealing HTML snippets from other websites to try to build things . . . to leading a team of 10 or 15 people who have very specific technical expertise around managing the code for this very complex and growing piece of software.

The museum technology professional was no longer working alone in the back room building websites with no one watching over their shoulder but coordinating projects and managing teams as an integral part of the fabric of the institution. While this was at times challenging, this transition was important; if museum technology professionals had waited for their institutions to catch up with the technology before going online—if they had waited for someone else to tell them to do this initial, invisible work—then they and their institutions would have likely missed the boat entirely. Staying on the cutting edge is important, even if no one is asking you to do it, expecting you to do it, or understanding why you are doing it, because it sets you and your institution up for future success. As Sam Quigley explains, if museum technology professionals had not taken the initiative and grasped the importance of this work early on, then museums would not have been ready to go online once everyone else caught up:

> I used to say, we had to stay within shouting distance of the popular culture, because at that point in time, this new thing, the World Wide Web, that was so obviously going to take over, and yet it wasn't until the summer of '96 or so, when it really took on efficacy with regard to commercial real estate, or commerce. Basically, if we hadn't jumped on beforehand, museums would have been left out of the picture entirely, I think.

As we heard time and again from our oral history participants, none of this was easy. Keeping current with constantly changing technologies places unique demands on museum technology professionals. Keeping up with the pace of technological change is hard, and predicting the future is impossible. Technology changes are often two steps forward, and one step back, with no immediately visible or obvious benefit to the individual or the institution. As Scott Sayre explains, the quality of images online, for example, was initially quite poor, and it took time for the images on museum websites to reach the quality of images on CD-ROMs:

> It was kind of going backwards. I mean, we were back to small color spaces, no animation, everything really, really, really, really limited. Half my team was

really rebellious against any attention being paid to the web, because we were working in these much more rich kiosk environments.

In the end, however, the actual technology itself does not matter; whether one is adapting to the introduction of CD-ROMs, the World Wide Web, mobile devices, social media, virtual reality, or artificial intelligence, one cannot skip to the end; one has to learn the technology as one uses it, dealing with all its fits and starts along the way. If we are to keep our heads above water as new technologies arrive in museums, then we need to work through the process of evolving along with those technologies, keeping up with increasing demands and new challenges as an integral part of that process. This mindset is essential if museum technology professionals are to keep current, and not fall behind, as the nature of their job changes along with the very technologies that enable them to accomplish their goals and help their institutions achieve their missions.

SUGGESTIONS FOR FURTHER READING

Bearman, David, and Jennifer Trant. 1999. "Interactivity Comes of Age: Museums and the World Wide Web." *Museum International* 51 (4): 20-24.

Besser, Howard, and Jennifer Trant. 1995. *Introduction to Imaging: Issues in Constructing an Image Database*. Santa Monica, CA: Getty Art History Information Program.

Bowen, Jonathan P. 2002. "Weaving the Museum Web: The Virtual Library Museums Pages." *Program: Electronic Library and Information Systems* 36 (4): 236–252.

Frey, Franziska S., and Stephen Chapman. 2001. "Developing Specifications for Archival Digital Still Images." In *PICS 2001: Image Processing, Image Quality, Image Capture, Systems Conference Proceedings*, 166–171. Montreal, Canada: Society for Imaging Science and Technology.

Giannini, Tula, and Jonathan Bowen, eds. 2019. *Museums and Digital Culture: New Perspectives and Research*. Cham: Springer.

Mirapaul, Matthew. 1999. "Taking Web as a Given, Museums Go After Net Audience." *New York Times*, March 16, 1999. https://archive.nytimes.com/www.nytimes.com/library/tech/99/03/cyber/articles/16museums.html

Salvador, Phil. 2016. "Bob Stein on the Voyager Company, Transitional Multimedia, and the Long Outlook on Information." *The Obscuritory*, February 5, 2016. https://obscuritory.com/multimedia/bob-stein-on-voyager/.

Samis, Peter S., and Mimi Michaelson. 2017. *Creating the Visitor-Centered Museum*. New York: Routledge.

Sayre, Scott. 2005. "Multimedia that Matters: Gallery-based Technology and the Museum Visitor." *First Monday* 10 (5). https://firstmonday.org/ojs/index.php/fm/article/view/1244

5

Creative Innovation

> With those early interactives . . . somebody had to go in and make sure those things were working, and the screen was clean, and that was our responsibility. . . . There was a lot of "boots on the ground" work that was really, really fun. Oh my gosh, I just said really, really fun, didn't I? Oh, it was so lovely. Just got to work with lots of lovely people. It was a great time to be a pioneer in technology.—Oral History of Holly Witchey

The history of museum computing, from the 1960s to today, is in many ways a story of the inspirational projects that drove the field forward, as museum technology professionals adopted new technologies, overcame barriers to innovation, and kept the spirit of creativity alive. Many of our oral history participants spoke about the power of technological innovation, inspiration, and creativity for enabling their accomplishments and their success. When we examine the growth of museum computing through the lens of these oral histories, we see how many of those technological advances were a direct result of the enthusiasm of the museum technology professionals who led the way.

A sense of delight pervades the stories we collected as our participants stressed the excitement of using new technologies to convey ideas and engage audiences in ways never before possible. Many of them described their time in museums as a Golden Age of Innovation, full of wonderful and unique opportunities, and powered by joy, enthusiasm, and inspiration. In many ways, the introduction of museum computing offered a freedom to innovate and a kind of delightful enthusiasm that encouraged creativity and new ideas.

The creative innovations that emerged as new technologies became available to museum professionals inspired new approaches to museum work that offered positive experiences for many museum technology professionals. Our oral history participants spoke frequently about how they were inspired by their love for museums, and how much they loved their jobs. Andrea Ledesma, for example, explains in her oral history what prompted her to pursue a career in museum technology:

> I like working with museum technology, because I love the Internet, I love museums, I love working with people, and it was just this perfect amalgamation of all that.

Many of our oral history participants talked about working with museum technology as being their dream job. Shelly Mannion, for example, describes her work at the British Museum:

> I worked for the Samsung Digital Discovery Centre for five years. . . . I absolutely loved my job as the Education Manager of the SDDC. It was literally the best job I've ever had. . . . It was really my dream job. I absolutely loved it.

Much of this love for their work was driven by the experiences they were designing for museum visitors and the tools they were building to support the museum visit. Jane Alexander recalls the thrill of applying for her job at the Cleveland Museum of Art:

> I love museums, and I had young kids, and the idea of giving people the tool sets to look closer, dive deeper, engage, understand when you go into the galleries, how do you look at art except for reading that didactic? I was really excited about this position, and from my first interview, was like, "Oh, I really want this." So, I felt super lucky. I called it my dream job. . . . I still call it my dream job.

Holly Witchey echoes this sentiment as she recalls her time designing interactive exhibits for visitors at the San Diego Museum of Art, and the creativity that these exhibits inspired:

> We did a lot of interactives at San Diego. . . . We did a beautiful one with dragon robes that was actually a Chinese cabinet where you could virtually pull the drawers out, and pieces would pop out. . . . It was just a really wonderful time. We were thinking about projects in depth. . . . People wanted more information. . . . There weren't any restrictions. . . . We really had the time to think through projects and go as wonderfully deep as we wanted to in discovering kingfisher feathers in Chinese jewelry.

Many of our oral history participants spoke positively and passionately about the inspirational power of museum interactives. Bruce Wyman, for example, attributes his love of museums to the interactive exhibits he discovered as a child at the Smithsonian Institution:

> I grew up in the D.C. area and would go to the Smithsonian all the time, and at the National Air and Space Museum, I was there for the opening in the late '70s, there was an interactive that sat near where the original Enterprise model hung in the galleries. It was a brain-dead, simple interactive. It was a grid of buttons. I think there were nine, and one axis was "size of planet", and the other one was "environment"—land, sea, or air. And you'd press the button at the corresponding intersection of those things, and you'd see on a screen in front of you a visualization, a NASA artist rendering, of the kind of creature that might inhabit that planet. . . . It was run off of a video display player, the height of technology at the time, but the thing that was compelling about it, and I would have been about ten when I first encountered this, is I recognized that I thought about it when I wasn't there, and it was those permutations that sat in the back of my mind. And years later, when I thought about the things that had influenced me, I thought so much about that, and what it meant, and how to apply that, and how that made me think about other things and learn other things. That kind of inspiring moment of really simple engagement is compelling! I'd love to do that for the rest of my life, and that is, frankly, why I started doing museum work.

These kinds of interactive experiences in museums inspired more than museum visitors; they also inspired museum technology professionals. Museums around the world were determined to figure out the best way to integrate computing technologies into their galleries, and the people in charge of these projects were constantly on the lookout for inspiration to strike. Nik Honeysett, for example, describes the origins of the Micro Gallery at the National Gallery of Art in London in the late 1980s, at a time when he had just started working for Cogapp in Brighton:

> Alex Morrison, CEO of Cogapp, was in a pub in Trafalgar Square right next to the National Gallery of Art. They had just hired what they called a Technical Project Manager to create a room in a new wing that was being built by the Sainsbury brothers that was going to be a computer information room. . . . And, literally, this Technical Project Manager in the bar is sitting next to Alex Morrison. . . . They happen to start talking and he says, "I've got this project. I have no idea what we're going to do. We've got to use computers to enhance the experience of the National Gallery." So Alex is like, "Come down to Brighton . . ." and they came up with this idea of a big color screen. We could put an image and some text next to it, and you could click on the text, and something would happen. . . . So we built this pilot, which was literally one screen. It took weeks to get a digital scan of an image. I mean, back then, it was a real problem. Throw up an image on a screen. Figured out how to do anti-aliased text on a Macintosh. And we just presented this screen, and were like, "What do you think?" And AmEx was a co-sponsor of this. And they were like, "What do you need?" So they wrote a check for a million dollars, and we were off and running building this, which was the Micro Gallery.

Groundbreaking projects like the Micro Gallery were not only expensive; they were inspirational as well, especially to young museum technology professionals. Nik Honeysett describes the launch of the Micro Gallery, and how even the Royal Family showed up for the exhibit opening, and were amazed by the potential of museum computing:

> When you launch these new systems . . . you have these big openings, like VIP openings. At the National Gallery, it was the Queen that did the opening. . . . I remember being there late one night, it was maybe half past nine. We were allowed to be there because we were the "computer kids"—that's what they called us, "the computer kids"—and we were trying to get this thing done on a tight deadline. I remember sitting at one of the desks late at night, and somebody came in. I thought it was a security guard, just checking around. And this guy said something to me. And it was Prince Charles. And he said, "What are you doing?" We had this conversation, and I explained what I'm doing. And he said, "I've got to tell everybody. I've got to tell Mummy about this . . ." And so, he disappeared off, and of course, I called up my mum and my sister and went, "I just met Prince Charles . . ."

Naturally, large-scale technology projects tend to involve numerous last-minute fixes and edits, a situation that can provide all kinds of unexpected opportunities for interpersonal interaction. As Nik Honeysett explains, when you are working behind the scenes as a museum technology professional, you never know when you might be called upon to demonstrate your exhibit:

> There was a week of VIP openings . . . and I remember, something had happened, and I had to fix it, so I'm up in this room doing a final tweak to some code and somebody comes in, and it's the Queen Mother, on her own . . . and she said, "What are you doing?" And I get a chair, and I show her what we're doing. And all she wanted to see were the portraits of horses . . . so, for maybe ten, fifteen minutes, I'm explaining this system to her, and I was kind of on one knee beside her, because she's barely five foot, and she's sitting down. So I'm on one knee, like I'm being knighted or something . . . and everybody else comes in and they're just all around. And they've been really quiet, while I was telling this, I had not been briefed on protocol with the royal family. And so, she said, "This was fabulous, dear. Thank you so much." And she stood up. She kind of looked around, and then she held her hand out, to kiss her hand, and I just kind of whacked it on my forehead. . . . And then, a couple of days later, the Queen came in, and I always remember the project manager was demoing the system to her on touchscreens, and he asked her to touch the screen on something that she was interested in. Of course, she had gloves on, and it didn't work. So it was this moment of panic, because that had been a big thing. We were meant to get pictures of the Queen touching the touchscreen, and it never worked. She was interested in horses too.

Groundbreaking projects like these naturally inspired similar projects, driving the field forward to new heights with each iteration. Holly Witchey explains how the wonderful and inspirational achievements at the National Gallery of Art in London with interactive computer technology led directly to the development of a similar exhibit at the San Diego Museum of Art:

> We had a trustee named Maurice Kaplan, and Maurice went to London, and he saw the Micro Gallery, which was the sort of first interactive installation on a large scale with the collection at the National Gallery of Art. And it had been created by a firm called Cognitive Applications. . . . And Mr. Kaplan, the trustee, called Steven Brezzo, the Director, in the middle of the night and said, "I want to do something like that at San Diego, and I'll pay for it, but you have to use this firm."

It can be hard to remember just how groundbreaking, and even futuristic, these projects were at this time. Holly Witchey describes the magical experience she had working with other museum technology professionals to design, develop, and install San Diego's Image (Interactive Museum Art Gallery Explorer) Gallery in the early 1990s:

> The magic was that everybody there really cared about art and art museums, and they like to look at things and they know why people like to look at things, so we built the Image Gallery, and we had so much fun. . . . We couldn't have the Image Gallery in the galleries with the works of art. You can't have the technology and the art competing. So they gave us a little room, just to the left of the staircase in the San Diego Museum of Art, and Mitch Gaul, the designer, built this fantastically Jetson-y installation for it, that had like two circular areas with flying saucers, and it wasn't until the night when we were installing that we realized that the guys were going to have to bench press these massive computers up into the installation. . . . The fourth member of that team was Nik Honeysett, who later went on to the Getty. Nik was the junior programmer that they left in place to help me do things, and to get everything finished, so Nik was bench pressing these computers into the installation.

The Image Gallery also featured a very early attempt to engage museum visitors with digital images in the galleries. As Holly Witchey explains, visitors to the San Diego Museum of Art were able to collect color printouts of their favorite works from the collection:

> The other thing Image Gallery had at the time that was remarkable was . . . an $11,000 dye-sublimation printer. It was the most expensive piece of equipment we had in there, and it would take five minutes, but it would chug-chug-chug-chug-chug out a full-color print of the works in the collection . . . and there were envelopes and people went away with their wonderful prints from

> the collection. . . . We had a desk in there with a full-time attendant to print and answer questions because people really didn't know how to use these touchscreens. . . . And I can remember in the first couple of weeks, more than one person came in and wanted to see the Mona Lisa. And I had to explain that the Mona Lisa wasn't there. Luckily, a few years later, the Internet came around, and people were able to see whatever they wanted to see.

Inspired by the success of these and other interactive exhibits, museum after museum started exploring how to offer interactive experiences to their visitors, even if finding suitable space for technology in the galleries was sometimes a challenge. Peter Samis describes the experience of bringing multimedia interactive exhibits into SFMOMA:

> Suddenly I was charged with leading this new effort to bring multimedia to SFMOMA, and the reason why it was relevant and urgent was we were about to move into a new building. The Mario Botta Building on Third Street gave us new spaces and new opportunities, and a new public, and a new profile. . . . There was a lot of energy around it in the community, and we were able to recruit a lot of interns and I was able to, with a slim budget, put together initial prototypes of three different programs. . . . We were really in this tiny little space on the second floor of the museum. It was revolutionary because we had a footprint at all. We had three computers set up in this little space, between the permanent Painting and Sculpture galleries, and the Architecture and Design galleries. . . . It was just by virtue of the emergency doors in this one tiny gallery that made it a space that neither department wanted, that we ended up having a footprint on the floor.

Once museum computing was established in this way, even if it was just a small experimental space, it was difficult to ignore the potential for multimedia in the galleries, and the way visitors responded positively to these experiences. Technological innovation and inspiration would irrevocably change the way museums interacted with visitors in the galleries. Peter Samis, for example, describes how the Compaq iPAQ Gallery Explorer revolutionized the way visitors interacted with the art at SFMOMA in the early 2000s:

> Sandy Pentland at MIT said, "Compaq is coming out with their new iPAQ Pocket PC Gallery Explorer and it supports video. How about just putting some videos on the Gallery Explorer and giving a mobile experience that way?" We thought, "Okay, but what videos do we want people walking around the galleries with?" And we thought, "Well, the only ones that seem important enough would be videos of artists." And so we culled all of our artist videos. We put three per gallery, basically, in this little HTML menu on these iPAQ Gallery Explorers. And people could check them out for free when they got off the elevator and use those, or if they didn't want to use those, they could just use the smart tables. And then, at the end of the show, after all of these

> different themes and smart tables and the iPAQ Gallery Explorer experience, they could sit in the learning lounge in the back, where there was the "Make Your Own Gallery" activity, an animated activity where, having seen the ways that the curators had organized and thematized the show, they could come up with their own themes and their own groupings, and recombine things and make virtual galleries, and write a little bit about it.

All of these groundbreaking technology projects combined forces to lay the foundation for a wide range of interactive multimedia experiences over the decades that followed. As museum visitors became more accustomed to the idea of interacting with multimedia in museums, museum technology professionals found they could be even more innovative with the experiences they developed. Jane Alexander, for instance, describes the design of Gallery One at the Cleveland Museum of Art, and how they intentionally developed their wall-sized interactive experience for visitors who would be inspired to engage with digital art in museums:

> When we first started Gallery One, there was this fear that this would intimidate visitors . . . so, I was like, "Let's flip it. Let's design for the people who use digital, and let's design it really well, and let's have it just kind of happen." We worked with Design IO for ArtLens Studio and one of the things that I just think is so fabulous is our Zoom wall. An object comes up, and your body's a magnifying glass, and your child's a magnifying glass, and if you get closer, it's a big magnifying glass. You're already looking at high-resolution images on a 20-foot wall, but now you've zoomed in, so when you see it in the gallery, you already know this object. You know where the horse is. . . . We're trying to introduce them to the collection. It's not about choosing the artwork. We have things that you can choose. You have the phone, you can look up any artwork—this is about, you don't know what you don't know. And it's been super successful.

The positive reaction that museums received from visitors engaging with digital interactives encouraged museum technology professionals to explore new kinds of immersive media experiences. Silvia Filippini-Fantoni discusses the importance of engaging audiences through creative technologies and the power of immersion when designing digital exhibits:

> Immersion is a great way nowadays to connect to people, and I think one of the greatest experiences. . . . Everybody has an Audubon collection in an American museum, so we created this experience, first at the Indianapolis Museum of Art for an exhibition, then at the North Carolina Museum of Art for the permanent collection, and now in the Newark Museum of Art, where we bring to life the World of Audubon. We use high-resolution images of his work . . . and put them into a kind of a world that no longer exists. . . . Some of these birds are no longer here, and the world that they lived in is no longer the

> same. So we bring it to life and immerse people in this reality, where they can hear the sound of these birds, see them fly around them in a kind of swamp-like or forest-like environment. And then we create a long-lasting memory.

The development of immersive multimedia experiences in museums helped encourage community engagement and build long-term relationships with a new generation of museum visitors. Museum curators and educators increasingly recognized the power of hands-on, immersive experiences in museums, as Silvia Filippini-Fantoni explains:

> We used technology to sort of recreate an experience that people cannot have nowadays, because that world doesn't exist anymore. . . . You know, a real part of understanding Frida Kahlo is understanding the role that Casa Azul, Blue House, had in her and her husband's life, as well as the cultural life in Mexico City, because Frida's family played a key role in the cultural scene in the city . . . and so we wanted to create an experience that sort of recreated, metaphorically, Casa Azul. We brought it to life through projections and sounds and animation that surrounded people and the 360-degree environment to immerse people in a world. . . . Same with O'Keeffe. You don't understand O'Keefe until you see the world that she lived in. She lived in these beautiful places in New Mexico, and she used that imagery very much in her work, but you don't realize that until you see what her house looked like inside and outside. So for an exhibition of O'Keefe, we sent people there, filmed in 360 degrees, recreated this environment, and then we overlapped the image of the work of art onto the images of the spaces around her and the details of the house, so that people understood how that the environment influenced her work. And the kind of comments that I received from people were like, "This experience brought it home for me. I get it! I get O'Keefe now. I didn't get her before, but now I understand her." And then we over-imposed a voiceover of O'Keefe. She gave an interview talking about New Mexico, so we took some excerpts that were relevant to what we were showing, and so this kind of combination of sound, of visual, and then the overlaying of the artwork really brought it home for a lot of people.

Many of our oral history participants spoke about the power of immersive media, and how the technologies used in creating immersive experiences in museums compared to those used in other environments, such as museum websites. Sarah Kenderdine, for example, described how her work shifted from developing virtual experiences online to building high-end interactive, immersive experiences in physical galleries at the Powerhouse Museum in Sydney:

> Intel came to the Powerhouse Museum three weeks before Christmas and said, "Hey, you're having the Olympic Games exhibition next year. What are you going to do? What can you showcase for technology?" And my boss at the time was Tim Hart. So we threw together a one-page statement, and

> suddenly we had a million dollars, which we had to deliver on. . . . It was a web outfitters service for Intel, so a very high-end website . . . and it included a complete virtual reconstruction of Olympia, hundreds of panoramas that were shot on long poles and all these kinds of things. It was very early, none of this stuff had been done before. And we put it all online. And it was very well received, and we made a CD-ROM. It went to all schools in Australia. It had many outcomes. But the outcome for me was not so much the website . . . but at that time, we also did this big virtual reconstruction of Olympia . . . and we made a big 3D installation inside the galleries with all the objects that came from Athens. They'd never left the country before. And it was at that moment, when I saw the real stuff and the digital stuff together, that I got off the Internet. I thought, "Ah, this is much more fun. The Internet's turned into a sewer, anyway. So let's get off the web and back into physical gallery space. So, in fact, that's what I've been doing ever since."

Naturally, creating these kinds of immersive experiences for museum galleries is not without its own challenges. Sarah Kenderdine explains the difficulties they encountered creating an immersive visualization of the Angkor Wat temple in Cambodia:

> I moved to build a very big eight-sided, rear-projected, immersive visualization system, which was very successful, five years at the museum. Now I'm building these really big machines with lots of hardware and software engineers. . . . I was also doing a lot of field work. I was still working in various countries, mainly collecting data now, not being an archaeologist, basically being a film/documentation hack, carrying tripods, taking photos in a myriad of ways, ambisonics, and stuff like that. I'm building big machines. We made many, many really great shows. . . . We went and shot stereographic panoramas at Angkor Wat for a show I was building for this machine. Now in those days there were no cameras for this, right? Nothing. Zero. No panoramic rotating cameras yet. . . . So the way we did it was a single camera with this massive 185-degree fisheye lens, and took 360 photographs in a circle. And then it took every second frame—a slice out of every second one—to create the left eye. And a slice out of the other one to create the right eye. This is big manual labor. But what's crazy about that, if you choose one of the world's most visited world heritage sites of course, is that tourists are walking everywhere. So poor Peter nearly had a breakdown at the end of that one because tourists are walking, we are stopping the shoot, they are continuing to walk . . . it was all hand done, you know, on a surveying tripod head. It was really, really arcane.

Nevertheless, as challenging as the work could be, technological advancements continued to offer museum technology professionals the opportunity to explore how emerging technologies can reshape the visitor experience. Holly Witchey, for example, describes the power of virtual reality systems for breaking down cultural barriers and providing access to cultural heritage resources in ways that were previously impossible:

> We have a group that developed the HoloLens here at Case Western Reserve University. They developed a really interesting application for anatomy students to look at the body, so you can put your lenses on and all look at a model and talk about things. . . . HoloLens had done a project with the Courtauld Institute of Art, and basically had some works in HoloLens, so you could put your lenses on, and it would look like you had a painting in your living room or a mummy . . . you could put a mummy on your coffee table. I had a conversation with them about digging deeper, and then the chair of my department, Elizabeth Bowman, who is a specialist in the Red Monastery in Egypt, which is closed, but she did 3D renderings of 3D scans of the entire interior and exterior of the Red Monastery, and now Art History students are using it to get close to places they couldn't see. You know, you can't get on a ladder, but with a HoloLens, you can go way up, and they can go places that women aren't allowed.

Emerging technologies in use in museums also include augmented reality devices, which have the potential to bring together the opportunities afforded by multimedia interactives, immersive media, virtual reality, and physical museum collections. Museum technology professionals have worked carefully to integrate augmented reality into museum exhibits in ways that complement but do not detract from the museum experience. Michael Haley Goldman, for example, reflecting on his work at the United States Holocaust Memorial Museum, talks about the challenge of building an augmented reality application that can provide additional educational context for their exhibits without intruding on the solemnity of the memorial space:

> Part of my job, specifically, is to think about these emerging technologies. How do you apply them in places like the Holocaust Museum? How do you not dishonor the memory of six million people who were murdered, but still try out things that could change the way you tell their stories? That's been a huge part of our work over the years. . . . I'm working on an Augmented Reality project for something we call the Tower of Faces right now. Tower of Faces is a part of our main exhibition. It's one of the more photogenic megafauna-type pieces of our institution, where, as you're traveling through the exhibition, you enter a tower that's about four stories tall, but it looks taller because of the way it's built, and there are photographs of individuals on all four walls around you, and they go up kind of to a vanishing point on the ceiling. These are all photographs of people from one particular community that was destroyed during the Holocaust. . . . When I talk to visitors about this space, often they want to know who the individuals are. They want to know a little bit more. You get the meta story. You get the story that these are all individuals from a single community, and you get the sense that they're going to be destroyed as

> a community . . . but we actually often know who these people are, and what they're doing, and we know the detail, the personal details about so many of these photographs. What if you could make that visible to people?

Innovative, immersive multimedia experiences also offer museums the opportunity to engage with their visitors even when the museum is closed, or when exhibits are inaccessible. Silvia Filippini-Fantoni describes an online, virtual escape room she created at the Newark Museum of Art, and speaks to the power of creating playful experiences to engage audiences:

> At the Newark Museum of Art, we have an historic property. It's a Victorian mansion from the late 19th Century, and it's inaccessible. . . . So how do we allow people to visit this, beyond the 360-degree renderings that we can do today? We created a game, so it's at the same time immersion as well as playfulness and participation. We created an escape room and set it virtually in this house. People can navigate from one room to another. They have four different rooms, even though the house is bigger, we limited it to the four main rooms on the main floor. They need to solve the puzzle within each room to be able to move to the next one, until they get to the last one, where they solve the mystery. . . . Some people manage to do it, some people don't. We divide people in groups, and they have about 45 minutes to an hour, but it's really fun and playful, and people seem to really enjoy it, and we offer it as a public program. . . . It's a source of funding for the museum, but also a great way to use technology to create a playful, immersive experience that connects people with the history of the house, and the history of the museum.

Over the past few decades, it has become increasingly important for museums to embrace innovation and technological change, and to use emerging technologies to devise new methods of meeting the needs of their visitors. In many ways, technology drives innovation. As Greg Albers explains, reflecting on the evolution of the tools available to support digital scholarship, changes to the underlying technologies available to museum technology professionals can help encourage experimentation and prompt new opportunities for innovation:

> Apple launched the iPad in 2010, and all of a sudden, there was a sort of amazing, beautiful device. . . . For museums, looking at the Kindle, which was an e-ink device, it's black and white, it doesn't do images very well, especially the early versions, they were very chunky, and kind of clunky. But here, the iPad presented this really beautiful, full color beautiful package that means that art museums especially began to see their publications and their artwork as being desirable on an iPad, on a device like that. Then all of a sudden, e-book publishing or digital publishing became sort of more appealing. . . . It was drag and drop . . . it made it a beautiful little package, you could do interactives, you could have videos, you can have different kinds of images. The design was really nice. It was easy to use, so it was appealing for museums

> who were looking to do digital publishing as a kind of easy way to get their content onto some nice package, and on a nice device . . . by learning just a little bit more, they were all of a sudden able to put an app out, a digital publication that looked like an app, and had kind of all the bells and whistles, and can be sort of shiny, and look beautiful and pretty.

This attitude and approach to creative innovation also opened up opportunities for museums to engage with technology in new ways, such as developing and sharing open-source software. The ability of museum technology professionals to engage in open-source projects, combined with the willingness of museum administrators to provide institutional support for these projects, was incredibly important for the development of new technologies. Greg Albers, for example, describes how his work with publishing software led to the creation of an online, open source, digital scholarly publishing tool to support the broader museum community:

> We've been working on what we now call QUIRE, which is a piece of software that is a multiformat software, that publishes online, but also in PDF and e-book as well, and it's really geared towards the kind of rich, visual scholarly publishing—citations and deep zooming images and videos and audios. We wanted to be able to handle all of that stuff. We've been working on that, and using our own books as prototypes in building out that software, and identifying what a digital QUIRE publication is, and where are the boundaries for that, and how do we manage that, and what do they look like, and all that kind of thing. We've been using all of our publications building QUIRE out with the idea that we're going to now work on open-sourcing this to the community so that others can also take advantage. . . . We felt that if we could provide software that was relatively easy to use, and that we could provide a certain level of support for that software, that we could help other institutions continue digital publishing, pushing forward that practice. . . . The more people we can get doing this, the better we're all going to be at it, the richer the experience is going to be, and the more new ideas are going to come out of that.

When one reviews the history of museum computing, one sees that the development and evolution of interactive technologies in museums represented a time of great growth for museum technology professionals working in an environment of constant change. As Silvia Filippini-Fantoni explains, museum technology professionals have had the opportunity to reshape the visitor experience in multiple ways, and it is important to keep one's focus on the positive outcomes and accomplishments that have accompanied those changes:

> I've had the pleasure, or the fortune in a way, to work on the three main aspects of how technology supports the visitor experience. I mean, technology supports museums in more ways than that, but my focus has always

> been on the visitor experience side . . . and when it comes to that aspect of using technology as a way to engage audiences on site in a kind of experience . . . when I look at the way technology has affected museums and changed museums, that's what I see as the most interesting change in the last few years. If I look at websites now and websites ten years ago, there is a different approach in the sense that the information architecture is more simplified, the design is different, but ultimately the same elements and the same functionalities are the same. And I'm sort of seeing the same thing with mobile technology, where I saw the most changes were really in experiences in the galleries. I think that ten years ago, fifteen years ago, the focus was very heavily on content, you know, using technology as a way to provide access to more content around the artwork, the objects, the stories that we were telling. And we're moving more away from that idea to creating experiences that are more immersive and playful. . . . You want to create an experience that people can remember and save and share that has some learning elements to it, but it's not heavy content, it's actually something that will check the boxes and connect with some key idea that you want to communicate, but will be experienced through multiple senses, and in a playful way. And I think that that's where I've seen the biggest and most interesting changes in the past few years when it comes to the use of technology.

Creative innovation is hard work. While the outcomes of these technology projects are truly inspirational, it is important to recognize that none of this is easy. There can be many barriers that stand in the way of innovation, and moving forward, we need to be careful not to lose the spirit of creativity, enthusiasm, and inspiration that made these projects possible in the first place. By recognizing the historical origins of the unique innovative spirit that pervades museum computing, museum technology professionals can continue to push the boundaries of creativity and experiment with new ways of engaging museum visitors, in the galleries or online.

SUGGESTIONS FOR FURTHER READING

Alexander, Jane, Jake Barton, and Caroline Goeser. "Transforming the Art Museum Experience: Gallery One." In *Museums and the Web 2013*, edited by Nancy Proctor and Rich Cherry. Silver Spring, MD: Museums and the Web. https://mw2013.museumsandtheweb.com/paper/transforming-the-art-museum-experience-gallery-one-2/

Carrozzino, Marcello, and Massimo Bergamasco. 2010. "Beyond Virtual Museums: Experiencing Immersive Virtual Reality in Real Museums." *Journal of Cultural Heritage* 11 (4): 452–458.

Economou, Maria. 1998. "The Evaluation of Museum Multimedia Applications: Lessons from Research." *Museum Management and Curatorship* 17 (2): 173–187.

Economou, Maria. 2016. "Heritage in the Digital Age." In *A Companion to Heritage Studies*, edited by William Logan, Mairead Craith, and Ulrich Kockel, 215–228. Sussex: John Wiley & Sons.

Kenderdine, Sarah. 2016. "Embodiment, Entanglement, and Immersion in Digital Cultural Heritage." In *A New Companion to Digital Humanities*, edited by Susan Schreibman, Ray Siemens, and John Unsworth, 22–41. New York: John Wiley & Sons.

Proctor, Nancy. 2010. "The Museum is Mobile: Cross-platform Content Design for Audiences on the Go." In *Museums and the Web 2010*, edited by Jennifer Trant and David Bearman. Toronto: Archives & Museum Informatics. http://www.archimuse.com/mw2010/papers/proctor/proctor.html

Rae, Juno, and Lizzie Edwards. 2016. "Virtual Reality at the British Museum: What Is the Value of Virtual Reality Environments for Learning by Children and Young People, Schools, and Families?" In *Museums and the Web 2016*, edited by Nancy Proctor and Rich Cherry. Silver Spring, MD: Museums and the Web. https://mw2016.museumsandtheweb.com/paper/virtual-reality-at-the-british-museum-what-is-t/index.html

Rubinstein, Ben. 1992. "The Micro Gallery at the National Gallery of London." *Archives and Museum Informatics* 6 (2): 5–10.

Thomas, Selma, and Ann Mintz, eds. 1998. *The Virtual and the Real: Media in the Museum*. Washington, DC: American Association of Museums.

6

Experimental Freedom

> We were kind of ahead of the curve. . . . We were really pushing what the use cases would be, and what it would mean, and so it was really powerful field-building work. . . . We were constantly in these intermediate spaces where we were making it up, and getting in trouble, and I don't know how we had the chutzpah to just keep going . . .—Oral History of Susie Wise

The history of museum computing, for many museum technology professionals, was a time of boundless enthusiasm. There were few preconceived notions about how things should be done; they were not bound by a rigid mindset of doing things the way they had always been done. Faced with the task of integrating emerging technologies into the museum experience, museum technology professionals combined a mindset of experimentation with a willingness to take risks. The freedom to experiment with new technologies and new ideas represented a powerful tool that encouraged cutting-edge museum technology projects and pushed the envelope for museum computing in innovative and creative ways.

The projects that museum technology professionals developed using emerging technologies over the decades were particularly exciting, especially as museums pushed forward with new concepts for online experiences, such as chatbots, artificial intelligence, and virtual reality. The museum technology professionals who championed these projects succeeded in large part because of the opportunities they had to take risks and figure out technology as they went along, often with the support of visionary directors who recognized the importance of experimentation, even in traditionally risk-averse institutions like museums. For many museum technology professionals, the late twentieth century was a Golden Age of Experimentation: a time for taking risks, experimenting with new technologies, and making things up as you went along.

This concept of experimental freedom was a pervasive theme for the museum technology professionals who contributed to our oral histories. The freedom to experiment with emerging technologies to improve the museum experience led to a sense of delight and enthusiasm that helped drive the field of museum computing forward. Many of our participants spoke about the importance of trying out new ideas for the first time and the fun that they had figuring things out along the way. Nik Honeysett, for example, in his oral history, describes working with museum technologies at a time when you had to build and figure everything out for yourself:

> That was a time when you had to build everything, had to write everything. There were no apps that you could download . . . in the late '80s, early '90s, you couldn't hire somebody who'd built interactive systems or websites or anything. You had to just kind of figure it out as you go along. . . . And I always remember the conversations of how do you figure out this stuff—user flow and digital experience and feedback and all those kinds of things. And I remember the endless conversations long into the night about what is a "button" on a screen, and what should it do?

Emerging technologies, almost by definition, were not typically part of the formal educational background of most museum technology professionals at the time. As a result, you often had no choice but to learn on your own and teach yourself the technology. Darren Milligan describes learning how to design and develop websites in the 1990s:

> My first job out of college was working at a nonprofit that did research on migratory birds . . . but this was the late '90s, and so . . . the directive came down: Figure out how to build a website, and figure out how to create an online shopping cart. And I think this is a similar story for most people from my generation in museums. . . . You couldn't go to school for these things in the '90s. You just sort of learned how to do it. You looked at the source code and you figured it out. You saw something cool on someone else's website . . . you copied it and modified it and taught yourself HTML and JavaScript and all the things you needed to do to be able to make things happen on your end. And suddenly, my job became less about biology and less about animal behavior, and a lot more about technology and more about building websites.

As institutions recognized the importance of working with new technologies and new tools, museum technology professionals were suddenly asked to do things they were not expecting to do, that they did not know how to do, and that they had no choice but to try to figure out how to do on their own. Many were being asked to work with new technologies for the first time, sometimes discovering they had to figure things out for themselves on the very first day of the job. Megan Forbes, for example, describes finding out at the last minute that her new job was not cataloging the museum's collections, but developing a collections management system:

> I ended up getting a job at the Museum of the Moving Image in New York City. . . . Contrary to its name, they don't actually collect film . . . they collect the material culture of film, television, and digital media—so movie cameras and action figures and costumes and scripts. . . . I thought I was applying for this cataloging job, where I was going to be cataloging films, and then on my first day, they said, "Oh, you're not cataloging films, by the way. And also we need you to develop a collections management system. Here's the developer's phone number." I had never used a museum collections management system. I had never worked in a museum before, so that was a surprise. . . . So really quickly, I had to figure out what a museum collections management system was, and why people would want one.

Teaching yourself technology and learning as you go is not an easy task. While the idea of not being bound by traditional ideas can be a powerful incentive for experimentation, this also meant that there was not a lot of precedent for museum technology professionals to draw upon to guide their day-to-day activities. Matthew MacArthur, for example, discusses how the relative newness of the digital field presented challenges for museum technology workers:

> The museum field has such a wealth of history and tradition to build on when you're talking about how to make an exhibition, how to present artifacts, how to care for and preserve and conserve artifacts. The digital space is so new. I mean, those of us in my generation, we're still like the first generation. We didn't have any classes to go to learn how to do it, or traditions to draw on, or things like that. We've been learning as we go.

Even something as relatively simple as putting collections databases online involved a lot of experimentation when you were figuring it for the first time. Paul Marty, for example, shares a story about connecting Filemaker Pro databases to the Internet at the University of Illinois in the early days of the World Wide Web:

> We're building these early databases, we're putting all this together, and we're connecting it to the web. And back then, in the mid '90s, there was no way to connect a FileMaker Pro database to the web without using various third-party tools. I remember I was working with a lot of developers who were developing these third-party tools. There was one in particular called Tango. . . . I can remember talking to them over the years, and they were very excited to have this museum collection connected to the web using their software. I even showed up in one of their advertisements at one point in some magazine. . . . People today would have no idea how hard it was to get a lot of those early databases online and talking to the web in '96 and '97.

In many respects, the idea that museum technology professionals were figuring these tools out as they went along—that they did not always know what they were doing—was liberating. When there is no path to follow, and you are stumbling forward with no preconceptions, you have the freedom to forge your own path. Megan Forbes describes what it was like developing their own collections management system, CollectionSpace, at the Museum of the Moving Image:

> Moving Image is probably organized differently than an art museum. . . . We were all sort of coming into this a little blind, naïve, whatever you want to say, in terms of what is the art world supposed to do? And instead, we thought, "Here is this object that has all of these fascinating relationships and stories to tell, and so, how do we develop a system that leads from that?" Rather than coming at it from a different direction in terms of formal art history, provenance research, or loans or anything like that. . . . None of us had ever worked at other museums, and we had no idea how it worked elsewhere. . . . It was a museum full of people who had either never worked in a museum or had never worked in any other museum. So, you know, liberating. Thinking about it now, though, I also see the awful mistakes that we made in the early days, and I think, "Oh my gosh, we spent so much time on the dumbest stuff."

This freedom to experiment may have been liberating, but it could also easily lead to mistakes. Museum technology professionals needed to be comfortable with the idea that they might do something that was both innovative and embarrassing at the same time. As Bruce Wyman explains, reflecting on his time at the New England Aquarium, innovative ideas might backfire, but that is how one learns what is truly important:

> We were working with a robotics team over at MIT that was keen to do some stuff. . . . We were going to have a Fiddler crab exhibit—Fiddler crabs are little crabs that have one claw that's bigger than another, and they signal to each other by waving this claw. Sometimes it's a threat, sometimes it's recognition, what have you. . . . They spent some real money on developing a prototype that had a little embedded camera, and the idea was you'd have a robotic Fiddler crab that could go into the exhibit. You could watch it there, and signal to other creatures, and see if they wave back to you, right? And we did a prototype of this, and it wasn't perfect, but it moved a little bit, and you could see some stuff and that was amazing! I mean, it was so cool to see the thing work, and actually have Fiddler crabs wave back at you. The humiliating part was we had an Educator there that cut out some pieces of paper, and had a paperclip, and made a little paper claw, and waved it at the edge of the tank, and the other crabs waved back just as much, you know, for a buck-fifty in materials versus twenty or thirty thousand dollars. . . . And that was that first point of like maybe technology is not always the best approach for this, despite how glittery and beautiful it can be. And even though I can rationalize, yeah, the crab-eye point of view is the important thing, it didn't matter. It just isn't a thing that needed to exist. And that kind of humility and kind of learning

early on, to always look for the inexpensive, non-tech solution, has been true over and over again.

In this environment, museum technology professionals needed to be comfortable taking risks, being bold, and accomplishing tasks in creative ways. Every new technology that came along carried with it some risk when implemented in museums, and museum technology professionals benefited when their creativity and willingness to experiment were encouraged by their director. Norbert Kanter talks about the risks he took when creating a bold design for the first website for the Kunst- und Ausstellungshalle der Bundesrepublik Deutschland museum in the mid-1990s:

> From the very beginning, we said, "We want to use this font because it was everywhere." It was on site in the museum, it was on all the print material. . . . We went through a number of iterations, and the whole design got reduced with every step. We got rid of the images, we got rid of other elements on the homepage, and we ended up with a white page and black font, and that was it. The building is quite iconic, and we wanted to do something outstanding—an iconic design on the web as well, which nobody has done before, which has a unique look and feel. In the end, it was just this font we used on the white page. . . . We used no images, and we constructed the homepage from the menu items: "Exhibitions," "General Information," and "Calendar." When we decided to do that, we finally had to deal with the name, "Kunst- und Ausstellungshalle der Bundesrepublik Deutschland. . . ." It really was a problem to fit it into a proper web design somehow. End of the story, the font size of the name of the institution was reduced to seven point. Super small! If you were shortsighted, it looked like just a black line, and not a name. And then the menu items, we blew it up to 70 point. . . . One of the poor designer guys probably spent a week in front of the computer, using Photoshop, typing in the whole alphabet in all the different sizes we needed, and then cropped the single characters to save them as a GIF. . . . If you clicked on the calendar menu, the calendar page opened, but there were like 400 little GIFs that needed to be loaded. Maybe all the "E's" were loaded first and appeared on the screen in random places. And then, all the "A's" and then all the "I's". In the end, it was like a piece of art. . . . It was annoying to some people, to be honest, but we were kind of relentless. We wanted to have it that way. That was the quite bold idea we had. We wanted to have it unique. We wanted to have it visible as the face of the institution. And we were sure that in the end the management and director would say, "Are you crazy? What are you doing? Here, go back, start again." But to our surprise, the director and everybody inside the institution loved it, so we went online at the end of '96. There were not so many museums or cultural institutions online in Germany back then. We got a lot of recognition. Very much of it was very positive. Sometimes it was very, very negative. I was pleased with that. It was not "average." Either people loved it, or people hated it. And I'm totally fine with that.

When it comes to experimenting, smaller institutions often found themselves at an advantage, because they were able to innovate and explore new ideas without a great deal of red tape. Many of our participants commented that smaller institutions can sometimes do quite radical things, as it is easier for small museums to be nimble, take risks, and respond to new ideas more quickly than larger museums. Rob Lancefield explains how the aspect of agility that came with being at a smaller museum allowed him to develop an open-access policy in the early 2010s—a task that would have been much more difficult at a larger institution:

> Open access was a case in which being at a really small museum offered a certain kind of nimbleness that the Davison Art Center was able to be a pretty early mover, and by virtue of that make Wesleyan a pretty early mover, in making highly accurate images of public domain objects in the art collection freely available for any use that people wanted. . . . I put together a one-page PDF that laid out why I felt that this move would be aligned with the University's mission, which is of course fundamentally educational, and how it, further to that, could help position the University as a leader in that area. And lo and behold: "Approved, go ahead." So okay, cool! We've got an open access image policy now. . . . In a larger museum with lots of departments, various concerns from various angles . . . would tend to make figuring that out a somewhat longer, slower process. So that was a case where being in a tiny museum, resource-constrained as it was, actually enabled something to happen really quickly.

In order to encourage experimentation, larger institutions would sometimes create smaller, more nimble innovation teams that could work in liminal, in-between spaces, and respond to new technological developments more quickly. Michael Haley Goldman, for example, describes the Future Projects team at the United States Holocaust Memorial Museum, which helped the museum embrace opportunities for innovation with emerging technologies:

> Future Projects is supposed to be a small kind of innovation group. We were created at a time when the museum was maturing . . . getting out of that kind of awkward period when the institution was young enough that we could often still kind of squeeze in innovation . . . but as the institution gets more mature, and as resources get more carefully aligned with mission, which is something institutions should be doing, the space to grab a programmer and get their time on something is much smaller. And so, our group was intentionally to build a little bit of additional space for this kind of innovation. . . . It's been a really great team. We were designed to be small. We have just actually hit our ideal size, which is four people. And everybody has a little bit of a Swiss Army Knife kind of background, so we can do a lot ourselves, although we really try to make sure everything we do is really in partnership with other parts of the institution. That's where a lot of the real energy comes from.

> We've had the good fortune to experiment with everything from games and spatial virtual technologies, all the way over to digital mapping, and a little bit of machine learning. . . . But our real work is really internal. It's really how we change the institution itself.

However museums approached innovation, a willingness to experiment with emerging technologies led to a wide variety of creative projects. Naturally, not all of these projects would enjoy long-term success, but each of them would improve our understanding of how museums can use technologies to engage their visitors in some way, regardless of their longevity. Personal bookmarking systems, for example, where museums offered their visitors the opportunity to personalize the museum experience by saving information about their personal favorites from a museum's collections, provide a useful example of a technology that might not have had a great deal of long-term success but nevertheless drove the field forward behind the scenes in the short term. Silvia Filippini-Fantoni shares her memories about the lessons learned from working on personal bookmarking projects at the Getty and other museums:

> I have been looking at the way technology could be used to personalize the visitor experience, instead of having the same content for everybody, how you can adapt the content, based on what people are interested in, and who they are. . . . The bookmarking story is an interesting one, because I think it was a main way in which museums were kind of implementing this idea of personalizing the visitor experience. . . . You would find them on websites—like, for instance, the Louvre website allows you to bookmark certain areas of the site and then access it again. You would find it on multiple mobile projects where you would be able to bookmark some information during your visit and retrieve it after the visit. And you would find it on a kiosk like the Getty Guide, where you would be able to bookmark certain information and access it after the visit online. . . . The results were kind of interesting because it wasn't . . . well-integrated into the experience. It was more of an afterthought, or something that wasn't really pushed or promoted, and it resulted in not much use. . . . Some people that used it, they used it more out of curiosity, to see what it would do more than just really wanting to invest more time. And I think that's the challenge. I think that one of the things that I have learned and something that I always remind my colleagues, even now, when you go into other contexts, that people are interested in engaging with your experience, then and there at the museum, and then, anything that's build content for later, it's really not as successful unless that content is something like a photo of you, or a video of you there, doing something that kind of fun and playful that you can retrieve and share with your friends and family.

Experimental projects offered museum technology professionals the chance to explore new kinds of interactivity and improve their understanding of the relative effectiveness of different technologies for connecting with museum visitors. Lessons learned about the willingness of museum visitors to engage with collections online, for example, or the willingness of museum curators to provide access to collections online, can easily outweigh the longevity of any one individual project. Seb Chan describes the lessons learned from an early project that used social tagging to encourage online users to help describe fabric swatch patterns at the Powerhouse Museum in Australia:

> The Electronic Swatch Book was a very early use of social tagging . . . the Curator of Fashion and Textiles, Glynis Jones, was showing us these old swatch books, these books in the collection that had fabric swatches in them. She was trying to figure out how to reduce the pressure on those because students from the fashion courses near us would come in and request access to them, and of course they're super fragile, and we were like, "Why don't we just digitize them, and then give away images of the swatches, because they're looking for patterns? They're looking to be inspired. . . ." Giv Parvaneh, who was working with me as a programmer, was looking at Etsy one morning, and said, "Seb, we should do this thing where people can tag those patterns just by what they reckon they're called. We should do that. . . ." So, we made a little tool that did that, and then we were using the social tagging from the users to allow people to search by "plaid" or "gingham" and things like that. And that happened before we put the Powerhouse collection on the web. It was really quite useful as a way of gauging, and building an institutional tolerance for, folksonomies with the curators directly.

Experiments with crowdsourcing tools such as social tagging were often driven by the needs of the museum's visitors, and the desire of museum technology professionals to better support those needs, particularly in terms of improving access to online collections. One of the most important experiments with the use of social tagging in museums was the Steve project from the 2000s, a multi-institution collaboration that developed open-source software for capturing user-generated content about museum collections. Koven Smith describes Steve's origins and inspiration:

> In those early days, the notion of accepting user submissions of any kind was unheard of, certainly in the museum space. . . . Public comments on web pages were not a new thing, but it wasn't something that everybody intuitively understood. . . . I attribute the Steve idea entirely to Susan Chun. Susan really had a vision; she understood that museums had a problem where all the metadata around objects was from a curatorial perspective, so that data might tell you everything about the object, except what it literally depicts. At the Met, we did have a couple of use cases where the curator actually did not know what a photograph was of. The curator could tell you everything else about the photograph: who made it, when, what style it was, the technique. But the curator would not know the name of the place being depicted in the photograph. And Susan's insight was, "Well, we might not know, but

> somebody probably does. Somebody might look at that building and say, oh, I know exactly where that is, or what that place is called, or what kind of car that is. . . ." Susan put in place this whole technical infrastructure for collecting user-submitted tags to help museums visually identify things.

The Steve project dramatically influenced the ability of museums to engage online visitors as active participants in the co-construction of digital knowledge in museums and helped to build an institutional tolerance for user-generated content and user-focused projects in museums. The museum technology professionals who worked on the Steve project conducted extensive research on how the availability of user-submitted tags could bridge the gap between museum curators and museum visitors, thereby improving access to museum collections online. Encouraged by the Steve project, Marla Misunas explains how and why social tagging was implemented at SFMOMA as part of their process of putting records online:

> The Steve project proved that crowdsourcing tags was really helpful. . . . Internally there was discussion about: Who's the audience? Are we getting our art historical experts to tag the objects? I think some museums were able to interest their curators in the experiment, but ours had other priorities. They felt their peers didn't need tags. Folks in the Collections Information and Access area, where I am, knew that it would eventually be helpful to have tags that a general audience could relate to. . . . As part of our process of reviewing the records against the paper documents, we put subject tags into each record that we were approving in the database. We were hoping someday those objects would go on the website, and that people would be able to find them, using the terms that we added.

As a proof of concept, the Steve project was revolutionary. The project's outcomes demonstrated the value of social tagging in museums, particularly for non-experts and especially when providing access to collections in situations where different groups will almost certainly use different terms to describe the same things. Layna White explains how the availability of tags helps drive collections access behind the scenes at SFMOMA:

> Tags are entered into our collections management system. They show up in our digital asset management system too, so there's an integration there, and can be searched there. Tags are not visible on the interface but are working behind the scenes in our online collection. They are being indexed. They aren't visible on the pages that our users see when they do a search on our online collection, but they are driving some of the results there.

While the software developed by the Steve project was ultimately not sustainable in the long run, the project had a considerable impact on the field that continues to influence museum technology professionals today. Diana Folsom, for example, describes how the radical ideas of the Steve project influenced her work implementing social tagging tools to improve understanding about the Tulsa Race Massacre Collection at the Gilcrease Museum:

> The Steve social tagging project was fantastic. . . . It was groundbreaking at the time. . . . It was so radical at that point, and that really appealed to my artist side as well. . . . It really stayed with me. . . . We've gotten a brand-new collection called the Eddie Faye Gates' Tulsa Race Massacre Collection. Eddie Faye Gates is a woman who was key in trying to pull together oral histories of the race massacre survivors. She's a real activist to help the community and improve understanding in Tulsa and even improve the way black citizens are treated, but also the way they are compensated for what happened during the race massacre. . . . I put together a plan where we will be pairing a young person, like a high school-aged person, and an elder from the north Tulsa community . . . and they will look at photographs in this collection that we're cataloging now. And they will also look at some of the oral histories that were recorded. And they will work on tagging together. So the young person will help the elder use the technology, and the elders will help the young person learn more about that time period and what happened and how it affected their community and their family members.

Like many experimental technologies, the benefits of social tagging were not immediately obvious. Just convincing museum curators or the museum's board of directors to take risks with emerging technologies can be challenging. As Bruce Wyman explains, a fear of technology can often keep museums from experimenting with new ideas:

> It's frustrating the number of times that museums have self-limited themselves because of their fear of technology. . . . Years ago, when we started the Steve.museum project where we're tagging our works . . . the animosity that was there, like, "What if somebody says that Manet is a Monet?" And, having been one of the authors of that, it's like, "What if they do? Is that bad?" I mean, if they get to the thing that they're looking for, that seems okay, right? You can teach them that it's not, but just that idea that there was a way to embrace inaccuracy and actually turn it to your benefit.

Experimenting with technology in museums is difficult because museums are inherently risk-averse. Naturally risk management is important, but institutions that place too great a focus on avoiding risk at all costs can get in their own way and stop themselves from innovating with emerging technologies. Seb Chan explains how a fear of taking risks at the Smithsonian Institution posed challenges to his team when they were developing the Pen, an experimental, handheld tool for personal engagement at the Cooper Hewitt Smithsonian Design Museum:

> You have to design the Pen so kids can't get the batteries out. There were things like, "What if the kids unscrew the top of the thing and swallow it?" All the overhead of Smithsonian risk assessment is intense, you know: "What if someone whacks someone with a Pen? They're heavy! What if Sammy hits Johnny with one of these, and pokes an eye out?" It's like, Oh my God, people! This is why these things are hard! This is institutions getting in their own way! It's madness!

While experimentation can be frightening, a willingness to take risks—that attitude of being willing and able to experiment with technology—pushed museums forward in many ways. Museum technology professionals needed to find a way to convince their colleagues that, instead of being afraid of new ideas, they could use new technologies to help them complete their work more effectively. Rob Weisberg, for example, describes convincing his editors at the Metropolitan Museum of Art that moving to digital publishing was worth the risk:

> The hardest part for me when I first got there was convincing the editors that this was going to work. We have very high editorial standards. The editors were used to having a lot of personal stake in the production process. They would walk around the office with X-ACTO knives so they could go to the galleys that were down on the flats, and if they didn't like the kerning, they could cut two letters out of the flat, and move them apart ever so slightly, or move them together ever so slightly. I had to win them over because I wasn't their manager or anything. I had to make them feel that this process was going to bring them the quality that they expected. . . . The first time I set galleys for our Quarterly Bulletin, all of the italics fell out of the galleys when I set them. The editor had given me a disk in probably WordStar at that point, and, when they saw the galleys, they said, "Well, I'm not sure this desktop publishing thing is going to work out. . . ." A lot of my work was convincing colleagues that the process would work, whether it was making galleys where all the formatting stayed in, or doing corrections really quickly and accurately for a lot of pages. And winning them over made me a victim of my own success, so the editors now could always walk down the hall and make another round of corrections. . . . That's always been the most enjoyable part of the job: winning people over to the process. . . . I learned a lot of good lessons in trying to win over those editors back in the early days of all the italics falling out and saying, "Trust me, these new tools are going to make things easier. They're not going to jeopardize the quality that's so important for us." It's always been about quietly moving us forward while still bringing everyone along.

Time and again, museum technology professionals led the way with innovative, creative projects in museums specifically because they had the freedom to experiment and the willingness to take risks, despite working in an environment that was traditionally risk-averse. Many of them were encouraged by their colleagues to experiment with emerging technologies in an effort to improve work practices at their museums. David Bridge, for example, discusses the importance of being creative, taking risks, and doing things that had never been done before during his time working with museum computing at the Smithsonian Institution:

> It seems to me that people were constantly asking me and probably other people to improve on something. Can we make that better? Can we improve it? Can we make it faster, more reliable? I was constantly being asked to do things that I've never done before. . . . Somebody comes to you and says, "You can do this, and this, and this. Why can't we do that?" So you say, "That's a good idea. Why don't we try that?" It seems to me that the people that paved the way were self-directed and creative and experimental and enterprising . . . that kind of, "Let's try it and see what happens" kind of thing. . . . We used to have a little test that we would do on things like, "What's the worst thing that can happen if we do this?" And if the answer is "Well, it won't work, and we're the only ones who will know that it doesn't work," then that's fine, right? But if it's going to bring down the whole network, maybe we should test that a little bit ahead of time. So we had to juggle the risks, if you will, of trying something.

It is important that museums do not create an environment that stands in the way of innovation when it comes to the use of technology. Factors that inhibit creativity and experimental freedom can lead to frustration on the part of museum technology professionals. Seb Chan describes his approach to managing expectations in museums, and the importance of museum leaders developing an appetite for taking risks, especially if doing so can help the museum improve its services and its use of technology:

> I think that this is risk appetite, and developing a risk appetite, and being comfortable with that risk appetite, rather than just risk assessment being about mitigating all possible risks. It's like, how much appetite have we got for risk? Okay, we don't have any appetite around people getting hurt, but do we have an appetite around systems being down for 24 hours? That's okay if it helps us do better stuff.

The more risk-averse we are, the fewer opportunities we will have for innovation. We need to be willing to take risks because when we are no longer taking risks, we are no longer as innovative. As Norbert Kanter explains, there are dangers in playing it safe, and true creativity only comes when museum technology professionals are willing to take risks and to be bold:

> Looking back so many years, it has been an unbelievable privilege to live during that time in an institution, and be tasked with bringing them online and working in the digital area. . . . If I compare it to what happens in the museum digital sector nowadays . . . the differences between web design back then,

> and web design nowadays. . . . It was risky. It was surprising. People were bold. Often, things were unique. . . . Sometimes it was provoking . . . and it was fun.

If we are to keep alive the spirit of experimentation that encouraged so much creativity with emerging technologies throughout the history of museum computing, then we need to continue taking risks and work to overcome the barriers that stand in the way of innovation. As Bruce Wyman explains, even with institutions as conservative and as risk-averse as museums, experimental freedom is essential for the future of technological progress:

> The thing I'd always advocate is, even if I think an idea is bad, I think experimentation needs to happen more often in the field than it does. We are a conservative field, to our great detriment, and I would rather see weird stuff happen more often, even if it has lousy results or good results. . . . When people ask me, is this field advanced, my answer is no. We're still so early and in the nascent stage of what it means to do stuff, and all of these things, frankly, are still experimentations because our storytelling method keeps changing. And so what we learned, even three or four years ago, is different from what we may do in two or three more years.

Experimental freedom drove the field of museum computing forward and resulted in fantastic new ideas and amazing experimental projects. The museum technology professionals who led the way with these innovations were successful in large part because of the enthusiasm they brought to the job—enthusiasm that stemmed from the excitement of learning things for the first time as a new field was being created. That sense of excitement does not last forever; discovering something on your own is very different from being taught how to do something in school. As the excitement of learning something new turns into a daily drudge of rote activities, it is easy to lose that sense of enthusiasm. But the Age of Discovery does not need to be over for the field of museum computing. Moving forward, it is important that museums keep pushing their use of technology into uncharted territory so that innovation, creativity, and uniqueness continue to be an integral part of the job of the museum technology professional.

SUGGESTIONS FOR FURTHER READING

Din, Herminia, and Phyllis Hecht. 2007. *The Digital Museum: A Think Guide*. Washington, DC: American Association of Museums.

Filippini-Fantoni, Silvia, and Jonathan Bowen. 2007. "Bookmarking in Museums: Extending the Museum Experience Beyond the Visit?" In *Museums and the Web 2007*, edited by Jennifer Trant and David Bearman. Toronto: Archives & Museum Informatics. http://www.archimuse.com/mw2007/papers/filippini-fantoni/filippini-fantoni.html

Marty, Paul F., Scott Sayre, and Silvia Filippini-Fantoni, 2011. "Personal Digital Collections: Involving Users in the Co-Creation of Digital Cultural Heritage." In *Handbook of Research on Technologies and Cultural Heritage: Applications and Environments*, edited by Georgios Styliaras, Dimitrios Koukopoulos, and Fotis Lazarinis, 285–304. Hershey, PA: IGI Global.

Ridge, Mia, ed. 2014. *Crowdsourcing our Cultural Heritage*. London: Taylor & Francis, Inc.

Terras, Melissa. 2011. "The Digital Wunderkammer: Flickr as a Platform for Amateur Cultural and Heritage Content." *Library Trends* 59 (4): 686–706.

Trant, Jennifer. 2009. "Tagging, Folksonomy and Art Museums: Early Experiments and Ongoing Research." *Journal of Digital Information* 10 (1). https://jodi-ojs-tdl.tdl.org/jodi/article/view/270

Wyman, Bruce, Susan Chun, and Jennifer Trant. 2006. "Steve.museum: An Ongoing Experiment in Social Tagging, Folksonomy, and Museums." In *Museums and the Web 2006*, edited by Jennifer Trant and David Bearman. Toronto: Archives & Museum Informatics. http://www.archimuse.com/mw2006/papers/wyman/wyman.html

7

Disruptive Technologies

> Computing was seen as a niche. It was seen as something done in the basement by people with a very specific kind of job. They ran the payroll. They took care of retail inventory. What they did was complicated and sort of mysterious. So why on earth would we—professional staff, curators, conservators, scientists, educators, administrators—why would we ever need this clunky computer on our desk?—Oral History of Douglas Hegley

New technologies can be disruptive in any setting, and the adoption of computer technologies caused disruptions for many museums. The creative innovations and experimental ideas that shaped the history of museum computing also disrupted long-standing, traditional museum practices in ways that posed new challenges, exposed latent fears, and surfaced underlying tensions for many museum workers. During the late twentieth century in particular, the rapid pace of change that accompanied the introduction of computers in museums, both in the galleries and behind the scenes, caused many to respond with fear, confusion, and frustration.

Many museum professionals were naturally suspicious of technology, nervous about computers, and resistant to change. Technology tends to change faster than most institutions, individuals, or societies can keep up, and as a result, there is often a tension between what can be done technologically and what is acceptable to do societally. When people do not understand the nature of technology, why it matters, or how it can help them accomplish their goals, it is only natural to be afraid of change. In this environment, museum technology professionals often clashed with museum curators and other museum staff members as new computing technologies were introduced into the everyday activities of museum professionals.

Meeting the increasing demands of museum computing required museum technology professionals to develop strategies for overcoming resistance to change in their institutions. They needed to recognize the obstacles to museum computing and figure out how to overcome them thoughtfully, carefully, and respectfully. Getting used to disruptive innovations takes time; jumping straight from no computers in any gallery to computers in every gallery, or from no collections data online to all collections data online, simply will not work. As Douglas Hegley explains in his oral history, efforts to force people to use computers when they are not ready to do so, especially when implemented with no support and no training, are just going to backfire:

> It was the Met, and they were having some trouble with resistance to the change. They were trying to roll out desktop computing . . . and the Systems and Computer Services guys—all guys, right?—all with their office in the basement, on the evenings and weekends were going around and moving people's books and papers off the desktop, and plopping down a computer, and then leaving it there. No real announcement, no follow up, no training, and no one to call if you didn't know how to use it, or if it broke. So these are the Ph.D. level professional staff, and of course, they were being treated without respect, so you know, as is human nature, they went back without respect, and these computers ended up in a hallway, on the floor, a couple of them in the dumpster. And this is 1997. A desktop PC from IBM was not a cheap investment, right?

With the introduction of museum computing, there was often a disconnect between museum technology professionals and museum curators, and bridging that gap required buy-in from both sides. In the face of resistance to change, one must try to understand and respect the needs of all the museum's stakeholders. This can take a great deal of time and effort, especially in institutions where one needs to work across departmental silos, each used to their own way of doing things. Sam Quigley explains the lengthy process required just to get a collections documentation committee together at the Museum of Fine Arts (MFA) Boston in the late 1980s:

> At the time, the MFA was about as much the MFA as it ever was. It was totally silos throughout the building. The Classical department had its own way of doing things . . . the Asian collection . . . the Paintings departments . . . everybody had their own collections documentation. . . . I remember going up to Alan Shestack, the Director, and suggesting that we really ought to do something about this. I pointed out that the Metropolitan had already started . . . a new program to try to organize their documentation. . . . He did one of his characteristic puckish things: He pulled out his pen, and said, "This is my word processor. . . ." However, he did recognize that I might have something worth talking about, so he suggested it would be a good idea if I would develop a proposal, and in the late 1980s, I got authority and a little bit of budget—a very tiny little bitty budget—to create this Committee on Documentation. . . . Nancy Allen, the Director of the Library and very much a strong voice in

Library and Information Science, and Linda Thomas, the Registrar, who was very technologically savvy and interested in these things, and Janice Sorkow, who was Head of the Slide Library. . . . We had those three very strong advocates for documentation, and then I recognized that there were very strong voices and many other ones who were going to need to be convinced. If they could be convinced of the value, they would be strong voices in favor of the process . . . so this group, this Committee on Documentation, met for months, I think it was at least a year or so. . . . We proceeded to have many, many meetings, large meetings, some of them, trying to garner support and get people's knowledge level up to snuff.

New technologies meant big changes for museum curators, especially behind the scenes, and getting them to understand how museum computing could help them organize information about their collections took time. Building momentum within the institution for technological change often required extensive planning and coordination with museum administration. As Sam Quigley continues, it eventually took a new director for the MFA Boston to create a department of information resources with a mandate to digitize the museum's collections:

Alan Shestack, who had commissioned the work, was handed his hat as he had exceeded the budgetary tolerances of the Board, and all of a sudden, nothing was happening. And I think this was around 1992, maybe 1993. Then a new broom came in, in the guise of Malcolm Rogers, as I recall, it was Labor Day of '94. We had a couple meetings of the senior staff of the curatorial departments in which he tipped his hand about how he was "shocked and appalled" about the fact that there was no centralized documentation; of course, in England, everything is very centralized, at the National Portrait Gallery, which is where he came from, and the British Museum as well, so he really couldn't imagine not having a centralized database. . . . By the end of January, it seemed like all the pieces were in place, and indeed, a couple weeks later, there was an event which some people refer to as the Valentine's Day Massacre at the MFA Boston because it was on Valentine's Day, 1995, that Malcolm Rogers laid off 90 people of the staff, and with the money that he was saving, created this new department called the Department of Information Resources, of which Nancy Allen was the department head, I was the new Manager of Collections Information, and a couple other staff members were appointed to it, and we formalized our work on February 15, 1995.

Given the disruptive nature of museum computing, it is perhaps unsurprising that obtaining administrative support to introduce computer technology into museum documentation efforts was just the first step in a very long process. Sam Quigley describes the challenges involved in creating databases and establishing procedures to digitize collections at the MFA Boston:

> We challenged ourselves to do two major efforts: one was to transcribe or digitize the information off of the comprehensive index cards for the collection, and for that, we created a physical space, which included nine computers hooked up to a database that was custom written by a guy named John Bastow. . . . He was amazing in translating my very amateurish needs requirements into this Microsoft Access database, which was then utilized by about 90 college work study students over the course of around four and a half years, who just came in for their shifts and pounded in data from the cards. . . . Simultaneously, we decided that we needed to try to capture and aggregate, through a whole series of normalizations, all these different little databases that had grown up in different curatorial departments using different programs . . . Shoebox . . . FileMaker . . . some Excel spreadsheets. . . . There was a broad variety of things that needed to be captured and aggregated and normalized. . . . I was particularly interested in doing the actual aggregation of the databases, and working with my colleagues to try to pull in their information. . . . We created some basic databases out of FileMaker Pro and then added to the data model incrementally, practically every night. And so it happened that bit by bit, we acquired, massaged, normalized, etc. all these various databases, and were maintaining this one basic Filemaker database on a single Macintosh G3 tower underneath my desk. We had 60 concurrent users at one point, off of that one G3.

This process of establishing digitization procedures happened in a wide range of institutions, and we collected stories about digitizing collections from many of our oral history participants. Martha Mahard, for example, shares her memories about digitizing the Prints and Drawings collection at the Boston Public Library in the 2010s:

> One of my former students who was then the head of the Digitization Lab at the Boston Public Library contacted me and asked me if I'd be interested in working on a special project to do an assessment of the Prints collection at the BPL. . . . They had begun digitizing images from the Prints collection when they kind of ground to a halt because there was no cataloging. . . . We went in and there were, you know, if you have a double row of shelves that has one shelving facing you and shelving behind, okay, so there's a double row, 25 of those in this huge room, and then another room they didn't tell me about until I got there, that had something like 900 boxes of prints stashed away in a non-air-conditioned room. . . . My first report, which was done at the end of April 2015, it took me a year to do, and that one identified the problems: the lack of intellectual access, the lack of control, the need to get some physical control over the collection, as well as intellectual control and standardizing their descriptions. . . . They had a curator who had been there for 43 years. He had been hired in 1961, and he didn't retire until 43 years later, and as a result, they completely missed working to digitize things. They missed the 1980s, when they could have been using the visual materials format to describe things. They missed all of that stuff. . . . BPL has an incredible museum-quality

collection of prints and photographs . . . but it really fell out of sight because it wasn't properly promoted, and it wasn't on the Internet anywhere. . . . I have never seen anything like this in my entire career and I, at that point, had been working for almost 50 years in this business.

Digitizing collections tended to be a lengthy process that involved a great many employees and was often internally disruptive to the institution no matter when or where it took place. As Martha Mahard continues, addressing the inventory control problems she uncovered at the Boston Public Library required the implementation of a major digitization project behind the scenes:

> In a period of four and a half years, I had over 50 different students who worked on the project. . . . And of course, once they saw that what we were doing was working, they kept throwing stuff at me. After a year, they said, "We've been given $10,000 to digitize some of the prints." And I'm like, "Really? Whoa! Super!". . . . That meant they had a whole other process to develop because now they're so security conscious that we practically had to have an armed guard when we took anything out of the collection and took it down to the basement, where the digitization lab was. We had to develop an elaborate "sign in, sign out, initial here . . ." just to get stuff upstairs and downstairs. . . . It was the peak experience of my career, I have to say. It couldn't have been more exciting to be part of that particular project. I got to handle prints that were original Goyas and Dürers . . . we found nine huge Toulouse Lautrec posters that had been laid on the top of a cabinet and forgotten about! Worth hundreds of thousands of dollars each. . . . In the four and a half, almost five years that I spent there, I think we encountered every problem that you could possibly encounter. We found mold; it wasn't active. We found bugs; they were dead. We found stuff rolled up so tightly that we couldn't unroll it to try to identify it. We found stuff stored in tin cans. We found a Whistler in the same box as a 1950s illustration for Little Women. How did this happen?

A reluctance to embrace digitization, and its accompanying technical issues, was not unusual. Change is hard, and it is understandable that people were afraid to integrate computers into their everyday work practices. As Marla Misunas explains, many people were never going to use a computer, no matter what you did to encourage them:

> There are always people in the institution who won't use the database no matter what you tell them, or how many times you train them. . . . We had one director, years ago, who wanted the entire database of object records printed on paper and shipped to his home. And we did it!

It took time and patience to convince museum professionals, particularly those who had been working in museums for many years, to make the move to computerized databases. Sam Quigley explains how they worked to alleviate concerns and reduce anxieties for the curators at the MFA Boston as they migrated the museum's card catalogs to a digital format:

> I was a strong advocate of the idea that we needed to work with the knowledge holders in using their knowledge and transferring it into a more standardized format. We needed to do that fairly carefully and gently, and with them being part of the solution, rather than tempting them to just hang back and not be part of the solution.... By doing that, I believe we made people feel more comfortable with seeing their data, their knowledge, their life's work in other words, in a completely new format.... I remember there was all sorts of, not acrimony, but anxiety, and grand concerns about how this crucially important information was going to be handled and cared for, so it was very important, as we made the transition, to work with them in ways that felt comfortable to them.... When we had the capability of doing whatever we wanted to with formatting, using the FileMaker database, one of the screens that they could view was actually a replica of the card, including the hole in the bottom center. And for some people, using Courier typeface too, by the way, that was a very comforting thing.

Even if you could convince people to use computers, many remained skittish and convinced that the technology was prone to failure for many years. As Douglas Hegley recalls, it did not help the museum technology professionals' cause when the world faced the Y2K crisis immediately after so many museums digitized their collections at the end of the 1990s:

> It ended up being a great big nothingburger, but it was an interesting adventure to go through with a museum, where people were really nervous about the whole thing. "You made us use computers, and now they're all going to break!" It was really fascinating.

One of the reasons for these fears was that disruptive technology, almost by definition, is unpredictable. It is difficult to recognize which technologies will be important or to predict what changes they will bring. David Bridge, for example, remembers how the museum community responded to introduction of electronic mail in the 1980s:

> I was also active with the American Association of Museums.... I proposed to give a talk on electronic mail to AAM, and they said, "Oh, that's way too technical for us." I kid you not! Turned me down! Rejected the proposal completely! And their idea was that, "Well, we only have email addresses for 20 to 30 of our people, so obviously it's not being used." But of course, they didn't ask them for their email address, so they didn't have them.

Likewise, at the start of the World Wide Web, it was not immediately obvious that this technology was going to be important for museums either.

Jonathan Bowen recalls the response he received when he started spreading the word about museums on the web:

> Once I'd started doing the Virtual Library Museums Pages, I wrote to the Museums Journal, all very excited. I printed out web pages, because then you had to actually physically write. They didn't have an email address or anything. I sent them these things saying, "This is going to be very exciting for museums." Of course, they didn't write back. I didn't hear anything. Until about six months later, when they suddenly realized that there is this thing called the Web. . . . Another slightly non-museums example is the Royal Society. I remember saying they should have a web page, and I remember getting a message back saying, "Oh, we don't do that sort of thing!". . . . It takes some of these organizations a bit of time to realize that there's something going on. Of course, now they have wonderful web pages and lots of stuff on it.

Similarly, when smartphones first became available, it was unclear what the value of investing in these devices would be for museums over the long term. Museum technology professionals often had to be strategic in how they helped spread the word about the potential uses of new technology. Nik Honeysett, for example, describes how the museum directors at Balboa Park in San Diego learned about the importance of the mobile revolution for museums:

> The Balboa Park Online Collaborative was set up to address this period in the early 2000s when all the institutions were understanding that technology was playing an increasingly important part, not only in how museum professionals can get their work done, but also to create engagement. . . . BPOC was bankrolled three million for three years. Hired Rich Cherry . . . and I always remember, because the trustee at that foundation always talks about this, he gets this invoice from Rich for 27 smartphones. And he's like, "This sounds a little weird." He was in the weeds on how the money is being spent. And Rich's argument was, "We're going to be talking about mobile." Because things were starting to happen on mobile. And he's like, "When I talk to the directors about mobile, they have no idea what I'm talking about, so I want to buy them all smartphones so they understand it." I mean, brilliant, you know, if you've got the money. Everybody immediately starts to understand this. . . . He already planted the seed of where things needed to go.

Another reason adopting disruptive technologies was challenging was that even when museums did recognize the value of a particular technology, the best way to use that technology was not always clear. Jeff Gates, for example, describes how the Smithsonian American Art Museum's efforts to use their new website to build an audience came with unpredictable results:

> During the early 2000s, the director decided that if we put on the front page of our website, "Free Gift," we could build a good-sized mailing list. The gift

> was a set of blank notecards with images from our collection. We had many of these cards, and we posted pictures of what they looked like on the site. After we did this, I began to monitor our traffic. At first, we had maybe fifty sign-ups a day. Then it went to one hundred a day, but suddenly it jumped to 3,000 a day. And then 10,000 a day. As I reported these stats, we all asked, "Where is this coming from?" We were going to run out of cards! Then what? I did some sleuthing and found a woman who had signed up right around the time the numbers had exploded. I sent her an email asking if she had passed on this information to anybody. She replied, "Yes, one card has a church picture on it, so I posted this on a religious website." By that time, we were getting 20,000 requests a day. Of course, our director was thrilled, and we had to find other gifts we could give. It was the museum's first viral moment. The moral: be careful what you wish for.

Misunderstandings about the appropriate use of emerging technologies were common. Museum technology professionals might work hard to integrate expensive new technologies into the galleries only to find that museum professionals and museum visitors alike were unclear on how those technologies were supposed to be used. Tina Shah, for example, shares a story about what happened when they unveiled the first multi-touch table at the Getty Museum:

> One of the projects that I worked on was our very first multi-touch table at the Getty Museum. Multi-touch tables were pretty new at the time. We had a gigantic table made from a company called Ideum, and we were one of the first museums to acquire this multi-touch table. My boss at the time was really rallying for it. . . . She was like, "We need to get one of these tables here. Let's do something really cool on it. . . ." That year, the AAM conference was happening in LA, and there was going to be an event at the Getty in the evening, so we decided to create an application that showed a map of cultural institutions in the area. You can touch points on the map and get more information about those cultural institutions, and view images of those institutions, and basically get your grounding. A lot of the people attending the conference weren't from LA, so we thought this would be a nice way to introduce the technology. We worked many late evenings and weekends. Got very close to my colleague, and my boss at the time. She even came with her kids during the weekends to show us support, while her kids roamed the museum. And we finally launched at this event. And it went great until someone—very high up in the museum—put their empty drink glass down on this table, thinking that it was just a regular table. Basically, putting their trash on the table. And the look on my face—I don't think my colleagues will ever forget—it's like, oh my God, all this time and energy, and some people don't even realize that it was an interactive table.

Museum visitors were often not ready to adopt emerging technologies. No matter how excited museum technology professionals might be to make some new technology part of the museum experience, they quickly learned that museum visitors were often reluctant to embrace change, especially when that change involved using new and unfamiliar devices. Richard Rinehart shares a story about the difficulties they faced introducing handheld computing devices to the Berkeley Art Museum before museum audiences were ready to adopt them:

> One of the first projects that I remember in the '90s was when we partnered with Apple Computer, and they were introducing a new device called the Apple Newton. . . . My great idea was to turn it into a new form of an in-gallery walking tour of the museum for visitors. . . . We worked together, the Berkeley Art Museum crew and myself and Apple, on these things for months. And, of course, this was invisible, behind the scenes. Very few other people knew what we were working on. Apple wanted this to be super-secret because they were going to use the event to promote the multiple uses for this new handheld digital device that would transform the world. . . . Trick is, they were ahead of their time, because when we unveiled the project to our public . . . for all of that effort and all of that glorious vision . . . it just went over like a lead balloon with the visitors. And it was, I think, primarily because people just weren't used to holding a computer in your hand. . . . We were just asking for too much for people too soon. Because if you're not used to this technology out in the world, and then you step into the museum, and they throw this thing in front of you that is so alien you've never seen it, that's too far advanced to have even appeared on *2001: A Space Odyssey*, there's just no familiarity with it. . . . Museum audiences are prepared to be challenged by the artworks. They're not necessarily as prepared to be challenged by the invisible furniture of the museum itself.

Innovations can be challenging when adopted too quickly, and museum staff members as well as museum visitors were often not prepared for the changes that came with new technologies in the galleries. Paul Marty shares a story about experimenting with digital image recognition at a time when few people knew what the technology was or how it worked:

> The Museum Computer Network conference in 2010 took place in Austin, Texas . . . and we're at the conference reception, which is being held at the Blanton Museum of Art. . . . Google had just released an image recognition tool . . . called Google Goggles . . . and I said, "I'm going to try this out." So I downloaded it to my phone, and I looked for something I could test it on. Well, at this conference reception, there was a temporary exhibit of impressionistic masters from the Walters Art Museum. . . . So, I pull up the app on my phone, I point it at a painting, and boom! Monet! It was perfect! I just pointed the camera in the app at the painting, and it immediately identified it. I went down the line: Monet, Manet, Degas, Seurat. . . . It was astonishing how well it worked. Of course, this being a museum technology conference, I soon had

> a crowd of people around me watching this work, and everybody was very excited to see how good it was . . . but, of course, this attracted the attention of the docents. . . . There were three of them in the corner of the gallery, looking at us and talking to each other . . . and then one of them separated herself from the other two, came over, and said to me, "Excuse me, sir. I'm sorry, but no photographs." And I looked at her, and I said, "That's okay. I'm not taking photographs. I'm digitally scanning these works of art for image recognition purposes." And she looked at me, and said, "Well, okay, then!" So she went back to her friends, and we continued down the line . . . marveling at what a good job Google did recognizing these images. But at the same time, I'm watching them out of the corner of my eye, and I see them talking. Then she comes back to me, maybe 30 seconds later, and she says, "Excuse me, sir, but I talked this over with my friends, and they think that's the same thing as taking a picture. . . ." So I stopped scanning then, but, astonishingly, nobody would have blinked twice if I had been scanning a QR code next to the painting. Nobody would have blinked if I had been typing in the name of the painting and pulling up a picture. It was just that I was using technology to identify the painting from the picture that caused people to blink. And that wraps up our entire history of technology in museums. . . . Technology changes so much faster than society does.

Given the potential technological disruption for museum visitors and museum staff alike, it was perhaps only natural that museum curators would initially resist the introduction of computer technologies into museum galleries. Holly Witchey explains how many curators, even today, still prefer to keep the technology separated from the art:

> We still see a lot of cases where technology is put somewhere by itself, and there may be artworks with it, but I still think it's fairly rare for it to be integrated into the gallery space. And that's because curators are interested in what they're interested in, and they don't want to go into their prized gallery and see everyone next to a screen.

Tim Svenonius echoes these comments as he recalls the challenges they encountered when bringing computers into the galleries at SFMOMA:

> The idea of having computers in the galleries was definitely . . . anathema for sure. . . . Everything was nestled in a corner or against a wall. . . . Any gallery kiosk couldn't really coexist with artwork. They were always in a corridor or in a lobby.

The resistance that museum technology professionals faced from curators who did not want technology in the exhibits often made innovating online much easier by comparison. Sarah Kenderdine explains the challenge of bringing technology onto the gallery floor:

> The space of the gallery floor is the most contested space in the museum. . . . Take the Rijksmuseum as an example. Brilliant online achievement. Lots of high-resolution images. Zero media on the floors of their museums. Zero. I think it's the last frontier.

Overcoming this resistance to technology in the galleries was a slow, transformative process. Museum technology professionals needed to be strategic as they worked to overcome fears, allay concerns, and convince curators that museum computing could add value to their exhibits without interfering with the experience of visiting a museum. As Holly Witchey explains, one of the best ways to do this was to work first with the curators who did want to experiment with technology in their exhibits:

> We continued to fight those battles, but I think even fighting those battles . . . another thing we learned to do was . . . work with the curators who were interested. If you could get an interested curator to do some sort of great project, then others would follow suit.

Bruce Wyman echoes this philosophy as he describes his process for getting buy-in from curators at the Denver Art Museum for integrating technology into the museum's galleries:

> I spent a lot of the first year that I was there working with curators to work through what the technology was and why we would do some of this stuff and making it exceptionally clear that—and this is true—I don't care about technology that much. I care that it's used well, but if it is better to do something on a piece of paper or a bit of laminate card, I would rather do that because it is so much more cost effective, frequently, to do it that way. . . . So a lot of the initial years there was building that sort of validation, so by the time we left, we weren't the ones initiating technology stuff. It was people coming to us, like, "We had this idea for this thing!" And we're like, "Yeah, we can do that!" Which was the right dynamic to eventually get to, which was rewarding in its own way.

As soon as museum curators saw the potential for technology to add value to their exhibits and reach their audiences in new ways, the use of computers in museum galleries grew rapidly. Scott Sayre describes getting curators on board with interactive multimedia at the Minneapolis Institute of Art in the 1990s and how positively they reacted once they saw the potential:

> I formed a team with the mandate of producing 15 interactive video kiosks that would be installed in the museum's galleries, which was unheard of, and highly problematic, because none of the curators wanted glowing computer screen anywhere near their galleries, and that's a huge story in itself of just the demonstrations and advocacy that we had to do to be able to incorporate

> technology in the museum. I ended up telling this story over and over again, sitting down with curators and saying, "Imagine we can just cut a hole in the gallery wall, and we can take people wherever, when they walk through that hole. Anything we can imagine, as far as helping them understand the collection better, we can do there." And once they really understood, "Oh, we can help you imagine this?" Once we had worked with a curator, then we couldn't keep them away, because they had so many ideas that we honestly had a hard time getting our jobs done because we kept having curators come into our area to talk about things: "Is it possible? Is it possible?"

Getting the curators on board with technology in the galleries was essential. No longer were museum technology professionals engaged in a one-way conversation to convince curators to experiment with technology, but a two-way conversation where radical, new ideas about the use of technology in the galleries and behind the scenes could be explored by all stakeholders. This represented a major change for many institutions. Peter Samis explains how his team worked collaboratively with museum curators to reshape the museum experience with technology as part of a new exhibit, Points of Departure, at SFMOMA in the early 2000s:

> Points of Departure was implicitly the Museum in Technological Times. What can technology bring to the way museums behave and interact with their public? . . . That was the whole idea behind Points of Departure. We were going to take the artworks that visitors often were most puzzled by, and turn, and make it a teachable moment in the galleries. . . . You know, "Why is this in an art museum? Why is this visual art?". . . . The idea was to deliver just-in-time information to visitors in the most accessible way via these smart tables in the galleries. And we gathered the curatorial voices down in storage. . . . We would schedule an hour for each theme, and bring the curators down to talk on the pieces we had selected for the exhibition that corresponded to that theme. . . . It changes the whole paradigm of what a museum exhibition is, how it functions, and how collaboratively it's developed.

Involving museum curators in the development process behind the scenes was a radical idea that helped surface hidden knowledge and bring important details to the museum's visitors. Susie Wise explains how Points of Departure at SFMOMA connected curators with visitors through technology in the gallery, honoring both the curatorial voice and the visitors' questions:

> What was happening in that exhibition was the bringing of that curatorial voice, and really also the visitor voice, because those questions of those themes and the whole literal interface of Making Sense of Modern Art were actual visitor questions. So there are just multiple layers of that kind of curiosity that presumably drives curatorial thinking, but also really drives great visitor experience, and how in those interfaces, particularly the technology-based

interfaces, we were attempting to surface that and honor it and make that visible. . . . Points of Departure got to be a kind of culminating moment where we've been doing all this technology stuff, but we're actually able to say that the stories we have captured, and the media that we've created, and the tools that we have at our disposal to do this, actually can help in a curatorial kind of way. And that we were far enough along that we could really kind of own that space in that way.

The more curators got involved with technology in the galleries, the more they saw its potential. New technologies suddenly seemed more helpful than disruptive, and new ideas continued to carry museums forward to embrace positive change at a rapid pace. Koven Smith describes this transformation at the Metropolitan Museum of Art, where the willingness of the museum's curators to incorporate computers into the museum's galleries increased dramatically as they grasped the benefits of digital collections and digital exhibits for museum visitors:

> Towards the tail end of my time at the Met [2007-2008], we started, after working on the curators there for years, getting requests . . . for actual interpretive technology to go into the galleries themselves. I can't emphasize enough how controversial that idea was at the Met at that time. The Met's curatorial divisions, with some exceptions, were highly conservative, with some making very bold pronouncements like, "There will never be computers in our galleries!" That sort of thing. . . . The first meaningful request was from the Greek and Roman department. Their galleries had been closed for renovations for years, and one part of the renovated galleries was going to be a study gallery—open storage, basically. They came to us because they had more objects they needed to show than they had space to identify them with any kind of physical labeling. They had cases filled with hundreds of pottery shards or coins and things like that. The head curator [Chris Lightfoot] came to us and asked, "Is there a way that we could have computers do this?" This was probably about as sophisticated as the request was, and I think Douglas [Hegley] and I were like, okay, this is finally our chance. Now we can really do something. We're not just doing experiments in the margins. . . . This is something that will go in the gallery and might be there permanently.

Over decades spent advocating for the use of computers in museums, museum technology professionals became very skilled at explaining how technology works, and how museum computing can help everyone working in museums do their jobs more effectively and efficiently. The overarching history of museum computing, and the changes that took place as new technologies were introduced into museums, is a story of positive growth and development spanning more than sixty years. For many museum technology professionals, the rapid changes that took place as museum curators and other museum professionals became more used to and accepting of new technologies, both in the galleries and behind the scenes, represented a kind of seismic shift in attitude toward computers, as Koven Smith explains:

> By the end of my time at the Denver Art Museum, my job had basically become showing up to Exhibition Committee meetings and asking, "Where do you want the iPads to go?" We had reached a point where there wasn't a lot of figuring it out anymore. We had an accepted way of doing this and now we were just executing on that. But that was a real change, just in that two- or three-year period . . . there's this very pronounced shift towards an acceptance of commercial technology that was not present before. The notion that a conservator would not catalog his or her work using a tablet seems asinine now, but we were working on a spec that was created before that existed. It was quite the seismic shift. . . . In a short amount of time, I went from working in the Registrar's office in the basement of the IMA, where one of the Registrars . . . was literally cutting out pieces of paper and pasting an exhibition checklist together, and not even five years later, we've got the Steve project, the stuff in the Met's Greek and Roman galleries and the American Wing, and I'm working on the Conservation Space Project. It was a total change in the scope of what tech does in museums.

Total change is hard, and it makes sense that museum professionals and museum visitors alike were not ready for the dramatic changes that accompanied the introduction of museum computing from the 1960s to today. Adapting to new technologies is also difficult, especially when they disrupt the status quo and change traditional operating procedures institution-wide. Whether they were advocating for the use of computers to support collections management or interactive exhibits on the gallery floor, museum technology professionals had to overcome fears, resolve confusions, and help people understand the value of emerging technologies. Through their efforts, they helped museum curators, administrators, and other staff members better understand the benefits of museum computing for improving access to digital collections and reaching their audiences through new technologies.

SUGGESTIONS FOR FURTHER READING

Chan, Seb, and Aaron Cope. 2015. "Strategies against Architecture: Interactive Media and Transformative Technology at the Cooper Hewitt, Smithsonian Design Museum." *Curator: The Museum Journal* 58 (3): 352–368.

Keene, Suzanne. 1998. *Digital Collections: Museums and the Information Age*. Oxford: Butterworth-Heinemann.

Parry, Ross. 2007. *Recoding the Museum: Digital Heritage and the Technologies of Change*. London: Routledge.

Parry, Ross, and Vince Dziekan. 2021. "Critical Digital: Museums and their Postdigital Circumstance." In *Art, Museums, and Digital Cultures: Rethinking Change*, edited by

Helena Barranha and Joana Simoes Henriques, 16-26. Lisbon: Universidade NOVA de Lisboa.
Peacock, Darren. 2008. "Making Ways for Change: Museums, Disruptive Technologies and Organisational Change." *Museum Management and Curatorship* 23 (4): 333-351.
Rogers, Everett M. 2003. *Diffusion of Innovations*. New York: Free Press.
Tallon, Loic, and Kevin Walker, eds. 2008. *Digital Technologies and the Museum Experience: Handheld Guides and Other Media*. Lanham, MD: AltaMira Press.

8

Radical Change

> How many times have we been queried about, "If we give too much information away online, will people still be inclined to come to the museum?" You know, it's, "Well, yeah!" Ever since they started publishing black and white images, it just engenders more and more interest. . . . In fact, these means brought more people's attention and awareness and hopefully their support to the museum.—Oral History of Sam Quigley

The introduction of museum computing brought rapid and dramatic changes to museums, especially as new ideas and new expectations about the availability of and access to digital representations of museum collections evolved in the twenty-first century. When one considers the range of information resources that museums regularly make available online today, it is astonishing how much has changed so quickly. In just a few years, the museum community went from having almost no information about their collections available on the Internet to massive, open-access projects with millions of records and images from museums around the world available online for public use. As an integral part of this transition, museum technology professionals needed to come to terms with revolutionary new ideas about providing online access to digital museum resources, encouraging creativity, and involving museum visitors as active participants in the co-creation of digital knowledge.

Access to digital representations of museum collections, including digital images, offered museum visitors new opportunities to interact with museum information resources in innovative, creative ways. But these changes also prompted rising tensions within museums as new technologies reshaped the nature of the museum experience and the responsibilities of museum professionals. Museum technology professionals had to manage a delicate balance between internal concerns and external expectations as the museum's digital infrastructure evolved. Changing ideas about what was acceptable in terms of providing access to digital images and collections data put immense pressure on museum professionals to determine how increased access to digital resources would change the museum experience for museum visitors.

As the museum's digital presence increased in importance, and it became possible to reach increasingly broader audiences around the world, museum professionals started asking difficult questions about the kinds of resources they should make available in digital format, their obligations to share digital images and collections data, and the effect that this might have on things like in-person museum visits. Concerns about putting collections data and images on the Internet clashed with new ideas about the evolving obligations of museums toward open access and open data. Few people, early on, had any idea how to respond to requests for digital data or digital images of museum collections. Deborah Howes, for example, shares a story in her oral history about what happened at the Art Institute when Bill Gates approached the museum in the late 1980s asking for digital images of its most popular works of art:

> The thing about the Art Institute of Chicago, being a public educator there, which I quickly had to learn how to do, is that they have a very well-known collection. And I couldn't believe that people were coming to my two o'clock general tours and saying, "I want to see this painting with a guy in a nighttime coffee shop, and there's a yellow light in the background." And I'm like, "Oh, Edward Hopper's Nighthawks. Sure, let's go see it." Or, "I'm looking for that painting with the pitchfork and the lady and the man—" you know, and so I'm like, "Okay, we'll do it." And then later I made this connection that those works of art were part of a board game we all played called Masterpiece, and I didn't realize that the collection of that board game was actually a big overlap with the Art Institute of Chicago. And the reason that's important is that it also meant that in the late '80s, when I was working there, and Microsoft's Bill Gates was building his amazing technology house in Seattle, he came knocking at the Art Institute of Chicago's door and said, "I have this idea that rather than buy art for my new house, I'm going to just project the images I love, and the images I love, many of them are at your museum." And I'm thinking Masterpiece! But the museum said, "Oh, Mr. Gates, we would love to have a partnership with you. What do you require?" And he says, "Well, can you send me, you know, my hundred favorite pictures in a digital format?" And we're like, "What's that?" You know, "What, what do you mean by that?" And Alan Newman was like, "We're not giving away the digital file! He has to pick. . . . The richest man isn't going to. . . . We need money for that!" And so, the Director, Jim Wood, was like, "Alan's kind of right. Why should we give away these images?"

Museums suddenly found themselves in a brave new world where experiments with digital images raised difficult questions for museum staff members with few clear precedents to follow, and many opportunities for misunderstanding. This was particularly the case as digital images of museum collections began appearing on the World Wide Web in the mid-1990s. While many institutions were familiar with issues of image rights and reproduction, the rapid adoption and spread of digital images online left many museum professionals feeling threatened and afraid. Richard Rinehart recalls how the Louvre Museum reacted to what may have been the world's first museum website, the WebLouvre, in 1994:

> The WebLouvre wasn't started by the Louvre at all, or anybody working for the Louvre. It was a grad student unaffiliated with the museum, Nicolas Pioch, and he started this thing on his own, and he was just using images that he could scan or grab from anywhere of works in the Louvre. I think that might have been the first museum website, which was kind of illegitimate. . . . At a certain point, the Louvre became aware of the WebLouvre that Nicolas had built, and apparently, they were not pleased. They were going through the French Minister of Culture to take action against him. . . . They wanted the website to stop and go away, and maybe there'd be some punitive action against him, because he had used their name and their images. . . . I wrote a letter to the Minister of Culture in France, and my main point of advice was, "Look, I get it . . . but instead of the Louvre punishing this guy, they should hire him." Really. He's already done the work for them, and he knows what he's doing. The website was extensive. And I was like, you know, take advantage of this kind of grassroots initiative, and grab on to it, instead of stamping down on it, setting the work back years, and then starting over again, which is what they did in the end. Anyway, I never got a response from the French Minister of Culture. I don't know whether he ever read the letter or not.

When it came to the opportunities for museums on the web, many museums did not recognize the value of these technologies or understand the potential vision for digital resources. As with any major change, it was natural there were underlying fears about putting digital images or data on the Internet, and many museum administrators saw the web as a danger and a threat to in-person visitation rates. Paul Marty shares a story about interacting with museum directors who were afraid of the consequences of putting images online:

> I would go into a museum, and the museum director would say to me, "I'm really worried about all this digitization, worried about all these museum artifacts being put online. Do you think it's likely that if people can see our artifacts on the Internet, they won't come to the museum?" And I got asked this so many times that I got really good at answering the question. I would put on my sad newscaster face, and I would look at the director, and I would say, "You know, it's a really good thing that you asked me this, because, yeah, it's a really terrible problem. You've got to keep a real close eye on this. Maybe you haven't heard, but ever since the state of Florida started putting pictures of beaches on their website, nobody vacations in Florida anymore."

Sarcasm aside, extensive research conducted as early as the late 1990s showed that these worries were unfounded. Data collected from museum visitors made it clear that the availability of online digital images actually increased, not decreased, traffic to museums. Nevertheless, overcoming these worries took time, and fears about putting museum images and other data online persisted for many years. Museum technology professionals had to work hard to help museum directors understand what putting images online really meant for their institutions. Howard Besser explains the origins of the Museum Educational Site Licensing project, and its importance in helping art museum directors improve their understanding of online images:

> The Museum Educational Site Licensing project actually grew out of some efforts that had been percolating a little bit before. . . . Geoff Samuels got a bunch of art museum directors to come to a meeting in New York City where they could look at museum images on a screen. I supplied the images. He got a workstation, and these museum directors were astounded at what it was like. They'd read about it or heard of it, but the quality of the images was striking to them. And Geoff really wanted to do something to kind of get over some of their resistance, because some of them had an attitude, "Well, if we put our images out there no one's going to come to the museum." These were the naive kind of notions that people had at the time, and no one really knew, and so Geoff really started pushing hard to do something to try to assuage the resistance from some of these art museum directors.

Naturally these concerns were not limited to museum directors. Marla Misunas, for example, remembers convincing artists that it was okay for them to share images of their work online:

> A lot of artists didn't want their images of their work online back then because they thought it would cheapen their artwork and make the actual object less impressive. Of course, it isn't true, and we have a lot of data on that. It reminds me of that old argument, "We can't put color plates in books because then no one wants to see the objects." We know that's not true. That kind of attitude was something we had to break through and get beyond.

It also took time for museum curators to understand what it meant to share collections data online. Misunderstandings about the nature of online collections management systems often combined with fears that access to the Internet would open the museum's sensitive data for the world to see. Megan Forbes explains how many people were initially afraid of managing their collections information online, a challenge that was especially tricky for the Museum of the Moving Image since the collections management system they were promoting, CollectionSpace, was fully web-based:

> When we first started, the biggest nonstarter was that CollectionSpace was web-based. People were really, really not ready to put their collections management system on the Internet. When they heard "web-based," they heard, "Our collections management system is going to be on the Internet for anybody to come in and see our valuations, and our anonymous donors, and you know."

Getting museum curators on board with sharing data over the Internet was particularly difficult because putting information online was often seen as a threat to their scholarly expertise. Much of the resistance that museum technology professionals faced from museum curators stemmed from worries that their collections data might be incomplete, and from an unwillingness to share potentially imperfect scholarship over the Internet. Cathryn Goodwin explains why the idea of putting collections information online was initially threatening to curators:

> Just the idea that all this information about objects that curators had been working on for their entire careers could suddenly be publicly available was incredibly threatening to curators at the time. . . . The mandate that comes from the Director that says, "You know folks, we have to share this information. It doesn't really belong to us. The collection needs to be made accessible, and so all the objects are going online. And you can come along and fix up your records and correct things as we go along." That striving for perfection was a real obstacle for a lot of institutions, I think. The notion that nothing could be online unless it was completely perfect, and all the research was done, which is just an impossible task, because everyone knows that cataloging museum collections is a never-ending process. Data is always changing. Scholarship is always changing.

Once again, even though these worries ended up being unfounded, overcoming those fears took time, and involved adjusting to rapidly changing internal and external expectations. It took time for people to shift away from traditional mindsets to new approaches to data sharing. As Sam Quigley explains, sometimes convincing curators to put their collections databases on the Internet required the museum director to get personally involved:

> By around 1999, [MFA] Director Malcolm Rogers had funded all this effort, had been patient, waiting for it to be coming along, and he wanted to see some tangible results. So, he started asking, "Okay, you've got this mfa.org thing. We have a website. When are you going to put the database on it?" And I said, "Well, we have to make sure that all the curators are fine about that." To which he rolled his eyes and said. . . . "Okay, you can try to convince people to authorize the publication of their data, but you can let them know that I'm pretty impatient about this as well." So, it was my job to go around and try to get people to sign off on things. . . . I think the first iteration of

> digital publication was something like 15,000 records, not all of which, by the way, had images even. Most were just what we now call stub records . . . just the bare tombstone information, but it was something. And something was better than nothing. That was our mantra, and eventually, we were trying to get more and more people to put more data out there. We started floating more images onto the database to make it a little bit more useful and visually appealing. And by this time, a number of museums around the country were doing similar things, and there was much more of a keen interest in seeing what was going on. . . . I think it was about a year later that, by fiat, Malcolm Rogers caused the rest of the 400,000 records to go online as well, in a newly redesigned website. Which is really, really quite good.

Sometimes getting collections data online was easier when there were museum donors involved who wanted information shared over the Internet. Deborah Howes shares a story about the origins of the Heilbrunn Timeline of Art History at the Metropolitan Museum of Art, and how the vision of the project's donors helped encourage the development of an online timeline:

> The development department identified somebody who had a reputation in the New York area as funding institutions for the purposes of making timelines. For example, when you visit the American Museum of Natural History, there's a timeline of the universe that is funded by the family known as Heilbrunn. And Philippe [the Director] was furious: "There is no way he's going to paint a timeline on the gallery walls! That is not happening! But education, if you find a way to use this money, go right ahead." The Heilbrunns were wonderful, quite elderly individuals, very dedicated to art, very open-minded about things, but had never even seen a computer. And so, my task was, "How do I get these lovely donors excited about an interactive timeline on the web?". . . . We invited the donors up to the nice conference room with a view, and Philippe was in attendance, and I put up my slides, and I was showing them all these different things that you could do on the web, and that it would go around the world . . . and they said, "People in India would be able to see this timeline?" And I'm like, "Absolutely! In fact, people in India are well connected to this technology!" And they were sold! And they became the donors for this ongoing project.

Sometimes overcoming fears about putting museum collections content online was easier during times of change and upheaval. Museum technology professionals working in institutions that are closed to the public, for instance, may have an easier time advocating for online initiatives as part of audience outreach. Jeff Gates describes creating the Smithsonian's first blog at a time when the Smithsonian American Art Museum was closed for renovations:

> One of my key tasks was to figure out how to bring a constant flow of new content to our web pages. Remember, this was the early 2000s, and websites

were hand-coded and static. . . . How could the SAAM bring the vast amount of content on our website to the surface? In addition, we faced a challenge: In 2000, the American Art Museum closed for a six-year renovation. While we were closed, how could we maintain a public face on the net? . . . We were thinking seriously about how we could keep our website fresh. And a blog could provide a way. But we had a couple of challenges: all departments were preparing for our physical reopening, and we were concerned about how a "revolutionary" new project—few knew what a blog was at that time—could fit into their workflow. Would there be resistance to one more unknown? The other challenge was convincing the director that this was a viable project. So, we had to be very strategic in our proposal. We looked closely at the pros and cons. It seems very pedestrian now, but it was a big deal back then. This was a new way of doing things. We had been trying to deliver fresh content via a "What's New" page, but we had no technology for quickly updating pages. Everything would have to be done by hand. . . . Every blog post had to be approved by the director. I remember being on a panel about blogs at the Museum Computer Network conference in 2006 with Phyllis Hecht from the National Gallery and Robin Dowden from the Walker. When I told the audience, "Every blog post has to be approved by our director," everyone's mouth dropped, and there was a collective sigh, and Robin said, "I don't know if our director even knows we have a blog!"

No matter the impetus or incentive, museum professionals worldwide were increasingly coming to terms with the idea that sharing collections images and data online was the right thing to do. There was a growing recognition, especially among public institutions, that museums had an obligation to provide greater access to their collections online. As Kate Collen explains, recalling her time at the Smithsonian Institution, if a museum has a public mission, then that museum is obligated almost by definition to push past their concerns and support access to images online:

I think there was a lot of resistance and a lot of fear. Now, a lot of museums are doing the same thing, but it was really groundbreaking at the time and really, really scary. . . . We were talking about watermarking images. And you can only release a very small file size. And what about copyright? And we'll lose control. But if the museum's collections are held in trust for the public, isn't it our mission to make that information accessible to the public? I would argue, it is. It's their collection. We hold it in trust for them, so we should make high-resolution images available when we can.

Many museum technology professionals argued that sharing collections data, if at all possible, was in fact the ethical thing for museums to do. As Sam Quigley put it, concerns about data privacy fell by the wayside when measured against the obligations many museums had to share collections that were held in trust for the public:

> There was real ambivalence . . . about the idea of making all this data, previously private information, and private bailiwicks of these little silos out there, and sort of mixing and mashing it all up. I mean, we're very skeptical and wary of privacy issues nowadays. . . . People were really worried and obviously, with very good reason. But at the bottom line, privacy of your own personal life is quite a bit different than privacy for collections held in public trust by museums, who receive tax-free status and all the other benefits that come along with it. I always felt that we were obliged to share our data, and in fact, we love sharing our data, so this is just a new way of doing it.

Overcoming those concerns meant coming to terms not only with the museum's social obligations but with the idea of the museum as a public good. As Greg Albers explains, the more museums shared their collections data, particularly digital images, the more museum leaders recognized the value of providing open access to museum information resources:

> Moving toward open access, open source, really thinking of the museum's public mission, a mission of public good, and trying to make their assets and their knowledge as open and accessible as possible. . . . I think museum leadership got really very positive feedback every time they released collection images, and that kind of positive feedback loop that came from users in the community, out in the world at large, from doing those kinds of things really helped museum leadership understand the value of that, and how that kind of open approach really blended well with the museum's overall mission . . . simultaneously with other museums opening their collections images, and really offering high-resolution images for download for free, and doing that kind of work as well.

Naturally, altruism was not the only factor at play here. While access to digital images was initially viewed as a potential revenue stream from offices of rights and reproduction, over time, museum leadership realized they were often losing money from charging people for the right to reproduce digital images. In other words, not only was open access the right thing to do, it was also the cost-effective thing to do. As Greg Albers continues, despite the fears involved with making these changes, museums administrators quickly realized that it was better to give away their collections images for free than to place barriers in the way of people using their assets:

> Museums often would charge for the rights to reproduce an image. . . . Many museums saw that as a kind of money-making opportunity in a way of helping the bottom line and sustaining their own practices in other areas of their institutions, which was sometimes valid, but oftentimes museums found that the cost of managing that process, of having someone write in and request an image, and then get it back, actually was costing them more than they were getting back in the fees, so now no one's winning. The museum's losing

> money, the people who are paying for the fees are losing money, so eventually, they started figuring out that it was better to just put them out in the open. It's goodwill, the images go much further, you get much better coverage of where your images are, and . . . you're better able to put out good quality images as well.

In the end, the fears that many people had about the unintended consequences of museums sharing collections data turned out not to be realized. In fact, the more museums opened up access to their collections data and images online, the more other institutions followed suit. There was a sudden rush of open-access images released to the public as museums worked to release images they were legally permitted to share without copyright restrictions. Diane Zorich describes this tipping point at the Smithsonian, and the hard work involved in convincing museum leadership about the risks and rewards of open access:

> The Smithsonian was obviously not first out of the gate . . . but that was okay, because those before us gave us the ammunition to show that they did it, and no one died. It was okay. Nothing untoward has happened. That was really important in convincing not only senior management, but legal departments, who are often, I mean, it's their nature to be risk-averse. . . . I think all of us in the trenches should pat ourselves on the back for the years of hard work on that. . . . It really was people in the trenches who moved open access forward. . . . The truth is we do have to be accountable to Congress and the taxpayers for the use of their money, so it's really hard to justify not making this stuff open. This is the American public's collection.

Once museum administrators realized that the world would not end if museums shared their collections online, they became much more receptive to the idea of adopting open data, open access, and open image policies for their institutions. Museum technology professionals soon found themselves asked to undertake massive projects intended to move collections data previously inaccessible to the general public to online collections management systems. It could be difficult to grasp the magnitude of effort required just to begin work on these projects. Josh Gorman, for example, describes the origins of the Smithsonian Institution's effort to digitize its collections, and how they grappled with the scale of the project:

> It all arose out of this really simple question, "Why aren't we sharing more of our pictures online?" All of this really got started, the apocryphal story is in 2011 or so, when the Secretary of the Smithsonian Wayne Clough, went on Fox News, and was talking about some exhibit or something, and out of nowhere, the anchor asked, "What are you doing online? Are you going to digitize your collections?" And he said, "Oh yeah! We're going to digitize everything!" And

> then he came out of the interview and asked somebody, "What does that mean?" Because there was really very little information about what we had—digitally, physically, anything. . . . So a collections advisory committee was put in place across the Smithsonian. And one of the things that they finally rolled out in about 2012 was a Collections Digitization Reporting System . . . through which all of the museums could report how many objects they have, how many loans they have, how many of those objects are described, how many of them have images taken of them. Which meant in 2013 or so, for the first time, there was this real accounting of everything that was at the Smithsonian . . . and what it revealed was that we had millions of digital images of our collections across all of the museums . . . and very, very few of them were available.

For many museums, the primary challenge to digitizing their collections was not getting the digital images in the first place, but working around institutional barriers to sharing those images. Before they could put digital images online, museum technology professionals first needed to identify those barriers and develop procedures to move past them. Josh Gorman describes the challenges they faced taking their existing collections information records and putting them online at the National Museum of American History:

> When I came to the American History Museum in 2016, I'd come from the Anacostia Museum, where I've done a lot of work really pushing everything online. It was a very small collection, fewer than 5,000 objects. . . . It was a much smaller enterprise than the American History Museum, which has plausibly as many as three million objects. . . . So coming to the American History Museum, I was really interested in trying to do more, because when I showed up . . . we were sharing not even one percent of collections in this space. . . . We had collections records in our database for over a million objects. More than 600,000 of them had at least tombstone data that we could share with the world, but we weren't doing it. And this had to do with sort of the authorities for how we were sharing things. If it was going to go online, it had to be specifically requested by a curator to go online, it had to be reviewed before it could be nominated to go online, and then my office, the Registrar's Office, had to make sure that we owned the object.

Museum technology professionals needed to figure out how to streamline the process of sharing information online, which often meant disrupting existing curatorial practices, and helping their institutions come to terms with managing risk in digital environments. Josh Gorman explains how changing ideas about what it meant for records to be available to the public at the National Museum of American History helped dismantle barriers to sharing data more broadly:

> We started unpacking different ways that we could share more quickly. The first thing we did was we just decided we're going to share everything that has

> been through what we were calling our legal title process. . . . We determined that we have achieved a minimum viable product at least with these objects because we've described while we photographed them, we know we own them, so we have zero risk sharing these with the world. . . . We were very rapidly moving past a position where curators had literally been the sole arbiters of every decision about what went in front of the public. We were very quickly dismantling that, and saying that, no, the decision about what goes before the public will not be made at the point of putting it in front of the public, but had been made at the point of acquisition. By putting something into a public collection, that became the moment at which something enters the public realm.

Slowly but surely, each of these changes led to new understandings about the importance of sharing collections content, and new philosophies about what was acceptable, or even necessary, for institutions to share. Many museums, particularly public museums, discovered it was often better to put their records online than to hide their records from the public. New ideas about open access helped museums better understand the benefits of open data and the value of encouraging broader digital participation through technologies like application programming interfaces (APIs). Mia Ridge, for instance, discusses lessons learned about the value of open data, participatory websites, and community knowledge at the Science Museum in London:

> While I was at the Science Museum, I worked with external developers to release an API to a subset about collections, based on work that we're doing with a new gallery. And just before I left, I did an Open Data release from the catalog as a CSV, and immediately, people sent me back improved versions of the records, which is amazing, and really proved the value to people in the museum, and I think also, just helped them realize that the world doesn't end if you can see a CSV, and people realize there are errors in your catalogs. But also, that was my first real intimation of the need for round tripping, so as soon as you release data, or if you put on a Wikidata, you enter into a really complex area of negotiation around who can update records, what correctness means in different contexts, the value of neat and tidy data visualization versus just having something you can consult as a curator. . . . I'd never been into the idea that museums are places of authority that exist as islands. They always have to be in dialogue with people. There's a lot of knowledge out there in the community. . . . There are these communities of passion who are really deeply knowledgeable about things, and they meet and they discuss and they generate knowledge and learning through their dialogue.

Naturally, it took time for these ideas to evolve and become broadly accepted. Museum technology professionals needed to work behind the scenes to get the pieces in place long before any opportunities related to the benefits of open access could be implemented. They needed the underlying collections data in place, in digital format, and ready to go; they needed the recognition among museum staff members that sharing something was better than sharing nothing; and they needed the right people in the right place at the right time who were willing to support and champion the value of digital participation in museums. But once those things are in place, once you can stop arguing about open access and instead start openly sharing your data, the possibilities for connecting information resources across domains are almost endless. Cathryn Goodwin, for example, describes how changing the way people thought about accessing collections data at the Princeton University Art Museum opened up new opportunities for connection, discovery, and innovation across the university:

> About a year ago, we were able, finally, to integrate the museum's collection with the library search at Princeton, so that anyone can go to the library and search their collection and find museum objects. This was a long, long, long term goal. . . . We were able to hire a developer, with one of the grants that we wrote, and that allowed us to write an API to our collections database, and to set up a IIIF server for image delivery, and subsequently, our data was open, our data was accessible, and all of these other things are possible now. Cross-discovery becomes a real achievable thing. And it's also great fun being in an academic museum with that kind of technology foundation because we have students who come to us two or three times a year, wanting to build projects on top of our API. And they go off and they create some kind of a little app that will help you discover all the paintings that are blue, or whatever it is that they're interested in, but it's been really, really fun. And we're starting to plan what will be an annual hackathon at Princeton for innovation around museum data . . . the work has proven itself over, over these decades, and now, what we're more likely to hear is, how can we integrate all of these cool functions into our own collection pages? Or how can we use all of the things that we've built to support this particular class that's happening at Princeton?

Despite their initial concerns about what this future would entail, museums faced their fears and embraced a spirit of boundless enthusiasm and the potential of open access. Once museums accepted the idea of opening their collections to the public as fully as possible, they almost immediately recognized the positive benefits of open-access initiatives and the value of providing tools like open APIs that let people from outside the museum work directly with the museum's content. New ideas about sharing collections data and images reaped numerous benefits for museum professionals and museum visitors alike. Tina Shah explains how open access to collections data at the Art Institute of Chicago provides everyone with a wonderful opportunity to learn from the museum's resources and explore their own creativity:

> Thinking about open access and being transparent about data and collections, I think mixing all of that together enables people to have access to things

> and gives them opportunities to do things on their own to be creative and to think about the possibilities. Like now, through our API, there's been a lot of Twitter bots that I've seen come along. We created a really cool Chrome plugin with our API that on every new tab that you open in your browser, you get a brand-new work of art. And that's just been amazing . . . and I think that the open access initiatives around being able to download works of art and being able to create things. . . . It takes work, of course, to spread the word and to help people learn how to use the API . . . but I think that the world is in a very different place now. And there's people that want to learn and want to be challenged. They want to do things in their own time and create some beautiful things.

The evolutionary changes that had to take place over the past sixty years to allow these ideas to develop represent a sweeping change in philosophy that was truly radical for many museums. Current attitudes toward providing open data, open access, open-source tools, and open APIs for museum collections are a far cry from what they were just a few years ago. In a very short period of time, the museum community went from telling people they could not have access to images or data (at least not without paying for them and with significant constraints) to releasing vast quantities of images and data online that were freely available for public use without reservations or restrictions. By recognizing the importance of open access to collections data as a public good, museums were able to face their fears and embrace the necessary changes to make their digital information resources broadly available for the benefit of humanity.

SUGGESTIONS FOR FURTHER READING

Barry, Alisa. 2006. "Creating a Virtuous Circle between a Museum's On-line and Physical Spaces." In *Museums and the Web 2006*, edited by Jennifer Trant and David Bearman. Toronto: Archives & Museum Informatics. http://www.archimuse.com/mw2006/papers/barry/barry.html

Chadwick, John, and Patricia Boverie. 1999. "A Survey of Characteristics and Patterns of Behavior in Visitors to a Museum Web Site." In *Museums and the Web 1999*, edited by David Bearman and Jennifer Trant, 154–162. Pittsburgh, PA: Archives & Museum Informatics. http://www.archimuse.com/mw99/papers/chadwick/chadwick.html

Hamma, Ken. 2005. "Public Domain Art in an Age of Easier Mechanical Reproducibility." *D-Lib Magazine* 11 (11). http://www.dlib.org/dlib/november05/hamma/11hamma.html

Kelly, Kristin. 2013. *Images of Works of Art in Museum Collections: The Experience of Open Access*. Washington, DC: Council on Library and Information Resources.

Marty, Paul F. 2007. "Museum Websites and Museum Visitors: Before and After the Museum Visit." *Museum Management and Curatorship* 22 (4): 337–360.

Matz, Robert C. 2000. "Bridgeman Art Library, Ltd. v. Corel Corp." *Berkeley Technology Law Journal* 15 (1): 3–23.

Simon, Nina. 2010. *The Participatory Museum*. Santa Cruz, CA: Museum 2.0.

Terras, Melissa. 2015. "Opening Access to Collections: The Making and Using of Open Digitised Cultural Content." *Online Information Review* 39 (5): 733-752.

Trant, Jennifer. 1996. "Enabling Educational Use of Museum Digital Materials: The Museum Educational Site Licensing (MESL) Project." *Art Documentation: Journal of the Art Libraries Society of North America* 15 (2): 25-28.

9

Digital Leadership

> I realized really early on that my role was to remove obstacles to let my team thrive . . . so that they could go forward and do what they wanted to do. And I still feel that's a large portion of my role on a day-to-day basis. Trying to find funds, trying to showcase their work, so people see the amazing things they've done, because often it's hidden labor, hidden products.—Oral History of Diane Zorich

The work of museum technology professionals has ranged widely from the 1960s to today, encompassing everything from struggling with computer networks as invisible workers behind the scenes to paving the way for innovative technologies in museums as technology managers and project leaders. Over time, as their day-to-day responsibilities shifted from the nuts and bolts of plugging in computers and installing servers to supervising operations and supporting digital initiatives in collections and exhibits, museum technology professionals increasingly needed to develop leadership skills. They became experts in building bridges and making connections between different groups, advocating for and inspiring employees within their institutions, and professionalizing the field of museum computing to ensure everyone has the knowledge and skill sets necessary to support museum technology projects.

As an integral part of this process, museum technology professionals looked to create institutional support for digital projects by identifying innovation champions and institutional leaders who could work together to help museums embrace new technologies. To have any chance at success, it was critical that museum technology initiatives be driven by visionary leaders who could provide guidance for digital projects, engage their colleagues behind an idea, and get the necessary buy-in and institutional support from museum administrators. As they pushed forward in pursuit of technological innovation, museum technology professionals needed to position themselves within their institutions in a way that provided them the opportunity to help museum leadership understand how implementing new technologies could enable museums to better achieve their goals—behind the scenes, in the galleries, and online.

One of the reasons this task was so challenging is that the individuals in these technology positions were defining the job and its responsibilities as the nature of museum computing evolved. While technology roles might have been easier to define in the corporate world, where there were more individuals with backgrounds in management information systems or business analytics, there was no precedent for this work in museums. Museum technology professionals needed to figure out for themselves what the job was and what it entailed almost in real time. As Cathryn Goodwin explains in her oral history, no one even knew what to call the work they were doing:

> Sam Quigley was at the Museum of Fine Arts in Boston, and I was at the St. Louis Art Museum, and we both had invented our own job titles, and were called Information Resources Coordinators, because nobody was doing this work in museums, nobody knew what to call it, how to describe it, how to write a job description for it, what kind of background was necessary. All of those things were challenging.

As museum technology professionals worked to integrate computers into the daily life of museum curators and collections managers, they often had to carve out their own space alongside the rest of the computing world. Sam Quigley describes the relationship between collections management and information technology in the Museum of Fine Arts Boston:

> It was a parallel universe, shall we say? The rest of the computing power of the MFA Boston was located in the I.T. department, but they viewed their mandate—probably because their boss told them—to make the cash registers sing in the Museum Shop, and to sustain basic office word processing throughout the building, initially using a Wang Mini system. And, in fact, try as I did to work with them, I found them to be just short of antagonistic to this idea of utilizing the computing power of the museum for collections management—imagine that! So it really had to be a parallel thing, and it was not all that pleasant, the interaction between I.T. and I.R., which is what we called ourselves, Information Resources. Even though we were using their network, there was very little else that we had to share. But we worked it out, and over time, they got a new director, a guy named Gordy Sands, who was much more sympathetic and helpful actually in helping make some of this stuff work.

The division between the people who kept the computers running, and those who were trying to integrate those computers into the museum's collections and exhibits, was often stark. It was difficult to explain to outsiders that this was something new, something that transcended plugging in physical devices and running network cables. Max Evjen describes explaining how his work at the Michigan State University Museum differed from information technology:

> I was working for the MSU Museum, which is a science and culture museum on campus, and my original title was "Exhibitions Technology Specialist," which really didn't quite encapsulate exactly what I did, because I did a lot of work in, yes, exhibitions technology, but also digital strategy, social media, marketing stuff, program stuff—it was pretty broad. I came into that job really focused on the visitor side of technology. They have an I.T. person who deals with all the backend stuff, and the servers, and making sure your email works, and the printers work, and all the infrastructure works, but they didn't have somebody thinking critically about the UX and humanistic ways of thinking about technology. And when I ended up getting in that role, somebody at the museum actually asked me. . . . "How does your job differ from I.T.?" And I was like, okay.

This was not an easy question to answer, especially given how quickly the job kept changing. For most of our oral history participants, the world of museum computing changed around them so rapidly that they were constantly facing one new challenge after another. Douglas Hegley describes the evolution of his job at the Metropolitan Museum of Art, and its relationship with information technology, as new technologies prompted new needs, and vice versa:

> "Douglas, there's some photographers who want to use digital cameras, and then there's the 'not over my dead body' film people. Do you think you could help?" Got in the middle of that, enjoyed that. The years are ticking by. "Douglas, can you come to the photo studio?" "What's wrong now?" "Well, here's our problem. . . ." Open the closet door, and there's 10,000 CDs and DVDs with digital images on them. "We can't find anything. There must be a system out there." "Yes, it's called Digital Asset Management, so okay, let's go do that." And these things rolled on and on. And through it all, my career kept moving away from hardcore I.T. I kept hiring managers and handing that off to them, and moving more and more toward digital, which would be more about content production and audience engagement, and really thinking about the mission of the institution rather than the infrastructure change management process. . . . I've gone from being the person primarily responsible for I.T., to being an internal customer to I.T.. . . . I really have to rely now on the I.T. operation, rather than lead it, and really lead digital, which is much more focused on getting all that content produced in an intentional and cogent way, getting it out to our publics, making sure that it's accessible, making sure that it's meaningful.

This shift from internal information technology work to external digital content production happened in museums across the board, and it was a difficult shift in perspective to make. As the responsibilities of the museum technology professional evolved in response to new technologies, and new ideas for using those technologies prompted new opportunities for museums, it took time for people to realize exactly how the very nature of the job was changing, or even to grasp that it was changing at all. As a result, museum professionals and museum administrators sometimes struggled to understand what the job actually was, or that when hiring someone to do technology work in museums, they were not just looking for someone simply to install and manage computers. Koven Smith, for example, describes what happened when the Indianapolis Museum of Art decided to hire its first chief technology officer:

> The IMA needed to make a personnel investment in technology. . . . I and others sat on a committee to evaluate possible hires for what became Rhonda Winters' position, the Chief Technology Officer. One of the people who advised us was Len Steinbach, who was, at that time, still at the Cleveland Art Museum. . . . Everybody at the IMA was still thinking in very kind of rigid, conservative terms like, "We need somebody who knows how to install servers." They were thinking very narrow, and Len came in, and was very much Len for two hours or whatever it was, and just blew everybody's mind. He was like, "No, no, no! You're thinking about this all wrong!"

As the field of museum computing evolved, the museum technology profession needed not only programmers and engineers but also leaders who understood how to use new technologies to offer improved access to collections content and transform the museum experience for visitors. This required the development of specific professional skills and new leadership philosophies. Leading digital initiatives is challenging work, especially as digital pervades museums, and it can be increasingly difficult to measure the specific impact of digital initiatives on the institution as a whole. Digital leaders need to be able to set a vision for the future of digital that can inspire their whole institution and empower their colleagues to make a difference as they move digital initiatives forward in museums. Douglas Hegley describes the leadership philosophies that can encourage museum professionals to embrace emerging technologies:

> I'm in a position of leadership which really is a position of empowerment, and going back to the day of helping a curator understand why putting a computer on your desk is actually a good thing, and why a collection information management system actually isn't just for your Cliff Notes, the blue sky version, the reason we're building these systems out, is that they will be publicly accessible one day. The schism between what people understood about their day-to-day work and open access in 1997 was wide, and in many ways, my

> job was not necessarily to say, "Go team! You can do it. You can learn how to use a mouse. . . ." My job was to try to sell what the future would look like in a way that was inspirational, but realistic and meaningful, and attached to what motivates people to work in an organization like an art museum. Why do you work in an art museum? It's one of those really interesting questions to ask someone and sit back and listen to the answer. At some point along the way, it almost always is going to include sharing. . . . The magic moment in the museum—and I went to museums as a toddler and I always found them magical places—is that jaw-dropping, heart-stopping moment of "Oh, my goodness! How did this ever . . .? How did someone make that? What does it mean? Oh my God, I get it!" And I think the second piece of that is they have to tell somebody—your "Mom, look at this!" kind of experience that's so wonderful in museums.

As institutional leaders, museum technology professionals need to be able to advocate for their work and explain to others how technology initiatives can help the museum. Digital projects such as building centralized repositories for collections information often involve working across institutional silos, building interdepartmental connections, and convincing others to participate. While serving as an evangelist for digital initiatives may not be explicitly part of one's job description, museum technology professionals need to be comfortable arguing for the support of their programs if their projects are to succeed, as Cathryn Goodwin explains:

> The most challenging and rewarding aspect of this work for me has always been this invisible piece, which is bringing along the rest of the institution. . . . You're required to build a bridge between the technology that not everyone has to understand and the benefits of that, and the people who are the content holders in their heads, or in their records, or in their work, and creating an environment where this work becomes a collaborative project that benefits the entire institution, and really proselytizing for the importance of centralizing information about works of art in a museum . . . trying to get all of those things to be consolidated into a central source of information that can create efficiencies for museums in everything they do, and again, that proselytizing piece around the museum is about the collection, and educating people about the collection, educating from the collection, and in order to do that, you have to have information about the collection . . . a centralized repository that makes the collections discoverable, so that others—researchers, students, the public—can know that they exist. And certainly now, this is how people know that collections exist in the first place. I think that's probably one of the things that I have done in my career, and I think most people who are doing the kind of work that I do, are charged with, but that isn't really in the job description. It's not in the job description that you need to be an incredible diplomat, and be able to bring people together around a common cause, and argue for your program.

Museum technology professionals in digital leadership positions need to advocate for their team internally as well as externally. Especially in large institutions, it is easy for people to be unaware of the technology expertise available to them in house. Diane Zorich describes advocating for the expertise of her mass digitization team at the Smithsonian Institution:

> People within the Smithsonian will go outside and say, "We need somebody to 3D scan something," but we have an in-house team that is stellar at that. They just didn't know it. So I'm always out there, trying to sell this group, even among the Smithsonian, especially among the Smithsonian actually, because it's a large organization. It has 6,000 people. You can't possibly know everybody. And you can't possibly know all the projects going on either, which is amazing, but it's also a liability, sometimes, especially with a team like mine, where we could help so many of these clients.

Serving as a champion for digital initiatives requires the ability to work across departments and bridge different communities. Our participants discussed the need to wear many hats and speak different languages, especially as they worked to bridge the gap between technology-oriented and non-technology-oriented groups. The most challenging aspect of any digital project tends not to be the technology, but the people involved with the project. Museum technology professionals who could work across silos, resolve conflicts, and gain buy-in from different communities found those skills in high demand. Douglas Hegley describes how his ability to communicate across professional communities led to his first job at the Metropolitan Museum of Art:

> I worked in the schizophrenia lab at the university, and I got myself betwixt the psychologists and some very early UX programmers. . . . The psychologists were trying to talk to the programmers about the pace at which this would happen or how to adjust it, but they couldn't speak the programming language. They just could not communicate. And I found myself in the middle of this, and it became this interesting niche for me. . . . The Chief Systems Officer at the Met offered me a job on the spot, I think, because I was talking about listening and communication and the need to support people who'd never used technology before . . . to think about working with other professionals, just like I did as an undergrad, who didn't really get it, but needed someone in between to help.

Diana Folsom similarly describes the importance of being a translator between different groups, and how that can support both technology initiatives and the voice of underserved populations:

> I tended to play the role of the translator or in-between person—between the high-tech guys and the regular staff in the museum. And that's still, I think,

> kind of the role I play. But now it's been infused at the Gilcrease Museum with my personal passions for learning about the content and bringing in Native peoples and underserved peoples to help us change the nature of our information of what we share about our collection.

In order to connect communities, museum technology professionals must understand both the technology and the culture of the institution in which they work. Domain knowledge is important when advocating for digital initiatives, and technical skills will not be enough if one does not also possess the museum perspective. Reflecting on his time at the Smithsonian, David Bridge reminds us that you cannot be a bridge between groups if you do not understand both sides:

> I had collected birds, I had done research with birds, working on a couple of books, so I knew how museum people thought, and the kinds of things that they wanted to do. . . . You might have somebody in Mammals who says, "I have this problem, I need something," and then I could say, "Well, the people in Paleobiology have the same issue, but they would put it in different words," and then I would take the consolidated, and expand it a little bit, and come up with a more generalized solution. . . . I had enough of a biology background. . . . Half the people in our I.T. unit have never been in a museum today. And I don't know how they can sympathize with and understand the issues when they don't have any experience with the professionals they're serving.

In order to get support for digital projects, museum technology professionals need to build consensus across multiple constituencies, including curators and administrators. This can be very difficult. Our participants shared many stories of times when they could have given up—having decided that they were never going to change this person's mind, or never going to get the director to sign off on their project, or never going to get this curator to participate—but instead they persevered and found the resources they needed to make their projects work. It is important to fight for that first experience, especially when trying to convince people to do something they have never done before, because until people see what you can accomplish, they will not really understand the argument you are making or the experience you are proposing. Silvia Filippini-Fantoni, reflecting on her time at the North Carolina Museum of Art, explains how one successful project can be the catalyst that leads to more successes in the future:

> How do we build a consensus around moving from content to experience? . . . I think that it very much depends on leadership, and what their thoughts and vision are about this. So, if they are on board, definitely, there's more consensus and it's easier to convince people. But honestly, the best results that I can get is seeing, when you actually get to implement one of these

experiences, how successful it is, and how people respond to it. So, the secret is really, create a room for creating an experience first. Evaluate the heck out of it, during the development, to make sure that the experience is as positive as you can have it, and look at the data after it's done. Like, I can tell you that in North Carolina, for instance, O'Keefe was a catalyst. We did it. It was very successful. People said that it was the best part of the exhibition. And that it made it easier to build consensus around implementing another experience afterwards. . . . When people saw it, it was like, "Oh my God, this is incredible," first of all, and second, when they looked at the evaluation results, it was a lot easier to build a consensus around doing more of that in the future.

The success or failure of digital initiatives also depended on the director's vision and institutional support. Museum technology professionals needed to have museum leadership on their side in order to accomplish their goals. Getting museum directors in your corner meant speaking a language that they understand and articulating the importance of technology for the museum. Director support was critical for project success. As Peter Samis explains, having support from the director was essential for successfully bringing technology into the galleries at SFMOMA:

> We were still testing out what technology we might bring to bear in the galleries, and we could do that because there was a Director and a Deputy Director who were firmly supportive. So the curators didn't really have a choice. . . . They couldn't just say "No technology in the gallery!"

Having the director on your side was also essential to finding the resources you needed to get projects started, especially in museums where funding was in short supply. Even a small amount of seed money to get projects started often provided museum technology professionals with the impetus they needed to find additional support in the future from other sources, such as federal funding agencies. Institutional support can allow one to start small, and then get further grant money to take projects to the next level. Rob Lancefield, discussing a digital imaging project at the Davison Art Center, explains how even a small token of support from the institution can make a huge difference in terms of long-term technology success:

> Happily, there was a really supportive Dean at Wesleyan who was able to direct one summer's worth of funding to us in 2013. That was something that really made all the difference, because I already had the project design roughed-out in my head. I was able to build that out more completely. And that then enabled us to write for IMLS grant support, and we were fortunate to get funding from the IMLS to run very similar projects—of course, each summer iterating a bit, fine-tuning things, but basically adopting the same model for three summers of that. And then subsequent to that, to do so for a second grant as well, that funded further imaging. And so, after that first

summer of a really scrappy startup mode, then we were able to turn that into a recurrent thing.

Naturally, as helpful as institutional support for seed funding can be, museum technology professionals need resources not just to start projects, but also to keep projects going. As Greg Albers explains, questions of longevity and sustainability trouble even successful projects:

> The Getty in 2009 launched the Online Scholarly Catalog Initiative, which was a multiyear initiative with eight museums . . . to explore the idea of putting their collection catalogs online. . . . In 2009, the question was: "Could these things even go online?" . . . The Online Scholarly Catalog Initiative wrapped up in 2015. At that point, all of the museums involved had published online successfully . . . but they identified a few remaining challenges. One was discoverability. Once we published these catalogs, how do people continue to find them? One was around longevity. . . . How do we sustain the practice of digital publishing within our museum? When the Getty's grant money goes away, how do we make sure that we can continue to publish books like this, when we can't continue to make hundreds of thousands of dollars of investment to publish these catalogs?

Sustainability for technology projects is difficult to achieve even at the best times, and finding the resources needed to support longevity can be tricky. As Deborah Howes explains, in some rare cases, you might find donors who are willing to endow major digital projects, such as the Heilbrunn Timeline of Art History at the Metropolitan Museum of Art:

> That prototype amount allowed us to build a 5,000-year history of the collection, primarily featuring the collection of the Met, but also including signature other pieces. It was an early addition to art history teaching, and as a result of that, everybody connected to it, and everyone continues to connect to it. It is the number one draw on the Metropolitan Museum of Art website, I'm told, today. . . . Before I left in 2009, it was honored with an endowment. It is the only electronic resource I know of in a museum that has its own endowment. The heirs of the Heilbrunn family decided that it had been so delightful for their parents to be part of this endeavor, that they gave it a very generous endowment, so it's still around today, and I think that's a lesson that we don't teach enough about how the sustainability of these projects really needs continuing funding, and care, and feeding.

Without the guarantee of continued funding, many digital projects face an uncertain future once funds that were initially provided to launch a project run out. This is especially true if the people who had been working on or advocating for the project leave along with the money. As Scott Sayre explains, one of the reasons that technology projects lack sustainability is that all too often, when a project's champions leave an institution, their project disappears as well:

> The dark side of museum technology is how much of it disappears when people move from Point A to Point B, and the person who was the advocate for it is no longer there, or there are political changes at the top of the organization. All these projects are pretty delicate, and it takes very little for a technology project to fade into the past without ongoing commitment and support. I think every museum technologist can tell war stories about things that they've done that were amazing in the past that you would have to search very hard for any evidence of them today. I had to admit to myself that the world I'm working in is very ephemeral, and most of my work will probably and has already disappeared, but still doesn't mean I don't get joy from it on a day-to-day basis.

The fact that so many digital initiatives in museums depend on the commitment and dedication of one technology worker pushing projects forward raises questions about the obligations of the institution to support those projects over the long term after that technology champion leaves. What is the institutional responsibility vis-a-vis technological innovation when so much depends on the contributions of one person? As Richard Rinehart argues, if technology projects, particularly experimental ones, are to have any chance for long-term sustainability, then the museum needs to find a way to provide ongoing institutional support for innovation:

> One of the lessons that I learned is just how much innovation comes from an individual evangelist in an institution pushing for something, and when that person leaves, that just stops. So you have this really sort of staccato rhythm of institutional innovation. Like Steve Dietz goes to the Walker Art Center and Boom! It's the center of the digital art world, and then he's gone, and then the brakes are on. . . . And to my mind, that's not a good place to be. I'm happy that the institutions allow for that kind of rapid change and experimentation, on the one hand. On the other hand, I feel, as institutions, especially long-term cultural heritage institutions, we should all be forward thinking in terms of interoperability and sustainability, not only in terms of our green footprint on the earth, but our information technology projects too. And if it's not going to be taken up, if it's not scalable . . . it leaves me questioning the role of the institution. What's the obligation of the institution in these scenarios, besides providing a time for the individual to do this, and the resources? The willingness to experiment is great, but I wonder about the conversation between the individual and the institution. . . . What's the institution's responsibility here? If I or somebody else on staff innovates and creates some terrific experiment, what is the institution's responsibility afterwards?

Providing this kind of stability, with long-term funding and ongoing support for digital initiatives in museums, is not a simple task. Keeping technology projects going is particularly difficult when your work is invisible to the people in charge, so accomplishing these goals is much easier if museum technology professionals are positioned within their institution to champion their work to museum leadership. As Jane Alexander explains, it is essential for the chief technology officer to have a seat at the table if technology projects are to succeed in museums:

> I started in 2010, and I had five directors by 2014. I was extremely lucky that they really understood the vision, and what we needed to do to move us into a different realm. . . . I always ask, who does the CTO report to—because it has to be at the table—and what's the budget, and what are your goals in the next five years for this department? That tells you a lot about whether this is going to be a success . . . and if they're ready to embrace a digital experience.

The more museum technology professionals moved from the server room to the board room, the more they realized that the field of museum computing was now a profession, with viable career paths to important leadership positions in museums. Instead of figuring things out as they went along, and stumbling into museum computing almost by chance, museum technology workers found themselves in an actual profession with opportunities for formal educational and professional development courses on the subject. Nik Honeysett describes the watershed moment when he realized that the field of museum computing was now a professional career:

> I think it was a Leicester student who had done this kind of formal analysis, and they were deconstructing the design of the Micro Gallery and saying, "Oh, you must have used this." And they had all these names of people . . . and I remember being massively impressed that there was actually discipline around it. Because then it still felt like we were making stuff up and just trying to figure it out. It wasn't generally accepted practice. It was just, "Well this feels right." You know, we'd test it. We'd bring in girlfriends and wives and cousins, and test it, and get their feedback. But I remember that was the moment when I realized that this was a career, if that makes sense. You know it was like, "Oh, this is real. There's a real course about it, and this is going to be in real jobs." Because at the time there weren't many people who were in real jobs in museums doing this stuff. And that was the moment where I was like, "Okay, I'm in a discipline." That was a watershed moment for me in where the industry was heading.

Museum technology professionals worked hard to professionalize their work within their own institutions. Dana Mitroff Silvers describes her efforts to professionalize the web development process at SFMOMA in the early 2000s:

> At SFMOMA, I was really interested in how to professionalize what we were doing because it was still pretty new. I was still doing a lot of the

> updates by hand. I don't think we had a content management system when I started. We had to use Dreamweaver templates to manage the website. I can't even remember if the collection was online. Maybe a section of it was online. These were the old days of this time.... I was there for 11 years. And a lot happened in 11 years. We did a couple of redesigns, and it was a real effort to start to professionalize the field and to recognize that this was more than just taking something from graphic design and marking it up in HTML and slapping it up there. There was so much that went into the web experience.

The desire to professionalize the field of museum computing evolved hand in hand with the importance of the museum's digital offerings. Matthew MacArthur describes his work to professionalize online projects at the National Museum of American History:

> One of the trends over the first ten years at the museum was our desire to kind of professionalize the work and the staffing around web projects.... We were trying to get above the level of early tinkering, and into this idea that if it's not something you would put on the wall of the museum, or on a banner on the outside of the museum, then it's not something that we want to publish on the website—that a website needs the same level of professionalism and care.... At that moment when our traffic crossed, when our digital presence started getting more traffic than our physical museum, at that point, everyone had to realize that more people see our website than the building.... We've started, with our leadership, using the language of the digital museum as a second museum. It has a presence, it has infrastructure, it has workflows, it has defined spaces, and it has real resource needs as much as having a second kind of museum campus.

Educational opportunities also helped museum technology professionals as they worked together to professionalize the field. Shelley Mannion discusses the importance of continuing education in the 2000s for defining the field and encouraging museum technology workers:

> I was in the inaugural class for the Technology-Enhanced Communication for Cultural Heritage program at the University of Lugano.... We produced CD-ROMs, we built websites, and for me, it was really the opportunity to spend time with some of the luminaries of the museum technology field, and really just absorb their approach to things.... It was a really fun, exciting time where there was a whole world of new practices that were going to define this era of consumer technology. Just the way that our lives were changing, and that people were researching this, and that there was a kind of a scientific side to it, as there was an aesthetic side.... It was such an interesting time in terms of what was happening in our industry, and we were hearing about it from the

> people who were the pioneers in a way. That's what it felt like for us. It was just such an incredible thing to have been a part of.

The chance to engage in professional workshops also helped bring museum technology professionals together to learn from each other and share best practices. Cathryn Goodwin recalls the importance of the workshops she attended in the 1990s, and how valuable these opportunities were for professionalizing the field of museum computing:

> I was really fortunate in those early days to be able to get involved in the MCN community, and I was in fact sent off in my early days at St. Louis to what was then called an Art and Architecture Thesaurus Workshop that was run by Elisa Lanzi and . . . Suzanne Warren, who worked with AAT early in her career, and Toni Petersen who really had been driving the development of the AAT, and it was all still books. It was books! It was volumes and volumes of reference, and this was prior to its adoption and stewardship by the Getty, so this was when the AAT was a project on its own. And I went to Chicago for a week-long conference on how to apply the thesaurus and authorities to museum cataloging, which was definitely fundamental in my career. Given that museum cataloging was not a field that had accredited training programs, these independent workshops and training programs were the ways that we learned how to do this work because there were no official training programs for this kind of work. . . . And following that, I was fortunate to be able to attend two different summer institutes for libraries, museums, and archives that the Getty hosted with UCLA. This was a very formative training program again for museum professionals in information technology, and that's where I first met Howard Besser, who was teaching us all about digital imaging. . . . It's been a really wonderful journey for me, being able to be in on the beginnings of all of these technologies, and the evolution of the field.

As the nature of museum computing changed over time, and the work of museum technology professionals increased in importance for institutions worldwide, new opportunities arose to reshape this position as innovation champions and leaders of digital initiatives. New ideas about the role of technology in museums encouraged museum technology professionals to develop new leadership skills and the digital mindset necessary to lead their institutions into a future where the use of computing will only become more essential to success. Given the importance of museum technology professionals for setting technology policies and supporting digital projects over the long term, it is critical that museum leadership invest not only in new technologies but also in the museum technology professionals who will be tasked with implementing those technologies and executing the museum's digital strategy. In this way, we can work together to encourage and inspire the next generation of digital leaders in museums.

SUGGESTIONS FOR FURTHER READING

Alexander, Jane, Anna Faxon, and Haley Kedziora. 2021. "From the Server Room to the Board Room: A Decade of Digital Transformation." In *Museums and the Web 2021*, edited by Nancy Proctor and Rich Cherry. Silver Spring, MD: Museums and the Web. https://mw21.museweb.net/paper/from-the-server-room-to-the-board-room-a- decade-of-digital-transformation/

Decker, Juilee, ed. 2015. *Technology and Digital Initiatives: Innovative Approaches for Museums*. Lanham, MD: Rowman and Littlefield.

Mu.SA Project. 2017. *Museum Professionals in the Digital Era: Agents of Change and Innovation*. Rome: Mu.SA Project. http://www.project-musa.eu/wp-content/uploads/2017/03/MuSA-Museum-professionals-in-the-digital-era-full-version.pdf

Schwartz, Mark. 2017. *A Seat at the Table: IT Leadership in the Age of Agility*. Portland, OR: IT Revolution.

Stein, Rob. 2017. *Museums and Digital Strategy Today*. Washington, DC: American Alliance of Museums. https://www.aam-us.org/2017/07/10/museums-and-digital-strategy-today/

Taormina, Francesca, and Sara Bonini Baraldi. 2022. "Museums and Digital Technology: A Literature Review on Organizational Issues." *European Planning Studies* 30 (9): 1676–1694.

Winesmith, Keir, and Susan Anderson. 2020. *The Digital Future of Museums: Conversations and Provocations*. Abingdon, Oxon: Routledge.

10

Professional Communities

> In the beginning, you know, you are a little alone in this, and one of the challenges was really to be able to sort of find a community of other people to talk to . . . to develop a common practice, develop common themes, and also common criteria, and a common place to support each other, and to validate work, which was pretty important at the time. —Oral History of Costis Dallas

The job of the museum technology professional can be a lonely one. With the exception of a few large and well-funded art museums that might employ many technology workers, the majority of museums have only a small number of employees—often only one person, assuming they have anyone at all—engaged in digital activities. When you are on your own to support the museum computing needs of your institution, when there is no one else in your organization who understands the nature of your work, where do you turn for support? Where do you turn for encouragement? Where do you turn to find a community of your peers? Prompted by a desire to escape this feeling of isolation and loneliness, and driven by the rapid pace of change as technological innovations reshaped the museum experience, museum technology professionals banded together to support each other in their work across institutions.

Our oral history participants frequently mentioned the importance of belonging to a professional network or community of museum technology workers who not only understand what you are trying to accomplish but can also help you articulate why it matters. Professional communities build connections between different groups, inspire new ideas, develop a sense of value, and provide access to a network of peers who can support you in your professional activities. The connections that were made across these professional communities led to powerful collaborations that helped solve problems and build relationships between museum technology professionals. Professional networks helped individual museum technology workers move from feeling like they had to do everything on their own to recognizing the importance of community networks for sharing resources and validating new ideas.

As the field of museum computing evolved, and more people kept pushing for innovation in museums, it was the power of community leadership, communities of practice, distributed problem-solving, multi-institutional consortia, and professional conferences that moved the field forward and shaped the future of the museum technology profession. As Greg Albers explains in his oral history, being part of a community is essential for driving innovation with technology:

> Museum technology doesn't happen in a bubble. It's technical work, it requires special skill . . . but the underlying drivers of that work are these bigger strategies and stances and tactics and ideas that float around the community that are really driving the work we do.

Being part of a professional community was central to the careers of many museum technology professionals. The ability to connect with other like-minded professionals offered strength in numbers and helped them share important knowledge, strategies, and ideas. Costis Dallas describes the power of community and the importance of being part of a network of peers:

> There is this community that really allows people to derive strength from interaction with others. . . . Those experiences—all our conferences and bar drinks, and after-session conversations—were so central to what has been happening in the field. . . . I enjoy being part of this process, and knowing all these people, and feeling part of that community. . . . It's really the centrality of community, and the centrality of common knowledge, and common perceptions that are created by people when they talk to each other, and when they apply things in practice.

One of the ways that museum technology professionals looked to build community was online through computer-mediated communication. Many museum technology workers were members of early online communities which helped them connect over the Internet to address shared challenges despite being physically located around the world. David Bridge provides an example of distributed problem-solving in online communities in the early 1980s:

> I was running a VAX computer at the Smithsonian, and we were part of the BITNET network . . . and on BITNET listservs, which are scattered around the world. So I come in, in the morning, turn on the computer at 8:00, and there's this email message from this guy in Crete in the Mediterranean, who says, "I've got this hardware, I've got this software, I've got this problem, I've got this communications, and it doesn't work." That's 8:00 in the morning. So later

> in the day, somebody from California pipes in and says, "I've got exactly the same hardware, and I've got exactly the same problem." And lo and behold, by the time I went to bed, a guy from Singapore said, "This is the solution to your problem. . . ." I know we take that kind of for granted nowadays, that if you get an error message that you've never seen, you just put it into Google and you'll get an answer, but that was kind of an eye opener back then, and what really impressed me and still impresses me, is that I am absolutely certain that the three people that I mentioned, they never knew each other or never met ever in real life, but the guy in Crete has a problem, and it's validated, and then the solution comes from somebody else, and they've never met each other.

Solving technology problems on your own can be frustrating, so just finding someone with whom you share challenges and problems in common can help provide peace of mind. Tina Shah explains how online communities of museum technology professionals can support each other by participating in online software forums:

> Last Friday, I was working on a particular thing for just one too many days. I was like, why is this not working? All I was trying to do was get some text to display on the screen. I sort of knew why it wasn't, but I couldn't quite figure out how to get it to work. I tried many different things. I probably tried the same thing several different times. . . . And I'm so tired of working on this. Like, this is just driving me insane. But you know, I put a question up on the software forum, and I was like, "Look, this is what I'm trying to do. . . ." And then I switched gears and worked on something else. I was like, "Let's see what happens. Let's see if I can get an answer to this by Monday." And I checked on Saturday and found an answer. Tried it, and thankfully it worked. But I'm just reminded that, "Okay, maybe you should have asked this question a little earlier before you started feeling like you were going to have a nervous breakdown."

Online communities can also provide a safe, supportive space for museum technology workers. Lori Byrd-McDevitt explains how museum social media managers started using social media to provide a safe space online for distributed communication and shared problem-solving:

> We were just chatting, a few of us, and we were like, "Why don't we have a space where we can be more supportive of one another, more proactively supportive, have each other's backs, share resources, and just have fun?" It's so hard being a social media manager. Even back then, it was hard, and it's even gotten way harder. So we started a Facebook Group called Museum Social Media Managers. And that was 2013, and it has grown and grown and grown and grown. . . . It's definitely a safe space. . . . It really has become a place where we've collaborated, and actually made an impact. . . . We've created countless social media campaigns across museums nationally,

> internationally, theme-based, organization-based . . . campaigns that had true impact and were organized in our group. And fun things, like in the moment, because we have a group like that . . . we can say, "Hey, you guys want to have a museum snowball fight? #museumsnowballfight." And then we do, and then it gets on major tech magazines because, "All the museums are having a snowball fight. That's worth covering," because we have that type of impact. . . . It's to the point where people have said, "Is there a secret society of social media managers and museums somewhere that are organizing these things?" And we're just like, "We've won. We won the Internet."

Another way that museum technology professionals looked to build community was through joining professional organizations like the Museum Computer Network or the Museums Computer Group. These professional communities provided opportunities for museum technology professionals to share resources, discuss ideas, and build connections that cut across different institutions. Rob Lancefield, for example, describes the importance of being part of professional communities that include multiple museums:

> I had found it increasingly valuable to become more and more active in MCN, the Museum Computer Network, serving in some leadership roles and finding in that organization a museum technology community that obviously transcends any one museum, because there were people there from all different museums.

As the needs of museum technology professionals changed along with the technologies they were supporting in museums, the nature of these professional communities changed as well. Cathy Heller describes the evolution of the Museum Computer Network (MCN) from a physical network of institutional members relying on shared software on mainframe computers to a professional community of individual members working with many different collections management systems on personal computers:

> The Museum Computer Network was born out of a cooperative computing project in the New York City area in 1967, under the direction of my father. The organization began as an informal grouping of museums with the goal of automating registration records. With funding from the New York Council on the Arts, MCN developed a prototype mainframe network that was shared by participants from 1968 to 1971. When the funding ended in 1971, MCN was formally incorporated as a nonprofit organization that has since attracted members from around the world. . . . Museums could join to receive consultation and advice about computerization projects or as full members with access to MCN software and hardware resources. . . . Originally conceived as a physical computer network, MCN was to become part of the growing professional network of related cultural heritage computerization projects. . . . During this period, MCN began to regularly host annual conferences. Initially, the

conferences were focused on issues relevant for GRIPHOS users. . . . Towards the end of the '70s, the operating systems found on IBM's mainframe computer were quickly becoming obsolete, foreshadowing the end for GRIPHOS, which had been tightly tied to those operating systems. . . . The computer revolution, which was changing the business world in the 1980s, was reflected in the rapid changes occurring at MCN as well. Cheaper desktop computers, along with more accessible software, made incorporating computers into their operations more realistic for some museums. . . . A different audience was looking for MCN for advice on computerization and for an affinity group of like-minded museum professionals. . . . During MCN's mainframe period, only institutions could become members of the organization. Reflecting the change to personal computing, the organization opened up membership to individuals for the first time in 1981. The organization soon attracted a broad spectrum of the museum community using a variety of different approaches to automating their collections. . . . Throughout the '80s, MCN moved further away from the original vision of a centralized system, choosing instead to emphasize the development of data standards that would allow the exchange of museum information between systems that met local needs. These efforts retained the spirit of the original network without forcing museums to adopt a single application or hardware platform.

The annual meetings of the Museum Computer Network provide an excellent example of how these organizations contributed to the development of the field of museum computing. Many of our oral history participants were involved with the Museum Computer Network and witnessed its evolution from a physical network to a professional community. Howard Besser describes a key moment in the evolutionary history of MCN:

> What I felt was a real turning point in museum computing was the MCN meeting in New Orleans in 1986. That was a real turning point. We had vendors who were showing that you wouldn't have to have a mainframe computer to do museum computing. There were vendors doing things on workstations. . . . That MCN meeting, I think, really, really set the stage for the future. In a way, you could say there was MCN before that meeting, and there was MCN after. And MCN after was much more populist, much more doable, much more affordable. . . . It felt like this was opening MCN to a much broader constituency.

Chuck Patch echoes these comments about 1986 being a pivotal year for MCN:

> The MCN meeting in '86 was my first year working in a museum in an official capacity. . . . At that point, there were just a handful of museums who had automated anything, and we were probably at this point, the only history museum in the country that had a system up and running for collections management. . . . The entire group fit into one modestly sized banquet room at a hotel in the French Quarter. There couldn't have been more than 50 people

> in attendance, maybe 60, but they didn't even fill up the room, and the big innovation for that year was an exhibitors' space, and this was a maybe 200 square foot area in the back of the room where pretty much every vendor that dealt with museum automation was showing their stuff. There were maybe five or six groups that had systems set up, and of course, it was all database stuff. There was virtually no image stuff going on. In fact, that was the fun thing when Alan Newman showed up with his Mac, which was like really exotic in 1986, and he was showing these nice color images that he had on a database that was running on a separate drive, and you almost had to beat your way through the crowd to get to his table to see what he was doing. At the same meeting, that was when Howard Besser presented his famous T-shirt collection. . . . He had a digital database that documented all of his T-shirts . . . and of course, he was wearing his T-shirt.

The more accessible these professional organizations became to a wide range of individuals and institutions, the more they could help shape the work of museum technology professionals. Professional organizations like the American Association of Museums, for example, established standing committees such as the Media and Technology Committee to help support the work of museum technology professionals and bring individuals together by organizing panels, sessions, and speakers at AAM's Annual Meetings. Indeed, one of the most important contributions of these professional organizations to the field was the opportunity they provided their members to meet each other at their annual conferences. Mia Ridge, for instance, recalls attending her first Museums Computer Group conference:

> While I was at the Museum in London, I found the Museums Computer Group in the U.K., and that was brilliant. It was like finding people that knew what problems I faced, who were familiar with all angles of the kinds of issues, in terms of the technology, the people, the institutions that museums are in terms of their resistance to change and innovation, but also their drive, their passion, and their under-resourcing, and all those kinds of common issues. So that was a really good moment.

Attending professional conferences brought museum technology professionals together with like-minded individuals from different museums around the world, including people that they otherwise might never have the chance to meet. As Lori Byrd-McDevitt explains, the opportunity to "find your people" was an important benefit for conference participants:

> It was MCN, and I'd found my people. And it was a whole bunch of other nerds that were just so nice and so welcoming, and they just happened to be from the Met, and the Smithsonian, and all these places, but they were not intimidating. It was amazing.

Thanks to the benefits that professional conferences offered the museum technology community, a variety of additional conferences naturally developed over time, bringing the community together around other important themes, such as Museums and the Web, and MuseumNext. Jonathan Bowen describes speaking at the very first Museums and the Web conference in front of a crowd of 400 people in Los Angeles in 1997:

> I got invited to the first Museums and the Web conference that David Bearman and Jennifer Trant set up in Los Angeles. I felt like royalty because he said, "You're coming along. You're going to be invited as the honorary chair, give a talk, etc." And he put me up in this, for me, at that time, as an academic, amazing Los Angeles hotel, in one of the top suites in it, and so on. But then he said, "You, as the honorary chair, we want you to say a few words." But he literally only told me that half an hour before. And I was used to little meetings, you know, a hundred would have been a huge meeting of people for me. The first Museums and the Web had 400 people! So, for me, not really having prepared much, and he says, "Stand up and say something!" And at that time, I wasn't quite as used to speaking in front of an audience as I am now, so it was a slight nightmare for me, but I really enjoyed the conference, and obviously kept going.

Many of our oral history participants told us that one of the reasons they kept going to these conferences was because of the community they found there. Much of the staying power of these professional organizations was due to the wide range of people who belonged to them and attended their meetings. Seb Chan describes the mix of people and the diversity of ideas that he would encounter at museum technology conferences:

> When I would go to Museums and the Web, there would be transformational moments because the networks that people were part of were really good. You'd chat with people, you'd go to this session, you catch up with them, there were good mixes of people.

As Rob Lancefield explains, museum technology conferences provided a space that helped everyone develop their work together, and kept the field moving forward:

> It's been kind of a mutually nurturing and restorative sort of space to be in from time to time, and to realize, "Okay, we're all in this together, each in our way, each in our institution." And not only can we share some things that we've learned with each other, but we can, by having those conversations, come to understand that there are a lot of us who are finding a way through these not just technical things, but the organizational positionings of those technical things, and the sorts of conversations that can be challenging to find ways through that to keep that work sufficiently resourced. . . . We are

> sometimes most visible to one another across institutions, and that wider community can be a key resource in keeping us going. Which is to say, in regard to the actual, like, "What is it that we do?" aspects of things, there's less invisibility sometimes when we walk out of our museum and talk with people who are at other museums.

Belonging to a professional museum technology community also helped individuals develop a sense of value for their own contributions to the field—something that they did not always get from their own institutions. Having access to a network of peers who are able to acknowledge our contributions within a shared community can help support us and keep us going even when we do not receive that recognition from our colleagues at home. Shelley Mannion, for example, describes the differences she observed between how her work with virtual reality technologies at the British Museum was received externally vs. internally:

> The frustration, I think, that a lot of us felt working in digital in museums is that we had established profiles externally amongst our peers at other institutions, but when we came back to our home institution, nobody cared. Nobody really valued that work, and they also didn't recognize the excellence of the work that was taking place in digital. They had no sense of how that work was breaking ground and being hugely significant within our field.

Belonging to these professional communities, attending these conferences, and participating in these professional forums kept many museum technology professionals from leaving the field of museum computing. Rob Lancefield, for example, explains the importance of the museum technology community to his own career:

> Those forums have been so important for a sense of community that, thinking hypothetically, were there no such a thing as MCN or Museums and the Web, I bet that I would have, at some point or other, walked away from this kind of work over the years.

Richard Rinehart echoes these comments, explaining how the community spirit that he found in the museum technology profession encouraged him to remain in the museum field:

> At the end of the '90s, when I was involved with MCN and the larger museum community, and I was teaching at UC Berkeley, I faced a split in my career, where I could teach, and do new media art, and go the academic route. . . . And really, the one most influential factor that took me in the other route, the route of staying within museums, was at the end of the day, I thought, "You know what? I like museum people better. I like going to museum conferences and

hanging out with them better. . . . After the day's worth of seminars, we'd go to the hotel bar and have some drinks and talk about metadata standards, and transfer protocols, and all this invisible technology. . . . There was a real spirit of community and collaboration during that period, and it was really special."

That spirit of community and collaboration did more than inspire individuals; it brought the entire museum technology professional community together to solve problems that were bigger than any one particular museum. Collaborative projects pursued by consortia of museums were instrumental in moving the field of museum computing forward, often prompted by important new technological developments. Eleanor Fink, for example, explains how the rise of the "Information Superhighway" led to the creation of several important museum collaborations:

> We all were pioneers in the early days trying to figure out and come up with recommendations to create documentation standards, but when the Internet came into being—I was at the Getty—it all started moving very fast. The Clinton administration took a keen interest in the Internet, especially Al Gore, and there was all this talk about the Information Superhighway. And when they talked about it, they didn't seem to understand it was not just about libraries or how it might affect the broader humanities and museum community. . . . So, AHIP, the Art History Information Program, tried to step in at that time, and help the administration understand that they should also use the word "museum" when they talk about the Information Superhighway. That effort in itself went on to the thought, "Well, we probably should have a presence in Washington, D.C., where policies are made, and that would be important." That led to NINCH, the National Initiative for Networked Cultural Heritage, to be able to stay on top of discussions that were going on in Washington, D.C., about the Internet, and to inform others that this was happening, and also to inform the people who create policy what the needs are of the cultural heritage and museum communities.

Projects like the Art History Information Program and the National Initiative for Networked Cultural Heritage were extremely influential and guided the development of metadata standards and new methods for sharing information resources. It is difficult for one institution working alone to effect change, and museum consortia can often accomplish things that individual museums cannot do on their own. Eleanor Fink explains the power of working together to solve problems through collaboration:

> It wasn't the Getty alone . . . it was a collaboration with other key organizations that resulted in being able to accomplish things. The idea of working with other organizations, I think is a very essential way to do these things, rather than just one institution. And that was really what was so exciting about working at the Getty. If there was a problem to be solved, you could bring together

> the best people and have a discussion and try to solve that problem. There are few organizations that can do that. When I worked at the Smithsonian, people came to see me even from other countries to find out what we were doing at the Smithsonian, and they sometimes were a little bit disappointed because we were prestigious and we were important, but the Smithsonian has limited resources. The Getty, on the other hand, had the resources to be able to convene and be a leader if they wanted to. . . . It really is a synergy that comes about by being active in organizations like the Museum Computer Network and the flexibility to be able to meet and convene people to discuss these things. That's what seeds vision.

Consortial projects were particularly important when solving problems that crossed national borders. The development of international metadata standards, for instance, provides a good example of the types of problems that require a collaborative approach. Eleanor Fink shares a story about the creation of Object ID, an international standard for describing stolen works of art:

> I was in Washington, D.C. at the FBI/Interpol headquarters—they share an office here in Washington—and at that very moment while I was there, a report came in about a work of art that had been stolen from a museum in the Netherlands. I was excited that this could happen while I was there, and I asked, "What are the next steps?" The person who I was seeing said, "Well, first we have to translate the report, and it's 15 pages long. It's the official curatorial record from the museum." And I thought, "Wait a minute, by the time this information is circulated to police worldwide, the thief could easily transport the stolen item across borders." Also, a 15-page report is not going to help a law enforcement officer like a customs official determine if something in front of him is the item described on 15 pages. What is needed is a very simple and precise description to easily identify the item, and not a 15-page certificate that you have to leaf through, you know, and figure out if this is the same. The goal was simple identification. What is the essential information that uniquely describes a piece of cultural property that the police or customs officials could use? That was the impetus. And then of course, came the challenge of building trust and getting key organizations involved.

Getting international organizations to agree to share information across national borders was a major challenge, but building an alliance of institutions willing to share data in a common format can have important, long-term outcomes for museum collections. Eleanor Fink continues the story, explaining the leadership efforts required to coordinate the development of Object ID:

> I first went to ICOM, then I went to UNESCO, then I went to the Council of Europe, then I went to Interpol, then I went to the United States Information Agency. . . . It was very difficult to get them to agree, because they competed with each other. ICOM said, "We're handling looting and theft." And the

> Council of Europe said, "We're handling looting and theft." And so forth. So, finally, I said, "Don't you realize this is much bigger than any one organization? We really need to band together to solve this problem." They finally agreed to form an alliance. . . . We sent surveys out to 32 countries to say, "Tell us how you document and send us that information." Out of that came an analysis that said, "Okay, out of these hundreds of ways of documenting, everyone has agreed on all of these categories. These twelve categories are the same across all these different methods of documentation." And that slowly became Object ID. . . . It's the core of the Interpol database and Carabinieri database in Italy. . . . Object ID is also the core of the Art Loss Register, and the U.S. Army handbook on reported endangered cultural heritage—so that when they go into areas where there is destruction of cultural property, they use Object ID to do reports.

These difficulties naturally were not limited to international efforts; convincing museums to agree to work together in the first place, no matter where in the world they were located, was often a challenge. Howard Besser explains how the success of museum consortial projects like the Museum Education Site Licensing Project (MESL) frequently depended on getting museum directors involved firsthand so that they could communicate the importance of these collaborative projects for their institutions:

> The Museum Education Site Licensing Project was a very elaborate one. It involved 14 different institutions, seven collections and seven universities. When we had meetings, which we had at least twice a year, those meetings had at least two representatives from each organization. . . . That meant that we had a minimum of 28 people at each of these meetings plus administrators. And there was a steering committee, which consisted of myself and Cliff Lynch representing the educational community, and David Bearman and Max Anderson representing the museum community. . . . Max was someone who was really critical in arm-twisting other museum directors to make this into a priority. He wasn't involved in the actual ongoing management administration functions, but he was really critical at certain points, intervening and trying to make things happen. . . . At one point we were looking at the application for the Houston Museum of Fine Art, and we were really concerned about something in their application, so he went to the phone, called his office, got someone to look at his Rolodex, and he called the director of that museum and kind of pressured him into making sure that they could indeed perform what we were expecting them to perform. That's just a sample of how Max really worked on this.

Once these consortial projects were established, however, they grew quickly and inspired additional collaborations and consortial projects. Howard Besser explains how the success of the Museum Education Site Licensing Project led directly to the development of several new projects, such as AMICO, the Art Museum Image Consortium:

> Mellon gave us a healthy sum of money to evaluate MESL with an eye towards putting something like that into place. They were constantly pushing us to focus on cost, and we were more interested in the mechanistic part. . . . We came out with an evaluation of the cost and use of digital images online . . . and that eventually became a planning model for Mellon's service that they created called Artstor. . . . The agreement was that MESL would last till 1998, and when we got to about 1997, everyone was worried about what was going to happen in 1998, when the contracts were up. Would all the museums continue to let these universities use the images? Would they want to charge for them? What would happen? And at that point, about '97, I would say, David Bearman started working on what became AMICO, and plotting out how AMICO would work. So the core for AMICO came from the museum side of MESL.

Consortial projects brought institutions together to work on solving common problems, like developing metadata standards that can work across different types of collections. Layna White explains how initiatives like the Museums and the Online Archive of California project were instrumental in establishing common data structures for museums, libraries, and archives:

> MOAC, the Museums and the Online Archive of California project, ran roughly from 1999 to 2007, and it had lots of good funding from the IMLS. . . . At its core, MOAC was about bringing together information about art, archives, and library collections into a shared space . . . the Online Archive of California, which is hosted by the University of California. . . . We were led by the Berkeley Art Museum / Pacific Film Archive, and that was Rick Rinehart and Gunter Waibel. . . . The challenge was that traditionally museums, archives, and libraries used different data structures for describing our collections, so what MOAC partners were really wanting to do is to explore and to experiment. The idea on the table was, could we all use the same data structure standard from the archive community to describe our collections and describe the things within our diverse collections? Specifically, we were experimenting with the idea of using the EAD, the Encoded Archival Description, to bring our stuff together into this shared space. And that, at the time, was a super novel idea and experiment. And in fact, that experiment yielded content that remains visible today in the Online Archive of California.

Belonging to consortial projects was particularly valuable for smaller museums that might not otherwise have the resources to engage in these activities. As Layna White explains, participating in consortial projects helped the Grunwald Center for the Graphic Arts put their collections data online in ways that they would not have been able to do on their own:

> One of the remarkable things that happened in this project was the Grunwald, at the time having really very limited in-house I.T. support, was able to get content into the Online Archive of California, in large part because of a tool that the Berkeley Art Museum team built. . . . And I don't think that the Grunwald would have been able to participate in a project like this without having a tool such as this that they made. So that made it super, super easy. . . . That project literally jump-started the Grunwald's ability to get a little bit of its collection on the web. That partnership really was key to getting that collection, at least part of it, onto the web.

Often the most important outcomes from collaborative projects were not the specific tools or technologies they developed, but the intangible lessons learned about the role of digital in museums. Participating in consortial projects helped museum professionals learn how to think digitally, apply technology carefully, and develop digital literacy skills. Deborah Howes, for example, describes how participating in the Museum Education Consortium in the late 1980s changed the way museum educators thought about the use of technology in museums:

> The Museum Education Consortium was a really early grant in the '80s from the Pew Foundation that encouraged seven museums with collections of impressionism to band together and make some kind of interactive digital experience . . . immersive experiences that were designed for K-12. . . . The value of that project was that the Boston Museum of Fine Arts, the New York Metropolitan Museum, the Brooklyn Museum of Art, the National Gallery of Art, the Art Institute of Chicago—those heads of education were taught to think digitally. And they went on to create and support, within their institutions, at a moment where it was really early to do so, all sorts of innovation that happened as a result of that. This is something that's wrong, I think, right now, with the way funding happens. Very often, we get funded for projects, but we should really be funded for professional development, or we should be funded for positions, because that's where the real change happens. . . . Whoever was lucky enough to mentor these leaders of their education departments like me had a lot of impetus and inspiration to go forth and do good things in the digital world, but we were just a handful. And I think that's something we really, really, really need to think about now, which is why I'm involved with MCN, spreading digital literacy, and just comfort. . . . I learned a lot being involved with that.

Consortial projects also helped museum professionals develop common frameworks that continue to shape the way museums share digital information resources today. Tina Shah, for example, describes the development of the International Image Interoperability Framework (IIIF), which allows museums to share digital images across institutional boundaries in ways that encourage and support open-access initiatives:

> One of the initiatives that I'm part of and really excited about is the IIIF Initiative. It's a software and hardware framework that enables institutions to share their media. I think a majority of institutions use it to share their images. There's a lot of work going on trying to create a protocol that is used by all institutions, the same protocol to be able to share their media, whether it's images, 3D models, videos, etc., and to share them in a way where someone from another institution could just grab that true Renoir image and not have to search all over the Internet for it. And to be able to use it to bring into another application where they can study it, annotate it, and share their research with other institutions. I feel like that initiative can be so useful not just for art historians, but also for educators. If I was an art history teacher, I could go to these different institutions and be able to access the media, and teach a curriculum about French Impressionism, and point out different details of artworks that I get to share with the students.

Time and again, we heard our oral history participants discuss the importance of participating in museum consortia and learning from collaborative projects that transcend multiple institutions. As Diana Folsom stated, consortial projects truly drove the field of museum computing forward:

> These consortial projects—AMICO was the first I was involved in—they helped us understand what the issues were and how to do things that we didn't know how to do. There were usually so few of us in technology, even in the larger museums, that we didn't know who to talk to. So this was a way to share information, to get to the experts that we would not be able to get to or pay for or even know about. . . . It was really the consortial projects that enabled me, and probably all of us in art museums, to begin to understand and learn how to digitize our collections, how to catalog, how to do this thing. So those consortial projects, I think, are key, were key, and they continue to be key and pivotal in the progress that we make in our institutions.

As we look into the future of museum computing, it is important to realize that even as the technologies we use change, the problems we are trying to solve remain the same—problems of sharing our collections resources, improving our ability to reach our audiences, and working together to enhance the museum experience for everyone. Belonging to a professional community can help museum technology professionals reach their goals, share lessons learned, and solve problems together through the power of conferences, consortia, and other communities of practice. We are stronger together than we are separately. Working together in professional networks, museum technology professionals will be able to guide their institutions in the adoption and strategic use of emerging technologies to meet their museums' missions.

SUGGESTIONS FOR FURTHER READING

Fink, Eleanor. 1999. "The Getty Information Institute: A Retrospective." *D-Lib Magazine* 5 (3). http://www.dlib.org/dlib/march99/fink/03fink.html

Knight Foundation. 2020. *Digital Readiness and Innovation in Museums: A Baseline National Survey*. https://knightfoundation.org/reports/digital-readiness-and-innovation-in-museums/

Lave, Jean, and Etienne Wenger. 1991. *Situated Learning: Legitimate Peripheral Participation*. Cambridge: Cambridge University Press.

Marty, Paul F., Barbara J. Soren, and Jackie Armstrong. 2013. "Building Community among Museum Information Professionals: The 2011 MCN Community Survey." *Museum Management and Curatorship* 28 (4): 394–412.

McClung, Patricia, and Christie Stephenson, eds. 1998. *Images Online: Perspectives on the Museum Educational Site Licensing Project*. Los Angeles: Getty Research Institute.

Rinehart, Richard. 2003. "MOAC: A Report on Integrating Museum and Archive Access in the Online Archive of California." *D-Lib Magazine* 9 (1). http://www.dlib.org/dlib/january03/rinehart/01rinehart.html

Snydman, Stuart, Robert Sanderson, and Tom Cramer. 2015. "The International Image Interoperability Framework (IIIF): A Community and Technology Approach for Web-based Images." In *Proceedings of the Society for Imaging Science and Technology Archiving Conference*, 16–21. https://library.imaging.org/archiving/articles/12/1/art00005

Trant, Jennifer, David Bearman, and Kelly Richmond. 2000. "Collaborative Cultural Resource Creation: The Example of the Art Museum Image Consortium." In *Museums and the Web 2000*, edited by David Bearman and Jennifer Trant, 39–52. Pittsburgh, PA: Archives & Museum Informatics. http://www.archimuse.com/mw2000/papers/trant/trant.html

Wilson, Kathleen S. 1991. "Multimedia Design Research for the Museum Education Consortium's Museum Visitors Prototype." In *Hypermedia and Interactivity in Museums*, edited by David Bearman, 26–34. Pittsburgh: Archives & Museum Informatics.

Yasaitis, Kelly E. 2005. "Object ID: A Model of Global Collaboration." *Museum Management and Curatorship* 20 (1): 21–39.

11

Changing Mindsets

> We learned a lot about why people use museum websites. I'd been doing museum websites for like ten years by that point, but in doing that study, I realized maybe I'd been doing it all wrong. I had focused on the wrong people. I was focused on the museum. I wasn't focused on the users. . . . That really changed my perspective, from being focused internally . . . to really looking outside. —Oral History of Marty Spellerberg

As their roles and responsibilities evolved over the past six decades, museum technology professionals changed the way museums engaged with their audiences in person and online. Prompted by new ideas about the importance of data-driven evaluations and user-centered design, museum technology professionals shifted the focus of their efforts from the museum and its needs to the museum's visitors and their expectations. This change in mindset drew upon evolving philosophies about the work of museum professionals and the role of the museum in the life of the visitor that helped institutions embrace new technologies and recognize the potential of museum computing to support the museum's overarching goals and objectives.

New ways of thinking about the visitor experience, and the difference that museums make in the lives of those who use museum information resources, led to several important cultural shifts regarding how museum technology professionals approached audience engagement and visitor outreach efforts. These new approaches included developing a culture of audience evaluation and data-driven assessments, with new metrics for measuring engagement and determining user needs; a culture of iterative design and learning from failure, with new methods for agile design and rapid testing; and a culture of user experience and human-centered design, with new techniques for engaging end users in the development of new technologies. Central to each of these cultural shifts was the recognition that the museum should have a presence in the lives of its visitors, whether they are physically in the museum or not.

With that recognition came new ideas about the museum's role when interacting with visitors, and new methods for meeting information needs. The more museum professionals learned about how their visitors used digital information resources, the more their attention shifted from thinking about the visitor from the perspective of the museum to thinking about the museum from the perspective of the visitor. Paul Marty explains the significance of this shift in perspective for the museum profession in his oral history:

> This is about making that transition from thinking about the visitor in the life of the museum, to the museum in the life of the visitor. The library world has been dealing with this for decades as well—if all you look at in a library is the record of the books that circulate, then you miss 95 percent of everything that's going on in the library. And it's the same thing in the museum world. We have to look at all the roles that museums play in the lives of our visitors, not just what they do when they walk through the door, and that's a difficult shift in perspective to make.

Embracing this shift in perspective is challenging in part because it requires extra effort on the part of museum professionals. Marty Spellerberg discusses the importance of museums engaging in the work required to understand their visitors' needs and motivations, and to demonstrate to their visitors the relevance of the museum in their own lives:

> In my view, we're making the audience do work that we should be doing. They have to make the association between the program that we're presenting and how that's relevant to their life. And the only reason we get away with it is because our programs are so compelling. But really, we should be taking on that burden, and understanding what's going on in their lives, what they're motivated by, and presenting our offerings as fulfillment of their needs . . . so that the visitor doesn't have to.

Helping museum visitors understand the relevance of the museum and its resources also means speaking a language that the museum's visitors understand. Jeff Gates explains the need to focus on two-way conversations when museums interact with their visitors:

> Those of us who were invested in the transformations that technology was bringing to the museum were trying to convey these changes to our coworkers. We were going from the traditional one-way conversation between the experts and our visitors to more of a two-way conversation. Even today, that's still a challenge: thinking of our visitors, not just as consumers of our content, but also people with valuable opinions. . . . I've always been interested in making sure that we're understood when we talk about ideas. If you want to be heard, one of my philosophies is to talk to people in ways they will hear you. Even if those ideas are complicated and variegated, there are ways to convey

that information in ways our public will understand, and in ways they can react.

Putting all of these philosophies together can be a powerful tool for museum technology professionals who are designing technology-enhanced experiences to engage visitors in new ways. Andrea Ledesma shares an example in her oral history of how the Field Museum combined visitor research methods, audience engagement techniques, and user experience practices to design and develop a chatbot for Máximo, the world's largest dinosaur:

> Máximo at the Field Museum is a touchable cast of the world's largest dinosaur ever discovered. . . . There was a very generous gift that came to the museum to promote this particular new specimen fossil, and knowing that we wanted to do something digital with it, the ask fell to our team, and we talked about SUE the T. Rex on Twitter . . . but that's a path that's well worn. . . . So then we started thinking like, "Well, how else might someone want to interact with a dinosaur?" The chatbot came up pretty early, like, what if we did this? . . . We then went to our Audience Insights and Research team, basically with the question, "We want to do a chatbot. We don't know if audiences are into it. How can we figure this out? Can you help us survey some folks about how they might want to learn about Máximo, or interact with Máximo if presented the opportunity?"

Designing an interactive experience like this for the first time involves a certain degree of risk, which underscores the importance of conducting research to figure out how to create an experience that works well for museum visitors. Andrea Ledesma explains the audience research they conducted as part of training their chatbot to answer visitor questions:

> We had a really awesome intern at the time, Sarah Anderson, and one of her final projects was to help us think about questions that people might want to ask the dinosaurs. She spent a day in Stanley Field Hall, the Field Museum's large open space, and just watched folks and looked at Máximo, and she's like, "Where are his feet?" Like, they were missing. And then, Caitlin Kearney on our team was like, "People always ask about the bathroom, so Máximo, because he's so big, obviously he's going to know where the bathrooms are. He sees everything from up there." So, it's like "Okay, what if we give them fun dino facts, along with some customer service tips, and let it run?" . . . Much of the work was essentially doing a map of all the content and thinking about what topics would he respond to? How would he respond to these things? How would people ask these sorts of questions? And how are they connected to each other? . . . And then from there, we just kept on testing it, both with visitors in Stanley Field Hall and our own staff because, of course, the more questions you ask a chatbot, the smarter it'll be, which was especially important because Máximo is a conversational chatbot.

Researching how museum visitors engage with artifacts through interactive technologies such as chatbots also demonstrates the importance of thinking about the museum visit from the visitor's perspective. Andrea Ledesma explains how lessons learned from this project challenged their assumptions about the kind of experience visitors want from the museum:

> When we launched Máximo, people loved him, and we were really glad to see the uptake. . . . Not to say that Máximo is human, but I did find that people really responded to a very humanesque voice, like stories and responses from the Field Museum with this product. . . . There's just something very joyful about that. I think museums spend so much time talking about how we are active community spaces that bring people together, and that is true, in many ways, but also the Field Museum is filled with literal dead things . . . so there's something to be said that this fossil cast in front of you is actually responding to the questions that you have, and hearing it straight from them, you buy into the allure of it, and it's just delightful. I think people resonated with that. . . . We learned a lot too about basic visitor services questions. . . . I made a joke about, "Where are the bathrooms?" We're like, "Maybe we should also throw in one about coat check in there, and our hours and tickets, because working in a museum, these are just things that you know about your space, and you have to remember that you are not your audience, and those sorts of logistics aren't always easy to navigate, so you always want to make it easy for people to come into your space. Beyond that though, we learned a lot about how we converse with visitors and people online in general. Our assumptions of what people might want to know, versus what they actually asked, was a good reminder to me that sometimes you don't need to overthink it, and you don't need to overcomplicate it, and sometimes the simplest answer is the most impactful one."

The recognition that you are not your users and that your assumptions about museum visitors may not be accurate, goes hand in hand with the need to find new ways to evaluate emerging technologies, and new metrics to assess whether those technologies are working as intended. Douglas Hegley explains how new approaches to engaging visitors require museum technology professionals to employ new methods for measuring audience engagement:

> Digital departments in museums, for the past decade in my opinion, have been far too focused on reach. They've been trying to justify their existence and describe their successes with metrics that are about reach: How many eyeballs? How many hits? How many unique sessions? "Look, we had X million last year, and we have 20 percent more this year. We're doing great. This is wonderful. Look how successful we are." But that's not the point of a museum is it? . . . I'm more interested in two other kinds of metrics: engagement metrics, and impact metrics. . . . It's not just about going viral. I want to help people find meaning in it, and want to engage with it.

Simply counting the number of people reached by any particular technology rarely tells the whole story and is unlikely to help museum technology professionals determine whether their efforts are truly making a difference in the lives of their users. Reflecting on his experiences at the Smithsonian Learning Lab, Darren Milligan explains the need to move beyond numbers to assess the true impact of the Smithsonian's educational outreach projects:

> We were moving to an era where we had to be more accountable for the budget that we had. It's very unique to have an office focused exclusively on educational outreach in a museum. So I think there was more pressure on our center to justify its existence. And I think to say, "Oh, we mailed out 80,000 magazines last week." I mean, that's like, "Okay, great. Did children's lives change? Are teachers giving money to the Smithsonian now? What was the actual impact of that from the student or from the institutional level?" And we couldn't answer those questions without extensive evaluation or other longer-term investigations.

Questions about impact often arise when museum technology professionals are asked to redesign an interface or improve some piece of computer technology, and they suddenly realize that, in order to do so, they need to learn much more about how their intended audiences are actually using those systems. Darren Milligan describes coming to the somewhat terrifying realization, while redesigning the SmithsonianEducation.org website, that they did not know how the extensive educational resources the Smithsonian Institution had created for use in elementary and middle school classrooms across the United States were actually being used by teachers:

> We had a portal that was very new when I came in. It had just launched when I joined. It was called SmithsonianEducation.org, which was sort of the central place for families or for teachers for the Smithsonian . . . and it was really a database of about 500 lesson plans from across the institution that were available digitally. . . . We published something called "Smithsonian in Your Classroom," which was a printed magazine. It went to every elementary and middle school in the country, so we were mailing between 80 and 100,000 of these out twice a year . . . and they were beautifully designed. They were usually 20-25-page magazines that included background information for the classroom teacher. . . . We might do an issue on whale migration, and the next one would be on Native American doll beadwork, and part of what I was doing was directing and managing that while taking on those webmaster roles. . . . That SmithsonianEducation.org website, which had launched in 2003, was starting to age pretty significantly. . . . Much of what was there were PDF versions of the "Smithsonian in Your Classroom" magazine, and I had for my mandate, "We need to redesign this and create a better user experience. . . ." And pretty quickly, I realized, with a lot of terror, that I didn't know how to do that because we knew so little about who our users were. . . . We could see

> what was being downloaded or Google analytics data about usage, but what does the teacher do in a classroom with a PDF of a 25-page magazine about whale migration? What is she actually doing, what does that actually look like, and how do we make that better? How do we improve that? I think I was really terrified at the time. I had to go to my leadership and say, "We can't do this. We don't know enough about what our role is, or who our users are, or how they use digital museum content, or how they use extensive lesson plans to be able to create anything that would be good, that would actually be more than just an improvement of the user experience."

Answering these kinds of questions involves extensive user research—including focus groups, quantitative surveys, and qualitative interviews—in order to understand the needs of the museum's users, and how best to meet them. Conducting this research is important because it is often the only way that museum technology professionals can ensure the digital information resources they are providing meet the needs of the individuals for whom they are intended. Darren Milligan describes how the user research they conducted at the Smithsonian Learning Lab about their "Smithsonian in Your Classroom" program opened their eyes dramatically to what the teachers who were using their resources were actually doing with them:

> Looking at the actual experiences of teachers who were using our material was astonishing. It was like 98 percent of users were not using the material in the way that we published it. Looking at "Smithsonian in Your Classroom," we would connect with people who were using it, and they'd say, "Oh yeah! We love that! I cut out the map that you had on the second page, and I blew that up for my bulletin board!" And we're like, "Okay, well, what about the lesson that went with the map?" And they're like, "Oh yeah, I don't think I read that. . . ." They didn't need the lessons. They didn't need the activities. . . . What we were publishing was useful to them, but we were publishing it as a PDF on a website that you had to know to go to and know how to find. We were making it almost as difficult as we possibly could to allow for that kind of customization and flexibility and mash-up behavior that we were quickly seeing was typical teacher behavior for how they create lessons. . . . And I remember at the time thinking, "Man, if we could just get our millions of images into these other external platforms that already have teacher communities of hundreds of thousands, it would be amazing! We would really see the results of that!" . . . It was at that point where we were really beginning to understand what teachers would want from museums like the Smithsonian.

Recognizing the importance of user research for determining the actual needs of their users represents an important philosophical shift for museum technology professionals, who increasingly found themselves creating information resources or technologies not because they met the internal assumptions of museum staff members but because they met the external needs of the museum's visitors. This shift in perspective went hand in hand with the development of a culture of data-driven evaluations in museums, where museum technology professionals increasingly relied on research data to determine the impact of new systems or technologies on museum visitors. Jane Alexander explains how her team at the Cleveland Art Museum used data-driven evaluations to assess the ability of their interactive exhibit, Gallery One, to engage museum visitors with art, and encourage them to spend more time in the museum's galleries:

> I'm a big fan of evaluations. I'm a big fan of data scientists. . . . We have 20 different dashboards that we look at each week, from our virtual events to our videos to our website, to ticketing, to our front page, what people are clicking on, what they're not clicking on. We change things around. I mean it's been really valuable just to be that connected. . . . We did an in-house evaluation of Gallery One. . . . It was easy to see that people were loving the engagement, but was it encouraging people to go to the galleries? That has always been the question. . . . There was a grant project that our evaluation team did that showed how people who came into that space, and spent at least five to ten minutes, left with more learning . . . that people who went into Gallery One, and spent at least 10 minutes there, spent at least 30 minutes to an hour more in the actual galleries. So that was the beginning of really seeing that this is working.

The more museum technology professionals relied on user-driven evaluation data to assess the impact of computing technologies in museums, the more they realized the importance of conducting data-driven evaluations in a timely manner. If you wait too long to acquire your evaluation data, you may be too late to implement solutions based on the results of your evaluations. Silvia Filippini-Fantoni discusses the importance of performing evaluations of technology-enhanced exhibits as soon as possible after a new experience is launched:

> There's always a phase of remedial evaluation, that's what we call it, where the experience has launched, but it's not finished. And that's a big step for museums because museums traditionally have had this idea that once you open an exhibition . . . things cannot be changed. It is what it is. And that's the hardest thing to convince my colleagues about. No, actually, you still have a couple of weeks to tweak things, and if you figure out that people cannot read the sign, you've got to redo the sign. . . . There's so much going on, and you have to move on to the next project, and there's sometimes not enough time to sit and think through is this working? Is it not working? So that's why I feel that always the first two weeks, when an experience is launched, you have to be there observing every time, doing a lot of research to tell you are people getting this or not? Because if you assume that they do, and then you look at the summative evaluation . . . at that point there's nothing you can do. So that's

> why the first two weeks of an experience, whatever it is, are fundamental to understanding that you can still do something to make it better.

Similarly, data-driven evaluations are not terribly useful if you are not asking the right questions of your audiences or gathering the correct data to evaluate the effectiveness of your technology initiatives. Bruce Wyman reminds us of the importance of asking the right questions when collecting and analyzing evaluation data in museums:

> When I was still at Denver, we had done a data warehousing product between all of our different business systems to try and pull up some analytics between stuff. And I find that nobody's ever asking the right questions to begin with. It's always something like, "How do we increase our revenue ten percent?" or, "On what days can we charge more for something?" as generic examples, and it's not until you spend time with the data and recognize that's not what it shows you at all. Either your data demonstrate something very different or, more fundamentally, you just weren't asking the right questions to begin with, and until you actually learn that you're asking the wrong things, you don't understand what the right things are.

In addition, museum technology professionals need to be prepared for the very real possibility that the evaluation data they gather may indicate that their technology initiatives are not working properly, or not reaching their audiences as intended. Seb Chan explains the need for museums to be comfortable with learning from failure when things go wrong:

> There's no perfect way to do any of this. If you're doing stuff at the edge of what's possible, then stuff's going to go wrong, and you just need to build that contingency in so that it's okay. It doesn't have to be a bad thing. But I think organizations have to feel comfortable that if you're doing new exciting stuff, there is no road map or plan. You have a direction you're heading, and things can and will go wrong. And it's your ability to adjust course as a result of that that's key.

The fact is that no matter how many times you test your systems and your technologies, something almost always goes wrong when you launch a new museum computing project. Museum technology professionals need to recognize that technologies rarely work as intended in the galleries, and they rarely perform in the same way that they did in the test environment. Silvia Filippini-Fantoni recalls what went wrong during the installation of an immersive media interactive where visitors could virtually try on high fashion dresses in a museum exhibit:

> We worked with a company who had created the software for malls where people could digitally try on their clothes. We tested it for about two weeks before it opened. We tweaked it, we fixed it, we spent hours and hours testing the thing. We opened the exhibition, and all of a sudden, it would get stuck. When people were standing in front of it for the system to scan their body to overlay the costume, it just wouldn't work. It would be all crazy. And we didn't know why it didn't work. We couldn't figure it out. And then we realized that, unlike during the phases that preceded the opening of the exhibition, there were a lot more people in the room, and the camera captured the people that were standing on the side, looking at the person being scanned, and the camera didn't know who to focus on, and so all of a sudden . . . we needed to start again. We had to completely reposition the whole experience so that the people walking by would not interfere with the camera view. And that resolved the issue, but that's again something that even though we did two weeks of testing, that's something that we didn't learn until we actually had a real-life situation with like 200-300 people in the room. And then we were able to figure out what the problem was. That was a very painful week in my life, spent with a lot of sleepless nights.

Many of our oral history participants shared stories about the high failure rate of museum computing projects and the importance of treating those failures as a learning experience. Richard Rinehart explains the personal value he ascribed to learning from failure:

> I have to say, I really did learn from my failures. Maybe they stuck in my brain more because we all are wired to want to succeed, you know. So maybe my failures stuck out for me more, but I think, as I got older, I realized, "Oh, you know, it actually is valuable to learn from your failures." There's no bad information. You can of course waste resources, and that's never a good thing. But as long as you have a good goal, and you're learning from what you're doing, that seems to be the important thing.

The importance of learning from failure goes hand in hand with the importance of iterative design, and the need to be constantly iterating when developing new systems and technologies. As Jane Alexander reminds us, launching any new museum technology project without planning for its continual iterative design is a recipe for failure:

> It's always been about iterating. Always. We're either iterating on the applications, or we're iterating on the infrastructure, or we're iterating on the outward-facing. When we put Gallery One up, I remember it was super successful, and I was putting the budget together for the next year, and the CFO at the time . . . he's like, "Wait. You just spent money. What's this money?" And I was like, "This is what I told you when I interviewed. It's not like you build it and leave it alone. That's why technology fails."

When it comes to successful iterative design, constant iteration goes hand in hand with constant user testing. It is important for museum technology professionals to develop a mindset where they are always testing, always gathering data, and always analyzing those data to assess new technologies and determine what works best to support the needs of museum visitors and museum staff members. Silvia Filippini-Fantoni explains the importance of being user-focused and developing a culture of evaluation and user testing in museums:

> My Ph.D. research was very much based on evaluation, so I had learned the basics of statistical analysis, but how you actually implement it, when you're developing a project from beginning to end, I learned that at Cogapp. Because their philosophy was very much "You've got to test. You've got to test. You've got to test." And the tools for testing . . . whether it's the wire frames, the design, the information architecture, the content that you're writing, you've got to test. And the tools that you have available to do that I definitely learned there. And ten years later, I'm still using some of the same approaches and philosophy that I learned there . . . that culture of evaluation.

Developing a culture of evaluation can be difficult, and user testing is hard work. There is no magic answer when it comes to designing usable information systems; you need to study what works and what does not work from the perspective of your intended users. Max Evjen explains the importance of user testing for museum professionals:

> We do so much in museums . . . but you don't really know if something's going to work unless you test it on somebody else. There's an axiom in user testing of "You're not your users," right? So it doesn't matter if *you* like it. It doesn't matter if *you* think it's great. Does everybody else?

It can be very difficult for designers in particular to recognize that the users for whom they are creating information systems and technologies may not be able to easily grasp how they work, or why they would want to use them. Scott Sayre shares a story about building ArtsConnectEd, a collaborative museum website between the Walker Art Center and the Minneapolis Institute of Arts, and the disconnect they observed between the designers of the website and its users:

> We built what I'm sure was the very first collaborative museum website between two institutions where we were merging their collections together, book-ending the Walker Art Center and the Minneapolis Institute of Arts. We also brought together our library collections and our curriculum collections and the art collections to one unified interface. And that was a huge learning opportunity for us because we thought, "This is the coolest thing in the

> world!" There was one search box, and this is right before Google came out, and we're like, "All you have to do is go to this page, and type in 'Rembrandt' and you're going to get not only images from the collection, and information from the collection, but you're going to get all the books we have in both of our libraries on Rembrandt, and you're going to get all the curriculum materials we have on Rembrandt. . . ." And we thought, this is the ultimate thing. And then we started to show it to people, and the end users were like, "What would I ever use this for? This is so confusing. It just blows my mind." And we all put our tails between our legs, and walked back home, and realized that we were kind of ahead of ourselves.

To overcome the disconnects that arise between the users and designers of information systems, many of our oral history participants emphasized the importance of usability testing. During the late 1990s and early 2000s in particular, museum technology professionals learned how to perform extensive user testing of their newly developed websites in an effort to make their interfaces less confusing from the perspective of the museum's end users. Scott Sayre describes what happened when they brought their ArtsConnectEd website to a usability lab at the University of Minnesota for user testing:

> We brought our website into the usability lab to do some testing, and this was revolutionary for us. . . . We brought teachers from all over the state and gave them scenarios that we wanted them to work through. . . . And our developers almost went home crying every day. They kept yelling, "Just click this! Click that!" They were realizing people weren't seeing anything that they had anticipated people would see in the user interface. But that was huge for all of us. It really brought us back home to think about our end users, how critical it was for us to better understand our end users, what they were looking for, and how our interfaces work for them. Obviously, I think everybody's very used to usability testing now, but in those days, it was huge.

The concept of user testing was revolutionary for many institutions, and it naturally took time for people to understand the importance of approaches such as usability analysis, user experience design, and design thinking for museums. Despite the personal enthusiasm that any one individual might have for embracing user testing and learning from their end users, museum technology professionals often faced resistance when bringing these ideas to their colleagues. Dana Mitroff Silvers explains the resistance she faced when trying to introduce the concept of user testing at SFMOMA for the first time in the early 2000s:

> I started to get really interested in the whole idea of user experience, user research, and usability testing. And people thought that was crazy, like, "Why would you do this? Because we know what our audiences want. . . ." But there was really no user research. Nobody talked to visitors. Nobody thought about

that stuff. It was just like, "We're the experts. It's our content, it's our collection, so why would we talk to people?" . . . I really tried to push for this idea of usability, user research, and really thinking about who's using this and what do they need versus what do we want them to need or think that they need. . . . People would come to the web team . . . and say, "I want you to make this or build that." And I would always say, "Why? Why are we doing this? Maybe you saw some cool thing on some other website, but why are we doing it? What's the point? You may think that it would be cool, but what visitor or user need does it meet?"

Applying the principles of user experience design in museums requires museum professionals to stop asking what *can* we do, and instead to start asking what do our users *need* us to do? Mia Ridge describes the difficulties the profession faced moving away from the perspective of the museum technologist to the perspective of the end user when building systems:

> Oh my goodness, all these debates about linked open data, and none of it was about the people, or about the difference that it made. It was about the acronyms. . . . If we could go back in time, and apply all the principles of UX—What need does this meet? Why are we doing it this way? Are there better ways to do it? Are there more creative ways to do it? But if all you have is technologists talking about it, then they're going to take a technology-focused view on achieving these goals.

Shifting perspectives to make information systems in museums more user-friendly and more successful means listening to our end users when they tell us what they need, and not just assuming that we know best simply because we are technology professionals. Reflecting on her time at the Smithsonian Institution, Kate Collen explains the importance of taking the information needs of their end users seriously when working to improve the usability of the collections management systems at the National Postal Museum:

> I feel like we were very innovative at the Postal Museum in that we tried to think out of the box in terms of pushing the collections management system to do things that maybe people thought it couldn't do. You just have to sort of think out of the box and approach it as a problem of, "How can I make this system work in the way that the people at the museum want me to make it work?" . . . A lot of times, I think that people sort of roll their eyes at collections management systems because they say, "Oh, this is this clunky database. I have to log in. I don't know how to search for anything." But if you make the system more user-friendly and go to the stakeholders in the museum and say, "What do you want the system to do?" And don't really discount anything they say: "I want to track the conservators' hours, the number of hours that she's treating an object. I want to be able to pull up a report that shows all of the treatment images for this one object." And then you just sort of think

> strategically of how you can work within the confines of the database to make that happen.

Embracing human-centered approaches to systems design, and being innovative with technology development, means setting aside one's own assumptions about the use of information systems and technologies in museums. As Dana Mitroff Silvers explains, the best way to do that often involves getting up from your desk, and talking to real people:

> One of the things that I really love about human-centered design and design thinking is that the process forces people in museums to get up from their desks, get out of their offices . . . actually get face to face with visitors who are not abstracted numbers in a survey. You're actually getting away from your desk and going into the galleries. . . . I have worked with curators who admit they never go to the galleries. They say, "I never talk to visitors. This is so eye opening for me. I never understood. I just didn't get it, like I didn't understand how important it is to have a place to sit. I just didn't understand why walking from this part of the building to this part of the building is such a huge ordeal because somebody's there pushing their elderly relative in a wheelchair." And it's these things that seem so obvious and basic but don't hit home until you have that first-hand experience. . . . This is why I was so attracted to human-centered design and design thinking—because you can have moments like this. . . . I worked on so many projects like that, where it was just really cool to see these light bulbs go off with staff members.

User experience design methods—such as developing user profiles and personas, rapid prototyping, and representative user testing—can help museum professionals break out of their preconceived expectations and see their systems and technologies through the eyes of their end users. Deborah Howes explains how helping museum staff members look at things from the perspective of museum visitors can be an important learning experience:

> You would be so surprised at the number of museums, and I'm talking about top level staff at major museums, who really have never put themselves in the shoes of those who have never been to a museum before. And it's a painful process for them, but also so eye-opening.

Understanding the museum's end users, discovering how visitors approach technology in museum exhibits, and learning why the user-centered approach matters are the first step in developing a culture of evaluation and improving the technology design process in museums. Dana Mitroff Silvers describes the magic of user testing and the "Aha!" moment that occurs when people first recognize the value of design thinking and user experience methods:

> I've had people say, "Wow, I never really watched anybody use our online collection," or "I never went into the gallery and talked to somebody while they were standing in front of an object, or while they were trying to use this kiosk we have. I never thought about it that way. Wow, this is really valuable. . . ." I think there's just something so powerful about letting "museum people" watch "real people"—visitors, users—use our stuff. . . . When you actually have a museum staff member watch a real human use something, that's where the magic happens.

When we examine the contributions of museum technology professionals over the past sixty years, we see that the history of museum computing has been driven less by the digital projects they designed or the innovative experiments they conducted, and more by the changing mindsets they had to adopt in order for those projects and experiments to succeed. On the surface, the memories shared by our oral history participants may appear to be stories of building museum websites, interactive exhibits, or online resources, but when we dig deeper, we see that they speak to the emergence of profound concepts that reflect new ideas about audience engagement and outreach, assessing information needs, visitor research methods, usability testing, and user experience design in museums. In this way, the history of museum computing is a story of changing mindsets and evolving cultures, where museum technology professionals embraced the ideals of data-driven evaluation, iterative design, and user testing in order to provide the best possible technology-enabled experiences for all their users—museum professionals and museum visitors alike—in all aspects of their lives. This is not an easy task, and there is still plenty of work to do, but by supporting museum technology professionals in these efforts, museums can ensure their institutions will continue to provide the most usable, engaging, and effective experiences possible for all of their stakeholders.

SUGGESTIONS FOR FURTHER READING

Anderson, Susan. 2019. "Visitor and Audience Research in Museums." In *The Routledge Handbook of Museums, Media and Communication*, edited by Kirsten Drotner, Vince Dziekan, Ross Parry, and Kim Christian Schroder, 80–95. Abingdon, Oxon: Taylor & Francis, Inc.

Cunliffe, Daniel, Efmorphia Kritou, and Douglas Tudhope. 2001. "Usability Evaluation for Museum Web Sites." *Museum Management and Curatorship* 19 (3): 229–252.

Dyson, Mary C., and Kevin Moran. 2000. "Informing the Design of Web Interfaces to Museum Collections." *Museum Management and Curatorship* 18 (4): 391–406.

Filippini-Fantoni, Silvia, Rob Stein, and Gray Bowman. 2012. "Exploring the Relationship between Visitor Motivation and Engagement in Online Museum Audiences." In *Museums and the Web 2012*, edited by David Bearman and Jennifer Trant. Toronto: Archives & Museum Informatics. https://www.museumsandtheweb.com/mw2012/papers/exploring_the_relationship_between_visitor

Harms, Ilse, and Werner Schweibenz. 2001. Evaluating the Usability of a Museum Web Site. In *Museums and the Web 2001*, edited by David Bearman and Jennifer Trant, 43–54. Pittsburgh, PA: Archives & Museum Informatics. http://www.archimuse.com/mw2001/papers/schweibenz/schweibenz.html

Marty, Paul F. 2008. "Museum Websites and Museum Visitors: Digital Museum Resources and their Use." *Museum Management and Curatorship* 23 (1): 81–99.

Marty, Paul F., and Michael B. Twidale. 2004. "Lost in Gallery Space: A Conceptual Framework for Analyzing the Usability Flaws of Museum Websites." *First Monday,* 9 (9). http://www.firstmonday.org/issues/issue9_9/marty/index.html

Mitroff Silvers, Dana, Molly Wilson, and Maryanna Rogers. 2013. "Design Thinking for Visitor Engagement: Tackling One Museum's Big Challenge through Human-centered Design." In *Museums and the Web 2013*, edited by Nancy Proctor and Rich Cherry. Silver Spring, MD: Museums and the Web. https://mw2013.museumsandtheweb.com/paper/design-thinking/

Teather, Lynne, and Kelly Wilhelm. 1999. "Web Musing: Evaluating Museums on the Web from Learning Theory to Museology." In *Museums and the Web 1999*, edited by David Bearman and Jennifer Trant, 131–143. Pittsburgh, PA: Archives & Museum Informatics. http://www.archimuse.com/mw98/papers/teather/teather_paper.html

Villaespesa, Elena. 2019. "Museum Collections and Online Users: Development of a Segmentation Model for the Metropolitan Museum of Art." *Visitor Studies* 22 (3): 233–252.

12

Inclusive Philosophies

> I think that's what really got me hooked on digitizing collections because I really do feel that it helps the world to share art and to share music and dance and all sorts of humanities ideas and to connect them together . . . to link our data to lots of other kinds of information—events and people and places—to enrich our information, which I think is part of the dream to make this important humanities and art information available to the world, and help us understand each other better. —Oral History of Diana Folsom

As the use of computers in museums became more common, museum technology professionals began to explore how access to digital information resources could help museum visitors make a difference in their everyday lives, no matter who they were, or where they lived in the world. Museum professionals increasingly realized that the true purpose of museum computing is not the management of technologies in museums, but the use of those technologies to help people—all people—achieve their personal goals and objectives. By making the museum's digital information resources available broadly to everyone, museum technology professionals learned they could help encourage new cultures of empathy, inclusion, humanity, and understanding centered around access to digital museum collections.

As an integral part of this shift in perspective, many museum technology professionals came to the conclusion that they needed to work to address inherent biases in their collections, make their collections more inclusive, challenge their implicit assumptions about cataloging, develop a culture of participatory design and inclusion, bring more diverse voices into their collections, and work to address societal inequities and encourage social justice through their museums' information systems and technologies. These changes prompted a new mindset for museum technology professionals where they shifted away from thinking about specific technology problems toward exploring more global philosophies in their work, and the difference that museums can make in encouraging diversity, equity, and inclusion worldwide.

Over the past few decades, in particular, many museum professionals concluded that their institutions cannot afford to remain neutral in the face of societal events of global significance. Museums are increasingly pressured to take a stand about their place in the world and the role they play during times of change. Museum leadership must determine how best to respond to questions about their institution's own biases, efforts to make their collections more inclusive, and what their collections say about their museum and its values. As Cathryn Goodwin puts it in her oral history, this is a challenging time for museum professionals:

> The leadership role that we take in conversations about inclusivity in description of works of art, and how we need to be thinking about the way we discuss artwork, the way we discuss artists, the way we label people . . . museums are obviously in a very challenging position right now. The ground feels a little shaky. The challenging aspects of accepting the fact that museums are not neutral, and that the things that we say have impact way beyond what we might originally have thought. There's going to be a lot of re-learning and repositioning and reprioritization for museums in general, and certainly for the technologists that support the missions of museums, and have a huge role to play in helping to break down those biases and opening the dialog in a much more fair and inclusive way.

None of these are easy tasks to undertake, and to make matters more complicated, museum technology professionals may find themselves wrestling with difficult societal issues that they may never have expected to arise as part of their job. An excellent example of how unexpected societal challenges can emerge from the development and implementation of new information technologies can be found in the "Send Me SFMOMA" service that the San Francisco Museum of Modern Art debuted in the 2010s. Marla Misunas explains how this service worked:

> Our digital technologist, Jay Mollica, came up with a texting service called "Send Me SFMOMA" which blew up the Internet and was amazing. . . . The awesome thing about "Send Me SFMOMA" was that you didn't need a computer, you just needed a phone. You could text "Send me something" to a number, and the service would go through and pull out an image—especially selected for you—based on whatever word or words you entered.

Individuals around the world loved this service and appreciated the ease with which they could request images on any topic at any time. As Layna White explains, the reason this technology worked so well was because SFMOMA had spent many years tagging their collections, and the Send Me SFMOMA service used those tags to select the best image to return:

> You sent the museum a text that started with "Send me . . ." and you filled in the blank with a word and, in return, SFMOMA sent you an image of an artwork that responded to that word. . . . It was such an unexpected and super beautiful payoff for that 12-plus-year concerted effort around tagging, and experimenting, and finding a fresh, new way of making art accessible in a way we hadn't even seen coming through texts and sending images. It was just really a delightful project.

While this service was a great way for SFMOMA to reach the general public, their success also came with some unexpected outcomes that revealed gaps in the museum's tagging process. In particular, as Layna White explains, Send Me SFMOMA made it clear that what the public looked for in museums was not necessarily what the museum staff had tagged in the system:

> The No. 1 request was "Send me love," and when a person texted "Send me love" to our number, Jay wrote an application that randomly chose an image of an artwork, based on the tags that Marla and Margaret and Ian and interns and many others around the building had added to the collections management system. . . . The thing with Send Me SFMOMA that was super valuable for us, and maybe you could see it coming a mile away, was that up until then we'd been tagging what we saw in an image, but here the No. 1 request was "Send me love," which we hadn't been tagging, because it was so personal, so interpretive. So the cool thing was that Send Me SFMOMA was super valuable for us because it surfaced absences in how we were tagging. It also underscored how important it is for us to take really fresh looks at what we're doing around tagging . . . what we're doing in terms of providing access to the collection online. Are we providing access to the extent to which people are actually desiring that? Are we providing access to the collection that is helpful, that is relevant to individuals who seek out works of art? The Send Me SFMOMA project, those queries . . . that whole project was incredibly valuable in that it also got us thinking about are our tags biased? Are our tags relatable? Are they relevant to our audiences and staff?

For the staff at the museum, analyzing the gaps in the tags that drove Send Me SFMOMA revealed important internal biases inherent to the museum's descriptions of its collections. In this way, the project demonstrates how emerging technologies can expose biases in museum collections, and underscore the need to make those collections more inclusive. Marla Misunas explains how Send Me SFMOMA helped the museum identify biases in how they collect and record information about diversity in their collections:

> We knew that there was bound to be bias in our tags. . . . We definitely had our own biases, and so did the institution. Biases and technical issues came into focus when we opened our new wing in 2016. There was a lot of hoopla around the new building, and everybody was really excited. The public had been hearing about it for a long time, and people wanted to see themselves reflected in the collections that we had in the galleries and online. We had to change our approach to tagging with the input of visitors and the people who were contacting us through the website. One correspondent emailed me and said, "I'm looking for images that I can show my kids of Black people represented in museum collections. How do I find that on your website?" . . . That person also searched "Send Me SFMOMA" for Black people, and what she didn't know and a lot of us didn't know was that "Send Me SFMOMA" could only search for one word at a time. It couldn't find two words separated by a space. So, when she searched for Black people on "Send Me SFMOMA," she got a picture of the United Nations' first meeting in the Veteran's Building where our museum used to be in 1945. There was this conference room full of white men in black suits. And she thought, "Well, that's interesting. It's not what I wanted."

To address those problems, museum staff members needed to challenge their assumptions about cataloging diversity in museum collections. Marla Misunas explains how the lessons learned from Send Me SFMOMA helped upend the museum's preconceived ideas about how their users would or would not search the museum's collections via social tagging:

> One of the reasons the person's search failed was that staff had never tagged or otherwise recorded what they might perceive to be the ethnicity of people in images. How would we know how people in pictures would identify themselves? And where that became a problem was the public wanted to find images based on someone's appearance. We hadn't known people would search that way.

Naturally, these assumptions are not unique to SFMOMA, or to any one museum. There are many assumptions in our cataloging activities—assumptions that stem from long-established practices that will take many years to correct. Martha Mahard, for example, describes the ambiguous data and assumed cataloging she encountered at Harvard University:

> One of the things we found when we were going from the old card catalog into the online environment was we had so many places where there was what we call "assumed cataloging." My first job had been at the Harvard Theatre Collection, and we had no subject headings for Theatre. . . . One of the special collections at the Houghton Library was the Teddy Roosevelt Collection, and all of the Teddy Roosevelt Collection had subheadings, but it didn't have anything that said "TR" or "Teddy Roosevelt. . . ." It was just "On a horse" or

> "In battle. . . ." The Schlesinger Library on the History of Women in America had no subject headings for women! You could go into VIA and do a subject search for "men," and find a lot of stuff because they always subject-headed when they had stuff about men, but they never . . . they actually had to go back and redo like ten thousand records. You know, this is the stuff people didn't think of. The card catalog still owned us in a lot of ways. It owned the way we thought about data, and it's taken a generation for that to change.

The act of cataloging a museum object—How do you describe something? What terms do you use? Who is included? Who is excluded?—is inherently a social justice issue. Many voices, including those of women and people of color, have been silenced as a result of the biases and assumptions in traditional museum cataloging practices. As Diane Zorich explains, overcoming these problems and addressing inequities in museum catalogs means challenging assumptions through activities such as reparative cataloging:

> Our American Women's History Initiative has taken that on as a challenge, to surface women in our history who haven't gotten the due they should. And that's been a fascinating project to watch. Because they are using a lot of machine learning to try to uncover from records, women's names, which are often recorded as men's names, or Mrs. Man's name, and they've unsurfaced so much, and brought so much attention to that work. One of the areas that I think we will be doing more work in, and this will probably be at the grassroots too that pushes us, is something we call reparative cataloging—to go back and look at our cataloging and see what voices aren't being exposed, the silences in the record. And we've got a team of people in the grassroots working on discussing how we can tackle that at an institution as large as the Smithsonian. What first steps can we take that get us some wins that help us go to the next step, and the next step, and the next step.

When it comes to art museum catalogs, if you were not white, and you were not male, you were often left out. For many years, the default assumption for many museum catalogs has been that, if not specified otherwise, artists were assumed to be white men. As Marla Misunas explains, increasing diversity data and identifying artist ethnicities in museum collections is a difficult problem to solve that will require extensive community involvement:

> People are asking, "Where is your work by Black artists? Where is your work by Asian artists?" . . . We have 6,000 artists for which the ethnicity has not been recorded, and after a long time working with the historic collection, I'm going to say most of those artists were white. . . . We are now intentionally collecting artwork by more diverse kinds of people than just white male artists, and I'm hopeful that direction continues. It's in our strategic plan, and it's something that we're all working on. I hope that in ten years, our collection and exhibitions continue to be more varied . . . but, honestly, finding a record that

> identifies someone as a white person or a person of color is very difficult. . . . As an industry, we have spent such a very long time collecting white artists that our records have only specified ethnicity—perceived or researched—when the artist was a person of color. . . . We need to push forward to greater representation, and hopefully as museums, we will be able to do that.

Moving forward with these corrections and overcoming centuries of implicit bias is not something that museum technology professionals can do on their own. Increasing diversity in collections records requires new approaches to increasing diversity behind the scenes in museums. Addressing areas of systemic bias in museum catalogs such as gender identity can be difficult, especially when working with artists who may no longer be alive. Museums need to develop a culture of participatory design and inclusion that prioritizes bringing diverse voices into their collections practices. As Marla Misunas explains, in order to improve access to collections records, museums need more diverse voices involved in tagging activities:

> We went back and tagged people, white people and people of color, but the other white lady and I didn't feel comfortable saying, "This is a Black person, and this is an African person." There were a lot of uncertainties. Some artists specifically make pictures of African American people, and we felt comfortable tagging those, if we knew the artist's intent. . . . We're getting statistics about what the public searches for, which helps make the case for getting more voices. I feel pretty qualified identifying a person in an artwork as white—and I might be wrong—but that's about it. That's where feeling qualified stops. . . . In a training session last week, somebody asked me, "What terms are you using to tag works by gay artists or members of the LGBTQ community?" And, we have not gone down that path yet, because even if it's public knowledge that an artist identifies as LGBTQ, that doesn't mean that their artwork shows an LGBTQ theme, and who's to say what that might be, or it could be that they think all of their artwork does or doesn't, so we're working with curators on that.

Getting more diverse voices involved in social tagging projects can raise awareness of issues of diversity, equity, and inclusion in museums and help amplify voices that are not normally heard. Recognizing diversity in collections records is not easy, and tagging for ethnicity brings its own challenges, but digital tools such as social tagging can help museums empower community members and encourage them to engage in collaborative activities with museum personnel, such as building folksonomies and controlled vocabularies with Native experts. Diana Folsom explains how social tagging projects can shine a light on diverse voices and help encourage museums to think about their collections from diverse perspectives:

> It's interesting that it's really turned into a tool that we've been using for the kinds of people in our community and in our collection and in our world, who have not been heard from enough and whose voices we want to amplify—they've been underserved, I think. . . . The perspective I wanted to learn from was, what words would they use to find these objects? What would they need to find these objects? The anthropologists who had already cataloged them used terms that don't make any logical sense whatsoever, most of the time, to someone who hasn't been exposed to them. . . . So we made this long vocabulary chart with all the possibilities. . . . We looked at art historical terms which weren't really used by the anthropologists, which is the way it had been cataloged so far. We ended up with this kind of long vocabulary in a chart that we used in an in-person committee meeting, like an advisory committee meeting with all the artists, and Holly Witchey was the wonderful facilitator, and we basically went through every term and they voted whether they would want to use those terms or not. So we kind of developed our own little folksonomy. And we also learned that Native peoples do not like it when we give a regular animal name to something that they see depicted on an ancient ceramic vessel because it's something that they may have seen in ceremony and it's not necessarily a regular kind of an animal. You wouldn't call it a hybrid of a dog plus a dragon or something because it's something very different. We learned a lot from that.

None of this can be done in a vacuum. Identifying and collecting diverse contributions involves building trusted relationships with community partners where museums recognize and value their expertise. When working with Native experts to address issues of metadata, for example, especially when there has historically been a colonial imposition of terminology, it is important to address these problems in a thoughtful way that involves people as active participants in a conversation where their voice is valued. It is also important that we pay for expertise; museums should not approach a Native community, ask them to give their knowledge away for free, and then leave, without giving anything back. Diana Folsom explains the importance of treating community participants as valued experts and trusted participants in the cataloging process:

> I do want to emphasize that it's really important to pay people to do this work for you. Because it is work for us. So often with Native communities, and Spanish-speaking communities, and Black communities, museum people will swoop in, and grab all their knowledge and information, and then we'll take it back, and process it, and put it online, or use it in our own intellectual ways. But it's really important to pay them. What they're doing is important work. It's key to what we do. And to use it in a more unedited fashion, in a more direct fashion, so that we really understand their perspective.

Encouraging community experts to contribute their knowledge to the museum's information systems requires a long-term commitment built on stable relationships and shared trust. Building trusted relationships involves developing a culture of participatory design and inclusion where museum professionals recognize the importance of finding new ways of thinking about their collections and working with their community partners. Involving outside experts in cataloging activities, for example, can be particularly useful in institutions that may not have many curators on staff. Diana Folsom discusses the importance of incorporating non-curatorial perspectives, and giving community experts a voice in documenting collections:

> We have a deep and wide-ranging collection, a very important collection, but just a couple of curators. We need experts to help us, so we take the approach of inviting all different kinds of experts. We're also working on another IMLS grant project now where we're working with ethnographic specialists and focusing on tribes, particularly those that are in this region—the Osage, the Cherokee, and the Muscogee Creek—and working with their ethnographic materials and photographing them, identifying them, and recording information from an expert—an elder in the field—who knows more about it than we do in the museum . . . and we are working with another expert on the ceramic vessels who reviewed our cataloging and fixed it and added more data that we did not have, which is then enabling us to have meaningful NAGPRA consultations . . . to work with Native peoples and improve our understanding of our collection and also to help them have a voice in what we say about these objects. . . . The museum curators are people who have studied these works, and studied these collections, and have a useful perspective, but it's not the only perspective. It didn't come from on high. So there are other critical perspectives that are equally important and sometimes maybe more important than ours.

Many of the projects discussed by our oral history participants involve new ideas about authority and expertise that challenge traditional operating procedures in museums and help give voice to underserved and underrepresented communities. These projects speak to the tension between internal and external expertise in museums, the difficulty of involving external experts in museum projects without taking them for granted, and the need to recognize the value of involving outside experts as active participants in the knowledge creation process. Holly Witchey describes her work with Native American communities on inclusive cataloging, and the importance of respecting physical cultures when creating digital objects:

> I've gotten engaged with the Native American indigenous communities through ATALM, the Association of Tribal Archives Libraries and Museums, and I heard a really interesting presentation a couple of years ago about Native American protocols for digital materials and physical materials. There are objects that are sacred, and if the object is sacred, the photograph of the object inherits those same tendencies, and the description of the object

> inherits those tendencies, so there's a lot of conversation about how do we let things die, naturally. . . . What does it mean to actively not preserve something for the right reasons? . . . We had a conversation once about a ghost drum that was going to be given back, and they build places where the ghost drum can be placed and where it can decay, and so the question was, "Before it goes, can we do a video or an animation of it being played?" And they're like, "No, you can't do that. . . ." If you're not supposed to see it, you're not supposed to take a photograph of it, you're not supposed to animate it, and I think that's hard for a lot of people.

Changes to traditional operating procedures often involve removing older perspectives in favor of newer voices and can be complicated by the introduction of, and ongoing changes to, legislation such as the Native American Graves Protection and Repatriation Act (NAGPRA). Despite the challenges involved, upending traditional notions of authority can enable museums to address inequities in their collections. Bringing new voices and perspectives into their collections databases is something that many museum professionals have worked to achieve for many years, as Kathy Jones explains:

> In the 1990s, the Peabody Museum had been through different iterations of systems. But we were at a place where we were talking as a group, and having conversations about how we were recording information. We were also, even then, looking at the language that had been recorded in ledgers and wondering if it was appropriate language to keep access to. Early curators might have referred to Native American groups in less than appropriate ways. So we're trying to manage that, but also keep the historical record. And I think that has been an important part of the work at the Peabody—even before NAGPRA, but also working on NAGPRA—and beginning to bring new voices and new perspectives into not just the museum, but also into the database.

The challenges of incorporating indigenous knowledge in particular into collections management systems are well known and speak to the inherent limitations of certain controlled vocabularies and nomenclatures in museums. Many museum professionals have thought carefully about how to bring new stories to the forefront without excluding other stories that have long been told. Megan Forbes discusses the need to integrate indigenous knowledge into collections management systems in ways that do not minimize or diminish non-traditional or personal contributions:

> Right now, most systems are asking us to describe our materials from a very Western art historical perspective. And there are of course lots of different ways to describe things. We are seeing a lot of interest in people wanting to incorporate traditional and indigenous knowledge management into a system where they can live side-by-side. . . . Thinking about the system as a way to capture the life of that object from its creator and their story, and how it came

> to the museum, and where it might be after. We're seeing in a lot of different communities this idea of traditional knowledge management, and how do we incorporate more of that, and support more of that in our systems. . . . We have implementers who have recently suggested within our name authority that we add a new section, where, if you are a creator, what do you say that you are? I have your ULAN record, but who do you say you are? Where do you say that you are from, or what is your gender, or how are you expressing information about yourself? Are we allowed to share that? Instead of an artist being sort of pinned to the wall, we're inviting them into the collections management system to say, "You tell us who you are, and how you would like us to express that information about you. . . ." How do we use this platform that we've developed, and this community that we've developed, to really turn a lot of what we have done on its head, to a certain extent, and think about how we can change things up and expand these traditional notions of authority?

As difficult as this may be, museum technology professionals have an obligation to address inequities and encourage social justice through their collections. The museum computing community can play an important role by encouraging inclusive cataloging, supporting efforts to increase diversity in the museum's collections, and managing the ethical stewardship of the museum's information resources. Kate Collen, for example, describes the importance of incorporating indigenous knowledge into the museum's records:

> Looking at past interpretations, and getting stakeholder buy-in from new generations, or maybe older generations of stakeholders like with indigenous groups, is very interesting to me. I teach an article by Jane Sledge who talks about a blouse in the Smithsonian collections that curators had put backwards on a mannequin. The indigenous groups came into the museum and said, "That's backwards. My grandmother never wore that like that. I've seen that in use." And the curator said, "Well, you know, we're not quite sure. We're going to look in the record. And we're going to make sure that that's actually really backwards." And it was. And so I think it is good to get outside groups coming in and adding to the knowledge base for our collections. Again, it is scary. It's a loss of control of the collections, but I think it's the right thing to do.

Evaluating traditional practices, examining our inherent biases, and reconciling social inequities may seem like a lot to ask of museum technology professionals, but it starts quite simply with the recognition that the purpose of museum computing is to put people first. None of the technologies we are building matter if potential museum visitors feel like they are not included, not involved, or not our intended audiences. If we are not using our information systems and technologies to make our institutions more inclusive, to underscore our commonalities, and to emphasize our shared humanity, then why do we have them at all? As Douglas Hegley reminds us, people are, and should always be, at the core of museum computing:

> I think what always motivated me was people, whether that was the internal staff and really seeing them come around to technology, to digital, to embracing it, to seeing its potential. And also the visiting public, whether it was launching the first app or building a touch screen and just seeing people in awe and wonder over this kind of magical experience that was both surprising and informing at the same time. . . . It's always about people. Somewhere at the core of everything that I want to do is about people, not necessarily about technology. Technology is a suite of tools, a suite of methods to help people accomplish their goals, learn something, whatever it may be, but I'm not an engineer, and I'm not interested, not motivated by the latest, coolest technology. I want to know if that makes people connect. If it makes people interested. If it makes people curious. If it satisfies a need that people have. Now I'm interested. . . . It's always about people. It's people first and people last. There's some digital in between—some of it works well, some of it backfires—but it's people first, people last, and if those are the bookends, then you can sort out what happens in between.

Museum computing is about building human connections. As Rob Weisberg explains, the job of the museum technology professional is a humanizing journey, and ultimately one that is more about working with people than working with technology:

> Whatever the technology role of my job was, it was really a human role. It was about being collegial, and I don't think that that's ever changed. . . . Even as my job description has changed, and even as the technology changed from floppy disks to XyQuest disks to Zip disks to CDs and DVDs to FTPs and now WeTransfer, the human element has always been the fun part of the job. And it's been the part of the job that I've really wanted to excel in, even if the technology is what's in the job description, it's what they think I'm being paid for. Being a human scale colleague, that's always been the part that I've really enjoyed. . . . When a new technology gets proposed to us, or I want to bring in a new technology, the first thing I think about is how is this going to affect the people? How is this going to affect my colleagues, my team, people I don't know yet who work in the museum? People who work in other museums? And our visitors, whether they're in the building or outside? So it's been a technology journey, but it's also been a humanizing journey, and that for me is the essence of museum technology . . . letting people do better work and letting people be more human inside of the institution. That's what I'm proudest about in my 27 years in museum technology.

Museum computing is about encouraging a culture of empathy and understanding for others. As the priorities of museums change along with the needs of humanity, the purpose of technology in museums should be to provide meaningful experiences that transform people's lives and their connections with others. Paul Marty explains how access to digital information about museum collections helped promote empathy and understanding at the University of Illinois:

> One of our main audiences was K-12 students . . . this museum was a major field trip destination for them. I was always cognizant of the fact that we're in Champaign-Urbana, Illinois. A hundred miles in any direction there's nothing but corn or soybeans. And for a lot of the kids that live in those rural communities, their once-a-year field trip to the World Heritage Museum at the University of Illinois was their only chance to learn about a culture other than their own. And it speaks to empathy, to the importance of what museums are doing as outreach . . . it speaks to the value of technology and museums for effecting change in the world, for building broader communities online, in person, building empathy, and emphasizing our shared humanity. My argument has always been that the more we can do to do broaden outreach, to get museums to present their information to a broader community, the better off we're going to be in general.

Museum computing is about helping people become better citizens in a global democracy. The more people have access to digital museum resources—the more we can bridge the divide between those who feel the museum is for them and those who feel the museum is for someone else—the more we can help people understand the commonalities that connect us and the future of humanity in a world of digital culture. As Darren Milligan explains, investing in digital museums means investing in citizenship, democracy, and cultural well-being:

> Investing in digital, and all the things that that means, lays the groundwork for us to have a greater impact, and I think most of us who work here, assume that that's possible, are optimistic that we have a role to play, that access to what we have, what we know here, is crucial to democracy, crucial to healthy citizenship, crucial to cultural well-being and satisfaction and joy. . . . All of us have drunk the Kool-Aid, you know, and I think there's been this bottom-up push for quite a while of people really making the case for that, building the evidence for that. . . . it's pretty exciting to be there at that moment.

If the outcomes of museum computing are to benefit humanity, it is important that museum technology professionals not get side-tracked by the pursuit of technology for technology's sake. Technology, after all, is not the core mission of the museum; the purpose of museum computing, instead, should be to create engaging, impactful, and meaningful experiences that are mediated by technology. As Douglas Hegley explains, museum technology professionals need to resist the allure of the latest trends, and instead think about how new technologies can support the museum's overarching goals:

> We're being pressured by funders and trustees to follow the latest trends. And right now in May of 2021, that's non-fungible tokens and can we make millions of dollars all of a sudden from NFTs? And it's AR and VR and "We heard that HTC released a new version of the Vive. How many are we going to buy? What are you going to do with them?" I think a lot of times the question for me is, "For what?" Like, "What are the people looking for? How does this connect with what people are looking for? And is this something that's core to our mission?" . . . I think we're missing a combination of a true North Star—what is it that we're trying to accomplish here?—as well as a really firm center of gravity—where do we stand? And where do we want to go? Those are the most important questions, not what is the technology? We should understand that we want to go, I think, toward delighting audiences, and where we stand is in really valuing the stories and narratives that we have, and inviting additional stories and narratives to come in. And digital can do all of this. It's not even that difficult for digital, if you set it up that way.

At the end of the day, the work of the museum technology profession is not to support technology in museums but to support the museum community writ large as they spread knowledge, enrich lives, and connect people. The more we can use our digital information resources to help people understand each other better, the more we can change the world for the better. Holly Witchey describes her passion for museum work:

> You know, we went into this with all the hubris that this is going to change the world and it did, in a few ways. Maybe not as much as we hoped. But it was so great to see. It's been so fantastic to see, I would say, the next generation, and the next two generations of fantastic people who are working in museums and making things happen.

Museums can change lives. They can be an amazing force for positive social change, with the ability to create meaningful human connections that transform people's lives and their relationships with other people around the world. As Costis Dallas explains, museum technology professionals are only now realizing the potential of the museum experience to connect people, objects, and ideas, in ways that are diverse, equitable, and inclusive:

> I think we've just only come to realize the transformational power that encounters with objects can have. Of course, I mean, we know it from theory, because theories talk about this kind of numinous or evocative power of objects, you know, the affiliate power of objects, their ability to link us with identities, and with others, and ideas, and with the past, and the sense of belonging, and the sense of being, sometimes. But I think we are only sort of scratching the surface again on something that is so seminal, it's so central. And it's so central in all our discourses of developing a reciprocal, equitable, inclusive reinterpretation of what the museum might be.

There is a magic to the museum experience that brings joy and wonder to museum visitors, in person and online, and leaves them smiling. As Douglas Hegley explains, the meaningful experiences that museums offer their visitors have the power to change their own lives and strengthen their connections with other people:

> Ultimately, I work in museums because I think museums can change lives. I really do. And you know, I don't think I'm naive in that way. I've experienced it myself. Museums can have the kind of impact on people that opens them up, that make us maybe feel a little smaller, and a little less self-important, but also more connected to a global arc of history, and to the best of what human beings can be. The most talented, most creative, most innovative things are on display in museums. Like, look what we can do. Look at our potential. So the impact for me has to do with things that are a little bit harder to measure: empathy, reducing narcissism, awe and wonder. . . . People who experience awe and wonder, it actually has a strong impact on them as human beings. It has an impact on their other relationships, which means you're not just impacting an individual, you're actually impacting the individual and their network of people. . . . I'm working with an individual, but I'm actually effecting change in the world, because every individual is connected to other individuals. And I don't have some kind of magical power that can change the world, but I can help this one person, and thus have a ripple effect across other people. And I think museums offer the same kind of potential.

Since the 1960s, computing technologies have transformed museums, and museum technology professionals have helped to make the world a better place. The more they worked to digitize museum collections and open up access to collections data and images, the more they realized the potential of information systems and technologies in museums to effect positive change in the world. As their work uncovered internal biases and implicit assumptions in collections data, museum technology professionals took the lead in solving these problems, righting historical wrongs, and making museums more welcoming and more inclusive. By embracing the power of museum computing as a force for empathy, diversity, and positive social change, museum technology professionals have the potential to change lives, and the magic to change the world.

SUGGESTIONS FOR FURTHER READING

Autry, La Tanya S., and Mike Murawski. 2019. "Museums Are Not Neutral: We are Stronger Together." *Panorama: Journal of the Association of Historians of American Art* 5 (2). https://journalpanorama.org/article/museums-are-not-neutral/

Bautista, Susana Smith. 2014. *Museums in the Digital Age: Changing Meanings of Place, Community, and Culture*. Lanham, MD: AltaMira Press.

Bearman, David, and Jennifer Trant. 2005. "Social Terminology Enhancement through Vernacular Engagement: Exploring Collaborative Annotation to Encourage Interaction with Museum Collections." *D-Lib Magazine* 11 (9). http://www.dlib.org/dlib/september05/bearman/09bearman.html

Cascone, Sarah. 2017. "How San Francisco's Museum of Modern Art Used Text Messages to Make Art Go Viral." *Artnet* (July 2017). https://news.artnet.com/art-world/sfmoma-made-art-go-viral-1023440

Coleman, Laura-Edythe. 2018. *Understanding and Implementing Inclusion in Museums*. Lanham, MD: Rowman and Littlefield.

Janes, Robert R. 2009. *Museums in a Troubled World*. London: Routledge.

Janes, Robert R. 2010. "The Mindful Museum." *Curator* 53 (3): 325–338.

Nash, Stephen E., and Chip Colwell. 2020. "NAGPRA at 30: The Effects of Repatriation." *Annual Review of Anthropology* 49: 225–239.

Topaz, Chad M., Bernhard Klingenberg, Daniel Turek, Brianna Heggeseth, Pamela E. Harris, Julie C. Blackwood, C. Ondine Chavoya, Steven Nelson, and Kevin M. Murphy. 2019. "Diversity of Artists in Major U.S. Museums." *PLoS ONE* 14 (3): e0212852. https://doi.org/10.1371/journal.pone.0212852

Afterword

DIGITAL MATURITY IN MUSEUMS

Analyzing 400,000 words of oral histories to identify themes that transcend sixty years of museum computing, determining which stories to share from each participant in this book, and then weaving more than fifty unique voices into one integrated history is not a simple task. As we worked on this project over the past four years, what kept us going was the sense of boundless enthusiasm that comes through each oral history—the inspirational spark of joy that we received from each of our participants' memories. Throughout each chapter, our oral history participants revealed the secrets of the magical, innovative, and creative spirit that drove the museum technology profession forward over the past sixty years. And if we are inspired by the stories we have collected and shared here, then perhaps others will be too. It is our fervent hope that this book has captured that spark of joy and creative spirit and will serve as a positive message to inspire and encourage the next generation of museum technology professionals.

When we consider just how pervasive and ubiquitous computing has become in the modern museum, it can be easy to take technology for granted and to become complacent about what the museum technology profession has accomplished. But the accomplishments detailed in this book really are amazing. They really are magical. We truly have come a long way. The more we understand the history of museum computing, the more we can shine a light on our shared accomplishments. Even though at times it may feel, as a profession, that the field takes one step back for every two steps forward, the overall historical sweep of museum computing remains one of positive growth with great potential for the future.

Our analysis of the oral histories presented in this book makes it clear that museum technology professionals faced many underlying challenges over the past six decades. They were invisible workers developing invisible infrastructures that were rarely appreciated as long as they worked but immediately criticized as soon as they failed. They faced misunderstandings about the purpose of technology in the galleries and behind the scenes, as well as the need for digital initiatives and strategies in museums. They spent their days struggling with technologies and information systems that needed constant attention and rarely worked as intended. They faced ongoing questions about the nature of their job, the relevance of their technical expertise, and who should be in charge of information technology in museums. They had to fight continually for the resources necessary to support the museum's information and technology infrastructures. And the institutional knowledge needed to sustain technology projects in museums was in constant danger of being forgotten, leaving each new generation of museum technology professionals to reinvent the wheel in a never-ending cycle of forgetfulness.

Throughout the history of museum computing, museum technology professionals had to find innovative ways to overcome a multitude of problems. They needed to be comfortable developing new skills, working in new ways, learning from failure, and figuring things out as they went along, with little or no precedents to guide them. They needed to serve as a bridge between diverse communities of museum stakeholders, including those that were comfortable working with computing technologies and those that were not. They needed to learn how to cope in an environment where the internal demands and external expectations placed on them increased constantly as technologies changed. They needed to work together to share lessons learned, document their accomplishments, and convince others to experiment with new technologies despite an ongoing risk of frustration, discouragement, and disillusionment. And they had to do all of this in an environment where people were resistant to change, suspicious of new technologies, worried about digitizing museum information resources, and confused about the purpose and value of museum computing projects.

Facing these challenges and overcoming these problems was not an easy task for the museum technology professionals who led the way in this history, but in so doing, they gained valuable insights into the unique leadership skills needed to guide museums into the digital age. They recognized the importance of encouraging and supporting innovation champions in museums who were able to advocate for museum computing projects, fight for those innovative digital projects and experiences, and have a seat at the table where they could champion the work of technology professionals to museum leadership. They recognized the importance of having access to professional networks of museum technology professionals that formed a community of practice that understands the challenges facing the profession, supports each other in solving common problems, and works to professionalize the field of museum computing. And they recognized the importance of having institutional support for museum computing projects from a director who understands the vision behind the museum's proposed digital initiatives, supports organizational change vis-a-vis museum computing, and can provide the top-down leadership necessary to make museum technology projects happen.

Thanks to the leadership abilities they brought to their institutions, museum technology professionals were able to encourage the development of new cultures and new philosophies that helped shape a more positive environment for museum computing. They led the way in developing new ideas that challenged our assumptions about the use of museum collections and promoted open access to museum images and information resources for the public good. They led the way in developing a culture of human-centered design, where thinking about how other people approach technology in museums is an essential first step in the development of new systems and technologies. They led the way in developing a culture of data-driven evaluation and assessment, where meeting the needs of the museums' users is a top priority, even when what users want does not match the assumptions of the museum professionals. And they led the way in developing a culture of empathy and understanding where museums prioritized meaningful experiences that transform people's lives and their connections with others, capturing and sharing multiple voices that involve all the museums' stakeholders, and using digital tools to build connections with communities around the world.

So where does this leave us today? As modern museums grapple with questions of digital maturity in a post-digital world, how can the history of museum computing enable today's museum leaders and professionals to better understand the role of technology in their own institutions and better advocate for digital initiatives moving forward? Must we fear our digital future? Must we keep making the same arguments over and over, and fighting for the same resources? Can we not build upon our prior work more successfully, prioritize our digital initiatives, and stop reinventing the wheel when it comes to museum technology projects?

The oral histories that formed the foundation for this book were recorded in 2021, while most museums were still closed for the COVID-19 pandemic. During these interviews, many of our oral history participants commented on how the challenges of the pandemic helped underscore the importance of technology for outreach and the need to invest in digital initiatives. With audiences unable to visit museums in person, and everyone forced to engage online, there was a sudden shift in perspective that hearkened back to the rise of the World Wide Web in the 1990s, revitalizing the online museum community. With the sudden rush to develop online initiatives, many museum technology professionals had the opportunity, often for the first time, to discuss digital strategies for their institutions in detail, which allowed them to build bridges and make connections with museum leadership in ways that were not previously possible.

But at the same time, our oral history participants raised questions about whether their newfound influence would continue moving forward.

They worried in particular that when museums reopened after the pandemic, museum technology professionals would lose their new voice in their institutions and return to their role as invisible workers behind the scenes. They are finally listening to us, many wondered, but once this is all over, will we again be forgotten? While the pandemic helped underscore the importance of being digital for museums suddenly unable to welcome visitors through their front doors, it also helped emphasize just how expensive those digital projects can be. A commitment to digital initiatives requires a corresponding commitment of resources across the museum, and many museum technology professionals questioned whether that commitment would continue post-pandemic.

The history of museum computing since the COVID-19 pandemic certainly indicates that these concerns were warranted. Despite the importance of museum computing to the success of museums during the pandemic, museum technology professionals were among the first fired as museum resources dwindled, and budgets needed to be trimmed. The pandemic exposed the invisible fault lines that underlie information infrastructures in museums and helped reveal the emotional labor that held so many digital projects together—projects that existed thanks to the invisible labor of invisible workers behind the scenes. And the museum technology professionals who had been trying for years with little success to get their colleagues to listen to them about the importance of digital strategies, database systems, metadata standards, museum websites, social media, and open access for museums were perhaps right to question whether their institutions' newfound commitment to digital initiatives would last moving forward.

The pandemic made it clear not only what museums need to do with technology but also the need for museums to invest in technology if they are to sustain digital projects in the future. Unfortunately, despite broad recognition of the importance of digital engagement for museums, and a clear acknowledgment that museums must invest in technology for the sake of their own digital futures, it appears that few museums, as of the time of this writing in 2024 at least, have lived up to the promise to follow through with new digital initiatives post-pandemic. One of the problems with institutions making organizational changes under duress, such as investing in technology during a global pandemic, is that once those same institutions are no longer under duress, they no longer need to sustain the changes they made. As a result, digital projects initiated during the pandemic were easily set aside once museums reopened post-pandemic.

Worse yet, many of the organizations that museum technology professionals relied upon for support and professional development are struggling to return to pre-pandemic operations. Well-established professional organizations such as the Museum Computer Network are operating under budgets that are a fraction of their pre-pandemic levels, while specialized technology conferences such as Museums and the Web are facing serious challenges and seem unlikely to recover. As professional organizations, networks, and conferences struggle to find their place in a post-COVID world, how will new connections be made, new ideas inspired, and a new sense of value instilled? Where will the next generation of museum technology professionals find their support communities? How can we keep the torch alive to inspire the next generation of museum technology professionals without the communities of practice that help preserve our invisible knowledge and our hidden history?

What then is the future of the museum technology community today? Despite the recognized value of museum computing and the role of technology in museums, questions of digital maturity continue to plague museums. For over sixty years, museums have been struggling to go beyond a simple digital infrastructure of servers and basic applications to develop a commitment to digital that reaches across the organization. Troubled by cost, personnel changes, and the ever-increasing pace of technological change, developing a long-term institutional commitment to digital continues to be a universal problem for museums.

If we want to see an improved, more positive understanding of the role of digital in museums moving forward, then we are going to have to work diligently to change the culture around digital in museums. A greater awareness of how digital connects people, processes, and technologies has the potential to spur changes regarding how the museum communicates, collaborates, and builds community with others. The act of achieving digital maturity is not a solitary act, but one that is collaborative. We need to consider relevant communication, collaboration, and community development strategies that can help museum professionals develop a commitment to digital initiatives for the long-term benefit of themselves and their institutions. Enabling a future where digital is supported appropriately across institutions means coming to terms with our differences and learning from our past in order to shape our future.

The more museum technology professionals struggle in a post-pandemic world, the more helpful it can be to look at the sweep of history covered in this book and to appreciate the positive effect of this history on the field as a whole. The amazing innovations that took place throughout the history of museum computing emphasize the power of the museum technology community to face challenges, overcome fears, and champion the potential of digital initiatives. Today's technology projects that are intended to provide new methods of interacting with collections data and engaging with visitors inside and outside the museum all have their roots in a history that goes back more than sixty years. Understanding this history is the first step in preparing the museum technology community to be able to face new challenges together, for it is this historical background that gives us the context, the knowledge, and the perspective we need to innovate, pull together, and effect positive change. Understanding where we have been and what we have done can help illuminate our path toward digital maturity.

The history of museum computing makes it clear that the museum technology profession has come back from hard times before. Organizations like the Museum Computer Network have seen their membership decline as economic downturns led to layoffs and financial worries, only for the profession to be revitalized by some new technology such as the World Wide Web that brought museum technology professionals back into the field. Despite the inevitable financial downturns and technological challenges, when we look at the overarching sweep of history over the past six decades, what we find is a period of great philosophical growth and positive change for the profession of museum computing. And with the appropriate investments moving forward, we can take steps to build upon the history of museum computing in a way that prioritizes positive change, growth, and enthusiasm for the future:

1) We need to invest in the technical personnel, the museum technology professionals who make museum computing possible. Museum administrators may feel that the people who manage technology in their institutions are interchangeable, but the history of museum computing shows that every individual plays a unique role in supporting the museum's digital ecosystem. Perhaps the best way to encourage and retain museum technology professionals is to help museum leaders understand the significance of technology projects for the future of museums and the importance of the institutional knowledge that is lost when the individuals with that expertise leave the museum.
2) We need to invest in the professional communities that support museum technology professionals across multiple institutions. Given the small number of institutions with more than one technology employee, it can be hard to understand the significance of professional organizations for the field, but the history of museum computing shows that access to professional networks and communities of practice is essential to developing and maintaining technological expertise. Professional organizations and communities can use their networks to support their members and advocate for technology work in museums as a core function that is key to institutional success.
3) We need to invest in the technical infrastructures that underlie and support museum computing projects. One might think that justifying resources for digital infrastructures would get easier as more institutions emphasize digital initiatives, but the history of museum computing shows that invisible work is expensive work, and the unintended consequences of building successful information infrastructures are that the costs to create and maintain those infrastructures are often completely hidden. By recognizing the integral nature of digital initiatives to the core mission of museums, we can help all of the museum workforce, from leadership

to volunteers, understand how technology infrastructures are used, managed, and supported from multiple perspectives.

4) We need to invest in a digital mindset where everyone recognizes the value of museum computing for the museum and its stakeholders. Given the importance of digital projects for modern institutions, museum leaders might expect that most of their employees are coming in with this mindset already, but the history of museum computing shows that the more digital permeates the museum, the more digital becomes taken for granted. Building a digitally mature museum means investing in digital holistically, and recognizing that museum technology professionals have unique skills that can help museums reach their visitors, online or in person, no matter where they live in the world.

Challenging times can be a catalyst for change. Overcoming problems and facing challenges can provide museums with a reason to invest in their own technology personnel and infrastructures, and push their institutions toward a new process of digital transformation. And so we close this book with one final quote from one of our oral history participants, Silvia Filippini-Fantoni, who describes how the COVID-19 pandemic encouraged her museum to embrace change:

> I started at the Newark Museum of Art in November of 2019. Four months later, we shut down for COVID. . . . This institution did not have any infrastructure to support technology when I first started. They never did any virtual programs before. . . . Within two weeks from the moment we shut down the building, we created our first virtual programs, and within nine months from that, we had 200 virtual programs, between social media and Zoom, that reached 95,000 people . . . and that was the catalyst for bringing a lot more changes along. Now we have a digital strategy. Now we have a web strategy. Now we have a new I.T. head. . . . It takes a lot of time, a lot of effort . . . but once you do it, then you build a consensus and build the understanding that we need to make these changes so that we can do more.

The museum computing profession is at a pivotal moment when digital initiatives are more important to museums than ever, but advocating for those initiatives continues to be extremely difficult. As a community of museum professionals, we can work together to lead our institutions into a more positive digital future, and encourage more museums to embrace organizational and technological change. It is essential that we invest in the dedicated personnel, the professional networks, the digital mindset, and the technical infrastructures needed to make museum computing a priority in our institutions. We hope that the lessons learned from the oral histories collected and presented in this book will shine a powerful light on the behind the scenes, invisible work of museum technology professionals, and help museum leaders, and the field at large, prioritize their work moving forward.

SUGGESTIONS FOR FURTHER READING

Geller, Stephanie L., Lester M. Salamon, and Kasey L. Mengel. 2010. "Museums and Other Nonprofits in the Current Recession: A Story of Resilience, Innovation, and Survival." *The Journal of Museum Education* 35 (2): 129–140.

Giannini, Tula, and Jonathan Bowen. 2022. "Museums and Digital Culture: From Reality to Digitality in the Age of COVID-19." *Heritage* 5 (1): 192–214.

Lindqvist, Katja. 2012. "Museum Finances: Challenges beyond Economic Crisis." *Museum Management and Curatorship* 27 (1): 1–15.

Marty, Paul F., and Vivian Buchanan. 2021. "Exploring the Contributions and Challenges of Museum Technology Professionals during the COVID-19 Crisis." *Curator: The Museum Journal* 65 (1): 117–133.

Parry, Ross. 2013. "The End of the Beginning: Normativity in the Postdigital Museum." *Museum Worlds: Advances in Research* 1: 24–39.

Petterson, Kate, and Katherine Jones. 2022. "The Digital Frontline." *New England Museum Association*. https://nemanet-archive.org/nemn/spring-2022/digital-frontline/

Index

About the Authors

Paul Marty is professor in the School of Information in the College of Communication and Information at Florida State University. His research and teaching interests include museum informatics; technology, innovation, and culture; experience design; and the information society. He has worked with museums, and in the field of museum informatics, since the mid-1990s.

Dr. Marty studies the sociotechnical interactions that take place between people, information, and technology in museums, and his publications explore the invisible work of museum computing, the evolving roles of technology professionals in museums, and the use of digital museum resources. He has served on the editorial boards and committees of national and international organizations including Museum Management and Curatorship, Museums and the Web, and the Museum Computer Network.

Dr. Marty has a background in ancient history and computer science engineering, and his PhD is from the School of Information Sciences at the University of Illinois at Urbana-Champaign. At Florida State University, he has served on a wide range of university committees, including serving as chair of the Honors Program Policy Committee, chair of the Innovation Hub Steering Committee, chair of the Undergraduate Program in Information Technology, and chair of the Milton S. Carothers Faculty Lecture Series.

Katherine Jones is program director for the Museum Studies program at the Harvard University Extension School. She has taught in the Museum Studies program at the Harvard Extension School since 1997 and has served as the research advisor since 2004.

Ms. Jones was assistant dean for Information Technology and Media Services at the Harvard Divinity School for nine years. Prior to that, she was assistant director at the Peabody Museum of Archaeology and Ethnology from 1994 to 2000 where she introduced the importance of websites and multimedia to all of the Harvard museums. She was responsible for raising funds for the various public-facing technology projects that were carried out during the time, including the virtual exhibit "Against the Winds: American Indian Running Traditions."

Her current research interests focus on applying artificial intelligence, machine learning, and natural language processing to museum databases in order to address challenges involving deaccessioning, visitor engagement, analyzing language used to describe collections to make it more accessible and less derogatory, and leveraging museum data to provide insights about climate change. Ms. Jones is editor of and contributor to two books on the use of technology in museums: *The Wired Museum* (1997) and *Museum Informatics: People, Information, and Technology in Museums* (with Paul F. Marty, in 2008). In addition, she has authored numerous articles on topics related to museum technology and given presentations at international, national, and regional museum conferences for the last three decades.

www.ingramcontent.com/pod-product-compliance
Ingram Content Group UK Ltd.
Pitfield, Milton Keynes, MK11 3LW, UK
UKHW012118150926
475560UK00002B/170

9 781538 183830